WATCHING THE WIND

WATCHING THE WIND

Conflict Resolution during
South Africa's Transition to Democracy

SUSAN COLLIN MARKS

UNITED STATES INSTITUTE OF PEACE PRESS
Washington, D.C.

The views expressed in this book are those of the author alone. They do not necessarily reflect views of the United States Institute of Peace.

UNITED STATES INSTITUTE OF PEACE
1200 17th Street NW, Suite 200
Washington, DC 20036-3011

First published 2000

Printed in the United States of America

The paper used in this publication meets the minimum requirements of American National Standards for Information Sciences—Permanence of Paper for Printed Library Materials, ANSI Z39.48-1984.

Library of Congress Cataloging-in-Publication Data
Marks, Susan Collin, 1949–
   Watching the wind: conflict resolution during South Africa's transition to democracy / Susan Collin Marks.
      p. cm.
   Includes bibliographical references and index.
   ISBN 1-878379-99-2
   1. South Africa—Politics and government—1989–1994. 2. Political violence—South Africa—History—20th century. 3. Conflict management—South Africa—History—20th century. 4. Aparteid—South Africa. 5. South Africa—Race relations—Political aspects—History—20th century. 6. Marks, Susan Collin, 1949– I. Title.

DT1970 .M37 2000
303.6'9'096809049—dc21

                                                            00-027275
                                                               CIP

For Peggy Levey, my mother—
one of South Africa's unsung heroes

CONTENTS

FOREWORD

Most books about peace processes, like most books about political movements and military campaigns, focus on the motivations, calculations, and actions of leaders at the highest levels. Autobiographical accounts of peace processes likewise tend to be penned by the men and—occasionally—women who held elevated political or diplomatic positions. This concentration on high-level decision making and decision makers is not only understandable (after all, the view from the top is usually more striking) but also instructive (the view from the top is usually clearer and broader).

The preoccupation with the upper echelons has two major shortcomings, however. First, it tends to isolate the reader of such books from the realities of life on the ground; too often, the reader is left with little or no idea of what the vast majority of the people in conflict-wracked countries were suffering, thinking, and hoping. Second, it presupposes that the negotiation of peace occurs only at the highest political levels and that the implementation of peace is largely an exercise in translating top-level dictates into local-level practice. But that presupposition is often wrong, especially in regard to the kinds of conflicts that have dominated the post–Cold War world. In the bitter and bloody civil wars of the past dozen or so years, states have either turned in upon themselves, pitting governments against peoples, or they have fragmented, pitting rival ethnic or religious groups against one another. In such conflicts, the traditional lines of authority break down. Decisions made at the highest levels are by no means certain to reach the grassroots level and are even less likely to be implemented without considerable renegotiation at the local level. In short, these days the negotiation and implementation of peace are no longer matters reserved for presidents, ambassadors, special envoys, and generals.

Watching the Wind captures the spirit of this radical shift in the character of peace processes by telling a personal tale of involvement in one of the most successful peace processes in recent years—the process by which South Africa journeyed from apartheid to democracy. The National Peace Accord, which was signed by all major political parties in South Africa in

1991, established a network of regional and local peace committees to help
reduce violence and boost political and racial cooperation as the country
moved toward its first majority democratic elections in 1994. The accord
linked grassroots activities with the highest decision-making levels, thus
forging a truly national peace process. Susan Collin Marks was a member of
the Western Cape Regional Peace Committee, and her book details the
efforts she and her colleagues made to encourage open political debate and
participation, to pacify potentially violent gatherings, to improve police-
community relations, and generally to stop violence escalating to ungov-
ernable levels.

Watching the Wind is a passionate and personal account. It conveys, as
very few books before it have done, a vivid and powerful impression of
what it is like to be a peace worker on the frontlines of contemporary conflict. It illustrates the difficulties and the dangers involved in journeying to
squatter camps, besieged city halls, and volatile townships to prevent or
mediate violent confrontations between desperate and bitterly divided
groups. It recounts the efforts made on the streets to negotiate between,
and sometimes simply to stand between, riot police and furious demonstrators. It takes us into council chambers and meeting rooms where peace
workers try to broker compromises that will satisfy or at least temporarily
assuage concerns about such distinctly palpable items as buses, houses, and
schools. And it takes us, too, into the hearts of the fearful and the revenge-
ful antagonists and of the doggedly determined peace workers, striving to
bridge interracial and intercommunal divides and steer their nation toward
a more equitable, harmonious, and peaceful future.

Susan Collin Marks has gone to great pains to present a balanced view
of the National Peace Accord, to reveal some of its shortcomings and to
explain why it failed in some areas to accomplish all that had been asked of
it. Even so, as Marks would be the first to acknowledge, her assessment of
what the regional and local peace committees were able to achieve is more
upbeat than the evaluations offered by many other players in, or observers
of, the South African peace process. Where Marks emphasizes the constructive, well-intentioned, and effective contributions made to the process by South Africans with different political and racial backgrounds, other
commentators have pointed to more ambiguous outcomes and perceived
shortcomings of the National Peace Accord. Some other writers might
also take issue with Marks's conviction that the principles of the South

African experience can be transferred to other countries plagued by deep-seated hatreds, structural inequalities, and pervasive violence.

Yet such differences of opinion are neither surprising nor, indeed, unwelcome. As with all books published by the United States Institute of Peace, our purpose in publishing *Watching the Wind* is to draw on the lessons learned in peace processes and to stimulate discussion about the best ways to resolve conflicts peacefully. Marks's book will, we trust, encourage open-minded consideration not only of how South Africa made the transition to democracy without succumbing to civil war, but also of whether the principles and even perhaps the effective mechanisms of the National Peace Accord can be replicated elsewhere. Furthermore, it will surely help to convince peacemakers at all political and social levels that we must pay no less attention to the grassroots than to the highest ranks if we wish to transform deep-seated ethnic, religious, and other "identity" conflicts into enduring examples of peaceful accommodation and acceptance.

Watching the Wind complements the Institute's previous publications in many ways. For instance, it illustrates the practical application of techniques and approaches similar to those outlined in John Paul Lederach's book, *Building Peace: Sustainable Reconciliation in Divided Societies*. It contributes another perspective on the challenges of contemporary mediation, a subject addressed by almost two dozen prominent mediators in *Herding Cats: Multiparty Mediation in a Complex World*, edited by Chester Crocker, Fen Hampson, and Pamela Aall. *Watching the Wind* adds to our list of memoirs by conflict resolution practitioners, a list that includes Mohamed Sahnoun's *Somalia: The Missed Opportunities*; John Hirsch and Robert Oakley's *Somalia and Operation Restore Hope*; Ahmedou Ould-Abdallah's reflections on his tenure as UN special representative in Burundi, *Burundi on the Brink*; and Paul Hare's insider account of efforts to bring peace to Angola, *Angola's Last Best Chance for Peace*. Susan Collin Marks's volume also enhances our already wide-ranging list of books on Africa. In addition to the books already cited, that list features volumes such as *African Conflict Resolution*, edited by David Smock and Chester Crocker; *Mozambique: UN Peacekeeping in Action*, by Richard Synge; *Ending Mozambique's War: The Role of Mediation and Good Offices*, by Cameron Hume; *Elections and Conflict Management in Africa*, edited by Tim Sisk and Andrew Reynolds; and Pierre du Toit's *State Building and Democracy in Southern Africa*. Of all the books published by the Institute, the volume that is closest in subject matter to *Watching the Wind* is surely Peter Gastrow's *Bargaining for Peace*, which offers an in-depth account of the negotiation of the National Peace Accord by a member of Parliament closely involved in the process.

The United States Institute of Peace awarded Susan Collin Marks a fellowship in our Jennings Randolph Program for 1994–95 so that she could report on her experiences as a member of the Western Cape Regional Peace Committee and thus provide present and future peace workers with a vivid sense of the nature, challenges, and rewards of their job. She has succeeded admirably. *Watching the Wind* seems certain not only to enlighten but also to inspire its readers with its story of the empowering possibilities of grassroots peacemaking and peacebuilding.

Richard H. Solomon, President
United States Institute of Peace

ACKNOWLEDGMENTS

In 1994, I was honored with a Jennings Randolph Peace Fellowship at the United States Institute of Peace, for which I am deeply grateful. Without that fellowship, I would never have written this book. My thanks to Richard Solomon, the president of the Institute, and Harriet Hentges, the executive vice president, for their leadership, and to Scott Thompson, a member of the Institute's board, and Joe Klaits, director of the Jennings Randolph fellowship program, for their unreserved support.

I have many people to thank for their part in this book's journey into print:

My research assistant, Jamie Frueh, who was fiercely loyal and supportive; my friend and colleague Melissa Baumann, who gave me the encouragement I needed and sweated with me over the first draft; my editor, Karl Signell, who brought a clear eye and a sharp pen to help me shape the final product.

USIP staff members Sally Blair, Barbara Cullicott, Kerry O'Donnell, Lewis Rasmussen, and Pamela Aall and fellow fellows Denis Dragounski, Rena Fonseca, Shlomo Gazit, Brook Larmer, Denis McLean, Vesna Pesic, Donald Rothchild, Mostafa-Elwi Saif, and Warren Strobel, with whom I had seminal conversations throughout my fellowship year and from whom I learned so much.

Many friends and colleagues who patiently and generously helped me with information, freely told me their stories, and advised me with insight and wisdom: Peter Gastrow, Andries Odendaal, Stef Snel, Chris Spies, Sean Tait, and Selma Walters as well as Craig Arendse, Elizabeth Becker, Linda and Peter Biehl, Val Rose Christie, Albert Dayile, Vincent Diba, Val Dovey, Jaap Durand, Chris Ferndale, Joanna Flanders, Kaj Stendorf Jensen, Ron Kraybill, Ampie Muller, Laurie Nathan, Gerrit Nieuwoudt, Ann Oglethorpe, Retief Olivier, Sakkie Pretorius, Wilfred Scharf, Hannes Siebert, Malibongwe Sopangisa, and Vladimir Zagora.

Lesley Fordred, who taped superb interviews with the six peacemakers highlighted in chapter 2; Doreen Scott, who worked nights to transcribe them; and Karen Zehr, who unstintingly supports me and all my work on a continuing basis.

USIP's Nigel Quinney and Dan Snodderly, who guided me through the final publication hurdles with kindness, tact, and grace.

My colleagues at Search for Common Ground, who inspire me with their commitment to making conflict resolution work in some of the harshest conflicts in our world.

My husband John Marks—my soul mate and my love—who believes in me, who unconditionally supported me in writing this book, and with whom I passionately share a vision of a world at peace and work to make it so.

And, finally, all the people who walk through the pages of this book, and those unnamed, who every day practiced the transformation, inspiration, and healing that made the National Peace Accord work and carried South Africa across the abyss from apartheid to hope.

To all of you: this is your book.

ACRONYMS

Sketches of South Africa's main political parties and groups, and of some influential individuals and ideologies, are provided in the glossary on pages 205–213.

ANC	African National Congress
APLA	Azanian People's Liberation Army (armed wing of the PAC)
AWB	Afrikaner Weerstandsbeweging (Afrikaner Resistance Movement)
AZAPO	Azanian People's Organization
BPC	Black People's Convention
CBM	Consultative Business Movement
CODETA	Convention for a Democratic Taxi Association
COSATU	Congress of South African Trade Unions
CTPC	Cape Town Peace Committee
GABS	Golden Arrow Bus Services
IFP	Inkatha Freedom Party
ISD	Internal Stability Division
ISU	internal stability unit
JOCC	Joint Operations Communications Center
LPC	local peace committee
LRC	Legal Resources Centre
MK	Umkhonto we Sizwe (armed wing of the ANC)
NEDF	National Economic Development Forum
NGO	nongovernmental organization
NIM	Network of Independent Monitors
NPA	National Peace Accord

PAC	Pan-Africanist Congress
PFP	Progressive Federal Party
PRO	police reporting officer
RPC	regional peace committee
RSC	Regional Services Council
SACC	South African Council of Churches
SACP	South African Communist Party
SANCO	South African National Civic Organization
SAP	South African Police
SDU	Self-Defense Unit (ANC)
SERD	Socio-Economic Reconstruction and Development
UCT	University of Cape Town
UDF	United Democratic Front
UMAC	Urban Monitoring Awareness Committee
WECUSA	Western Cape United Squatters Association

PROLOGUE

How to describe the transformation of a nation's psyche? How to convey the essence of a process so powerful that it carried a whole country across the abyss of self-destruction to the realm of hope? How to put spirit into words?

I remember a high summer's day among the hills of the undulating game reserve Hluhluwe, which lies at the heart of what is now kwaZulu-Natal. I had clambered into a cool hollow among the roots of a great wild fig tree dominating Hilltop Camp and looked out on the bush world spread below.

That day, the wind was powerful, and I watched hawks wheeling without moving a feather, riding the updrafts, swooping into the angle of the wind that gives the most lift; the ebb and flow of an open field of sour grass; leaves skittering, dry and scratchy, in the pale shadows under the thorn bushes; clouds caught in a running tide.

That day, I was watching the wind. The wind itself was invisible, but I saw its effect, its force and impact, its power and artistry.

This is the essence of South Africa's peace process. Nelson Mandela and F. W. de Klerk had, for different reasons, opted for a negotiated settlement. The National Peace Accord, invisible like the wind, swept powerfully through our land, blowing into troubled communities, turning upside down the established order of oppression and division, blowing the roof off structures rooted in centuries of separation and prejudice.

The results were miraculous: respectful meetings between bitter old adversaries, black and white—African National Congress (ANC) and government, community and police—to jointly resolve the common problems we faced; unprecedented and wide consultation by local, regional, and national authorities around decision making; facilitated meetings and mediation instead of force and bluster to resolve crises; relationships built across formidable barriers; the discovery of the Other that legislation had denied.

These were the wheeling hawks and the undulating grasses of the peace process. The peace process was invisible, but we could see its effects.

The National Peace Accord was launched in September 1991 to close the gap between the condemned political system of apartheid and a new future. I was one of many peacemakers, each with a story to tell. This is my story. It takes place in the context of the Western Cape Regional Peace Committee, established to serve the Western Cape province, at that time a vast area that radiated out from Cape Town north up to the Namibian border and east halfway to Port Elizabeth. It is a story that could be told by any peace worker in the other ten regions of the time. It is the story of how we South Africans made peace work on the ground, day by day by day, until the new South Africa emerged triumphant, President Mandela at its head, in April 1994.

I believe that our experience, in principle, is useful to other troubled societies, that they can sift it, extract what works in their context, adapt it, and make it their own. My hope is that this book will inspire others to say, "So there is another way to respond to conflict. Peace is possible. We can do it too."

We can make peace instead of violence. We must. We will.

WATCHING THE WIND

INTRODUCTION

The Reinvention of South Africa

My story, like many others, begins with Nelson Mandela.

I spent Sunday, February 11, 1990, on the Parade, Cape Town's central square, squatting in the thin shade of a date palm, waiting for Nelson Mandela, silent and unseen for twenty-seven years, imprisoned by the Nationalist government for fighting against its minority rule. Eighty thousand of us waited there for him to be released from prison. Our heads swam in the midday heat. Evening approached; the air cooled.

Around seven o'clock, Mandela finally strode onto the balcony of the City Hall, magnetic, smiling, waving, real. This lone black man and this great black crowd speckled with white looked at each other for the first time. He heard us roar our approval and acclaim. We cried, laughed, danced, waved, and shouted our welcome. He laughed and waved back. Parents picked up their small children and held them high above their heads so that they, too, could one day say, "I was there the day Mandela was released."

※   ※   ※

Nelson Mandela's release was a momentous event in our country. Afterward, when President de Klerk and Mandela began their difficult dance toward multiparty democracy, when violence threatened to tear the guts out of our hopes for the future, then we understood how easy it had been to cheer Mandela and how hard it would be to remake a nation. To save the day, our leaders approved a National Peace Accord. Hundreds of us rolled up our sleeves and pitched in to make it work.

My country has produced beautiful writers, and in writing this book I do not attempt to stand alongside them. I want only to give an account of the remarkable peace process that underpinned South Africa's transition from apartheid to democracy. It is a good news story from a country that for decades gave the world only bad news. It is also a story that didn't make the

3

headlines, perhaps because peacemaking is not usually recognized as the heroic undertaking it is.

For South Africans, those years of 1990 to 1994 were not only heroic but also dramatic and revolutionary. The international community had expected bloody revolution, accepting it as the only way out of apartheid. Instead, we stunned the world with a "negotiated revolution"[1] that cost thousands of lives, each of them precious, but did not even begin to look like the bloodbath that had been predicted. The world saw it as a miracle, and like most miracles it was rooted in visionary thinking, a leap of faith, and hard work.

The bedrock for that miracle was the political will generated by two men, F. W. de Klerk and Nelson Mandela—one the president of the country, the other recently released from jail. Their joint decision to negotiate a collective future supplied the leadership necessary to create a climate in which the National Peace Accord could be born and could thrive by means of a network of peace committees across the country. The purpose of this Peace Accord was to stem the bloody flow of violence that threatened to overwhelm the negotiations. Violence had erupted when the lid of oppression was lifted, and the struggle for power at every level began.

Along with hundreds of others, I worked in the front line of the Peace Accord, meeting violence every day, finding ways to use the methodology of conflict resolution to transform it. Without the Peace Accord, it is doubtful South Africa would have made it to the election. The story I want to tell is about how a growing band of peacemakers from all sides of the political and color spectrum took the skeleton of an idea, the National Peace Accord, and made it work.

❊   ❊   ❊

Nine days before Mandela's release from prison, de Klerk opened Parliament with a speech that electrified the nation. Sentence by sentence, he committed his government to negotiations for a democratic future. He said, "It is time for us to break out of the cycle of violence and to break through to peace and reconciliation. The overall aims to which we are aspiring," he continued, "include a new democratic constitution, universal franchise . . . and equality before an independent judiciary." He announced the unbanning of the African National Congress (ANC), Pan-Africanist Congress (PAC), South African Communist Party (SACP), and other banned organizations;

the release of political prisoners; the lifting of restrictions on thirty-three organizations; and the imminent release of Nelson Mandela. (Sketches of the major political parties and groups, as well as of key individuals, organizations, and terms, are provided in the glossary on pages 205–214.)

Around the country, South Africans looked at each other incredulously. De Klerk's speech meant the beginning of the end of apartheid. The majority of South Africans celebrated this lifting of the heavy yoke of oppression. The minority white government and its supporters felt uncertainty, fear, and a deep sense of impending doom. For all of us, in the time it takes to make a speech, the future was irrevocably transformed.

It hadn't been an easy decision for de Klerk—or a quick one. P. W. Botha, prime minister from 1978 to 1984 and then president from 1984 to 1989, had tried to reform the system earlier in the decade, but it had been too little too late, and his halfhearted measures served only to inflame black opposition groups. De Klerk would not repeat this mistake. It had to be all or nothing. He knew it was time. South Africa had hit rock bottom— internally, and in the eyes of the international community.

He also knew what few of his fellow South Africans knew. As Allister Sparks describes it in his wonderfully written book *Tomorrow Is Another Country*,[2] the government had been meeting secretly with Mandela for a number of years, the Broederbond had come to the painful conclusion that apartheid couldn't work, and Afrikaners at the highest level had been meeting quietly with the ANC at safe venues outside South Africa since the 1980s. De Klerk knew that he had to act, and act decisively. He chose the opening of Parliament as his venue, and he chose his words with care.

In the months that followed "the speech," everything in South Africa changed, yet everything stayed the same. The majority of black South Africans still lived in conditions of poverty and deprivation, the white minority government was still in power, and the security forces continued to act with an oppressive, heavy hand. Yet every day the media presented images of the ANC and government conferring, images that before February had been unthinkable. Together, de Klerk and Mandela began to lead their constituencies on the long march toward . . . what? The people of South Africa stepped with their leaders into the void. Like them, we didn't know what was waiting over the horizon, and no one was sure how to get there.

There were few sources to tell us how to make this transition from an authoritarian state to democracy. One book did say that political transitions are by their nature conflictual,[3] but we were discovering that truth for ourselves. There were those, mostly whites, who wanted to hold on to the old order, fearing loss of life, property, lifestyle, nationhood, power. They desperately wanted to stop the overwhelming progressive momentum forward to an unknown destiny. At the same time, long suppressed and deeply felt black needs, frustrations, resentment, anger, and pain were erupting, often violently. The shape and form of the incoming power structure were also hotly disputed within the progressive ranks, adding to the conflict. The struggle for power dominated the discourse as leadership at every level tried to negotiate slice by slice what they perceived to be a finite cake.

By the middle of 1990, the storm clouds had gathered, throwing shadows of violence across our land. The centuries of oppression, discrimination, and deprivation erupted in a burning rage. Political opportunism found violence useful, and new images of opposing political factions rampaging and killing filled the media. The crime rate skyrocketed, the political death count rose, gangs proliferated, and marginalized youth went on the march. Euphoric release from the cruel past gave way to endless crises. Everything was stark, extreme, sharp edged.

Violence permeated South African life. In the black townships it was an inescapable daily trauma. Political and criminal violence intermingled. A man was killed, some said in a fight between the ANC and the Inkatha Freedom Party (IFP), some said over a woman. The truth slid into the earth with his blood. Hostel dwellers lived in terror, holed up in the midst of inhospitable townships. Township residents lived in terror, barricaded in their houses in the shadow of brooding hostels. Others lived in terror in the bush, preferring primitive discomfort to the townships and hostels and gangs.

In the white suburbs, white people terrified one another with stories of increasingly violent robberies, murders, and rapes that the media headlined day after day. Security became a growth industry. Burglar bars and alarms, electronic garage doors and automatic lights, high walls, vicious dogs, and security guards provided an illusion of safety. All this violence and fear devastated our country.

The institutions of apartheid were crumbling and apartheid legislation was being wiped from the statute books, creating uncertainty and confusion in the absence of any new institutions or legislation to take their place. But the clamor for structural justice could not be resolved until a new government and a new constitution were installed.

NATIONAL PEACE ACCORD

In 1991, the South African Council of Churches (SACC) tried to take the lead in dealing with the escalating violence. At an upbeat conference in the town of Rustenburg in the Transvaal the previous November, under the leadership of the Reverend Frank Chikane, the SACC general secretary, and Louw Alberts, a highly respected Afrikaner layperson, the SACC had issued what came to be known as the Rustenburg Declaration, which "denounced apartheid, called for a democratic constitution and a more equitable distribution of wealth, and urged churches to condemn all forms of violence."[4] It also made provision for a peace conference to be held in March 1991.

The conference planning was already well under way when IFP leader Mangosuthu Buthelezi launched a broadside attack on the "busybody" churchmen, singling out Chikane for particular venom. Buthelezi was convinced that the SACC supported his archrival, the ANC, but the impact of his statement went much further than personal affront. Chikane and Alberts realized that if one of the major parties did not trust the church, then it would not be able to act as a facilitator. They abandoned the conference, as it was clear that the IFP would not attend. Who, they wondered, had the clout and credibility to pull everyone together to address the issue of political violence?

At the same time, the Consultative Business Movement (CBM), an alliance of progressive business leaders, was exploring its own response to the violence. Under the directorship of Theuns Eloff, a progressive former minister of religion, it convened a number of low-key meetings with a spectrum of political leaders. The meetings were inconclusive, and the CBM was pondering next steps, when in April President de Klerk called a summit on the violence to take place on May 24 and 25. Some sectors welcomed his initiative; others, primarily the ANC, rejected it. They felt strongly that an independent party, not one of the players, should convene any conference on the violence.

The president was unmoved and began to plan his peace summit anyway. The government and the ANC were set on a collision course. Something had to be done. Everyone knew that if the violence was allowed to shatter the dream, the country would fragment too, breaking up into small, bleak pieces of what could have been that would take decades to mend.

The church and business representatives decided to join forces, and over the next six weeks they worked out a plan that hinged on positioning the conference as a part of a broader process to respond to the violence. This would allow the ANC and others to view the conference as a starting point and to participate from then on. The government and the ANC agreed to this formula, and the summit went ahead. Its most important outcome was the creation of a committee, balanced for race, gender, and political leaning, and including all the major players. Groups on the far right and left of the political spectrum declined to participate, and although it would have been preferable if they had, the consensus was that the process could proceed without them.

In addition, the summit appointed church and business leaders to facilitate the process that would follow. The facilitators worked quickly, and on June 22, calling itself a "think tank for peace," the committee met and hammered out the skeleton for what was to become the National Peace Accord.[5] Over the next three months, this core group brainstormed with the broad political and community leadership in every sector, searching for mechanisms that could redirect the violent energy into constructive channels.

They drew on their personal experience. Jay Naidoo, secretary general of the Congress of South African Trade Unions (COSATU), played a key role, as did Theuns Eloff. Both had cut their conflict resolution teeth in the business sector, from trade union and management perspectives, respectively. Neither was a theoretician; both were schooled in practical experience on the street and through training courses and seminars. And since the mid-1980s, they had also been involved in trying to prevent violence as their workforces exercised new political muscle, organizing marches and demonstrations and clashing head-on with the police.

"While the committee made no attempt to operationalize theoretical models of conflict resolution, key individuals involved in drafting the National Peace Accord brought their direct and personal experience to bear. We had people who not only benefited from training courses, but had experience in the practical side," says Peter Gastrow.[6] Their study of the literature was reflected in the original naming of the peace committees as Regional and Local Dispute Resolution Committees.

Gradually a plan began to emerge from sketchy notes on the backs of envelopes and more formal deliberations. It was a daring idea; nothing like it had ever been tried before anywhere in the world. Could it work? The consensus was that it had to be tried, and on September 14, 1991, the plan for a National Peace Accord was unveiled at a National Peace Convention. It was an extraordinary moment for South Africa, one that would in hindsight be recognized as a major turning point.

The National Peace Accord was a pact between South Africa's major players to try to stop the violence. The twenty-six signatories included the principal political parties and organizations, the government and security forces, the leadership of the independent and self-governing states (so-called homelands under apartheid), and business, trade union, traditional, and church leaders. They committed themselves to a multiparty democracy and promised to support and abide by the mechanisms laid out in the Peace Accord.

The Peace Accord didn't replace the rule of law; it added to it. It was an alternative forum for resolving political and community conflicts that would have fallen through the ever-widening cracks in existing legislation. It was built around conflict resolution methodology as we knew it in South Africa at the time, and it applied to South African society as a whole.[7]

The Peace Accord drew to itself just about all the peacemaking efforts that were bubbling around the country. It was a grand attempt to address the violence, and we had to give it a try.

Conflict resolution is a relatively new field of practice and research that handles conflict in a collaborative way. Violence is such an automatic response to conflict in most of the world that we forget that violence is merely one response to conflict among many. Using conflict resolution methodology, we can replace this violent, adversarial tradition with nonviolent, nonadversarial approaches. The Peace Accord proposed an amazing and unprecedented experiment to transform South Africa's culture of violence into a culture of conflict resolution. It was the first time that conflict resolution had been tried on this scale anywhere in the world.

Unlike most peace accords, ours was not only an agreement on paper. It also mandated a countrywide structure with peace committees operating at national, regional, and local levels. In the interests of defusing the violence, people from nearly every sector were willing to work together with adversaries on peace committees. Soon there were hundreds of peace workers from all sides, working with, rather than against, one another.

The adversarial stance had been necessary. Apartheid had to be opposed by all means that could be mustered. South Africans of color and conscience had bravely fought against it to bring an era of tyranny to an end. Their stories stretch back in the history of a country built from the start on the flawed foundation of racial discrimination.

Now it was time to build a new society, and as the peace process got under way, something extraordinary happened. The forces of democratization adopted and adapted the conflict resolution tools, the problem-solving techniques, and the facilitating skills that form the essence of the peacemaking process. Conflict resolution spread as an agent of change on a mass scale at multiple levels.

The peace process set in motion by the launch of the Peace Accord provided a rickety way across the divide between apartheid and democracy.[8] Yet little is known about this process, without which South Africa would probably have never made it to the April 1994 election. This book tells how a band of peace workers made the Peace Accord work on a daily basis in one of South Africa's eleven regions (as demarcated at the time—see page 21), the Western Cape province, whose capital is Cape Town, from February 2, 1990, to April 27, 1994.

Some Lessons about Peacemaking

We learned a number of things as we went along:

- If peacemakers exist in a community they are likely to be used.
- Often, conflicts cannot be resolved without a third party.
- Crisis can provide the opportunity for peacemaking.
- Peace structures are in themselves mechanisms for conflict resolution.
- When people discover humanity in their enemies, they usually find it more difficult to remain enemies.
- You cannot change others; you can only support them if they want to change, and safe places like the peace committees provide the space for not just change, but transformation.
- Forgiveness carries awesome power.
- Each of us has his or her own truth (including my truth in this book).

Later, when I was able to think about it all, I sifted out four principles of peacemaking.

1. *Top-down and bottom-up mechanisms need to be incorporated into a peace process.* The South African transition depended on the political will

generated by both F. W. de Klerk and Nelson Mandela, on the one hand, and the active involvement of a vibrant civil society, on the other.

Even in established democracies in the West, there is always a gap between the bottom and the top, between the people and their leaders. The question is how to bridge it. In the upheaval of transition, who and what constitute the top and the bottom change, and the gap becomes a place for dialogue, creativity, and experimentation. Arrows of expectation can be shot up from the grass roots and find receptivity among decision makers. The roots of ideas can be extended downward to be tested. The transition is a fleeting moment that needs capturing before new arrangements become entrenched.

Conflict resolution and collaborative, participatory processes can play a key role initially as agents of change. Subsequently, they provide the techniques that keep alive ongoing communication between the top and the bottom, left and right, traditional and progressive, hawks and doves.

2. *All the stakeholders must be invited to join.* In South Africa, the stakeholders included the political organizations and parties, civic organizations, minority groups, security forces, businesses, trade unions, churches, and the government. Anyone left out would be unlikely to support the process and might well sabotage it. The peace committees of the Peace Accord served a convening function and became the key venues for stakeholder meetings. Forums played a similar role.

Inclusivity also needs to extend to the peace workers themselves. In the South African context, people working through the peace committees, peace desk officers of political and civic organizations, nongovernmental organizations (NGOs), community organizations, church groups, police-community liaison officers, academics, and others actively involved in day-to-day peace work had to find ways of cooperating for peace.

3. *Relationship building and healing mechanisms must be included.* Conflicts tear people apart, and when the divisions are as entrenched and sharply defined as in South Africa, they require active healing. In South Africa, we were so successfully divided by apartheid that we found ourselves strangers in our shared land, living parallel lives in which we rarely met as human beings.

The Peace Accord structures provided a place for people to build relationships, and the tools of mediation, facilitation, monitoring, and training provided the means to extend that healing into the greater community. Reconciliation must take place not just at the negotiating table, but in the hearts of the people.

4. *Socioeconomic and political development must accompany any peace process aimed at institution and nation building.* This is tricky, a catch-22 rule, because development requires peace, peace requires development, and development is inherently conflictual as communities compete for resources and the concomitant power. The peace process can help create the conditions in which development can flourish and can provide conflict resolution mechanisms to ease the conflict. However, more is needed. In South Africa, during the transition period, officials and citizens actively engaged in a series of forums to design alternative economic, educational, and health systems appropriate to the new democratic order. These forums acted as participatory think tanks for the future and generated an optimism that we, the people, could shape the rainbow nation to come.

These four principles—top-down and bottom-up, inclusivity, relationship building and healing, and socioeconomic development—form the basis for a transformative peace process. Collectively, they represent an approach that offers distinct advantages. The outcome is sustainable because it is participatory and legitimate; unlike wars, the peace process is constructive rather than destructive; real healing can take place within this kind of framework; real needs can be met because they are able to be articulated; and the process provides the basis for nation building.

CRITICISM OF THE PEACE ACCORD

At the end of 1994, the newly installed Government of National Unity closed down the Peace Accord nationwide. Members of the government saw it as competing for power and funds and, most of all, control. They were intent on focusing on the new democratic structures embodied in the constitution. But instead of drawing on the wisdom and experience of the Peace Accord, they abandoned it, and the people who had made it work, with little explanation.

Even during its short life, the Peace Accord had come in for a lot of criticism. Expectations of what it could and would deliver were unrealistic.

It could not resolve structural injustice. It could not change apartheid legislation. It could not remodel the apartheid institutions that had lost their legitimacy. It could not defend itself against sabotage by the forces that were trying to stop the peace process. It could not reach every community in the country. It could do little or nothing about many of the causes of the escalating violence, even though it had to keep trying to cope with the symptoms. In many cases, it could provide only a Band-Aid, not a cure, and it was blamed for this deficiency.

Some criticized the Peace Accord as a top-down structure. This was true in some regions, although it was more a flaw in execution than in design. Each signatory organization was responsible for keeping its constituency informed and involved, and in many cases these organizations neglected to do so. Either they did not have the means to do so, or their own internal information systems failed.

Some said the peace structures were too white. In the beginning, whites dominated the peace process. Whites had cars, access, and resources. They had time and guilt. And, in the best (old) South African tradition, whites were initially appointed to practically all the key posts within the peace structures.

It was also male dominated. The signatory organizations consistently selected a preponderance of men to represent them on the peace committees at the national, regional, and local levels. At the national meeting of police, political, and civil society leadership convened by the National Peace Secretariat at Johannesburg airport in June 1993 (see chapter 7), of the 150 delegates, only 10 were women. I stood up and addressed this issue. Although to my discredit my voice was strident, an ANC leader apologized from the floor and urged his fellow delegates to find ways to redress this balance when they went back home.

Despite its flaws, the Peace Accord changed South Africa and South Africans. It provided a place where former enemies got to know one another and found the humanity behind the stereotypes that for decades, if not centuries, had kept South Africans apart. It provided a buffer against violence that allowed the 1994 elections to proceed and catapult us into democracy. It formed a bridge between the old world we were breaking down and the new world that had not yet been born. It introduced conflict resolution methodology into the fabric of South African society. For many of the thousands that it touched, it was the most transformative experience of our lives. It was a means by which thousands of South Africans found our voices as champions of community and political peacemaking, voices we did not even know we had.

1
THE PEACE ACCORD

Peacemaking in Action

In 1990, to the surprise of the international community, South Africa's apartheid regime decided to negotiate with the ANC and the ANC decided to negotiate with the regime. In this process, a unique peace pact was born. The major stakeholders in South Africa agreed to cooperate in stopping the violence that threatened our chances for a democratic future by signing a blueprint called the National Peace Accord. Nothing with the scope and vision of the National Peace Accord had been tried before in the world. In one of the great paradoxes of our times, a pariah country whose government had legalized racism, divided its people into master and servant classes according to color, and consigned black people to lives of squalor and hopelessness created a multicultural peacemaking model for the world. From the terrible mess of apartheid, something new and beautiful was trying to be born.

The National Peace Accord was an idea conceived in desperation. By the middle of 1991, the escalating violence catalyzed by the upheaval of an entire social and political system was threatening to overwhelm the negotiations process. The leadership figures on all sides involved in negotiating the future recognized that democracy cannot take root in a context of violence, intimidation, and fear and realized it was in their joint interest to find ways to stop the violence. They had to figure out how to get old enemies to stop fighting and instead start seeing one another as partners in the peace that would, inevitably, someday come. Through a long process of brainstorming, consultation, and research into what had or hadn't worked in other countries, and with a dash of vision and faith, a group of respected church and business leaders, with the blessing of the political leadership, devised the National Peace Accord. On September 14, 1991, the major political parties, the government—which included the police and the army—and business, trade union, church, traditional, and homeland leaders signed it. That day, the twenty-six signatories collectively set in motion a peace process that would underpin the national negotiations, harness the energies of most South African peacemakers, and provide the framework for all South Africans to work together.[1]

All Peace Accord signatories bound themselves to a code of conduct for political parties and organizations, a code of conduct for every police officer in the country, guidelines for community reconstruction and development, and mechanisms for the implementation of peace committees. They affirmed fundamental rights and freedoms, and endorsed the establishment of a commission to investigate the causes of violence (which became known as the Goldstone Commission after its chair, Justice Richard Goldstone).

The Peace Accord provided an organizational framework for reducing violence and solving problems collaboratively. Its guiding spirit was peacemaking in action. It was conceptualized as a living structure, a system of peace committees in which everyone—Afrikaner and African, policeman and community activist, business mogul and factory worker, liberal and conservative, from top to bottom, from shore to shore—could meet together often and regularly to find ways of trying to stop the violence that was erupting among them.

Peace committees were put in place at the national, regional, and local levels. The peace committee members and staff mediated between the ANC and the government; intervened in the deadly taxi wars; improved relations between black communities and the police; brokered deals among warring African factions; and intervened in violent confrontations. The job of the peace committees was to monitor and intervene when violence occurred, to anticipate when violence would occur and find ways to prevent it, and to try to resolve the problems that were causing the violence in the first place. Sometimes these peace efforts worked, sometimes they did not; but the cumulative effect was to defuse enough violence and build enough relationship between former adversaries to get the country through the elections.

South Africans had never met one another before like this, face-to-face, and over time we learned to turn away from our habit of fearing one another and instead began to face our common problems and jointly find solutions. Instead of seeing ourselves locked in a zero-sum, win-lose competition in which only one side could win, we started to see ourselves as partners in a problem-solving relationship (see figure 1.1). This simple act changed the way we dealt with our problems—and one another—and the basis for much of the peace work that we undertook. And as we got to

Figure 1.1. From an Adversarial Relationship to a Problem-Solving Partnership

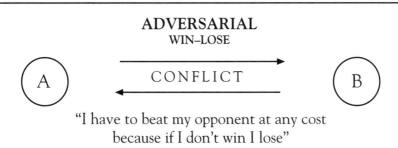

ADVERSARIAL
WIN–LOSE

A   CONFLICT   B

"I have to beat my opponent at any cost
because if I don't win I lose"

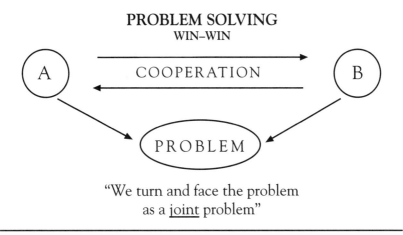

PROBLEM SOLVING
WIN–WIN

A   COOPERATION   B

PROBLEM

"We turn and face the problem
as a joint problem"

know, and even trust, one another, as relationships were built one-on-one between the human beings that inhabited the mythology of "ANC" and "Government," the bitter stereotypes of "police" and "black," as former adversaries found one another's humanity throughout the country, so the foundation began to be built for a place where we could one day all be human beings together, which we vaguely called "the new South Africa."

Building human relationships, seeing our conflicts as joint problems, consulting together to arrive at the best solution, taking joint action—this is the stuff of conflict resolution methodology, and the Peace Accord,

Figure 1.2. The Structure of the National Peace Accord

The structure of the Peace Accord shows a carefully crafted and thoughtful design at national, regional, and local levels.

National Level

National Peace Committee (NPC)	Functioned as a "council of leaders" that oversaw the Peace Accord at the highest administrative level, facilitated its work, and resolved disputes. Composed of representatives of the signatories. Made decisions by consensus.
National Peace Secretariat (NPS)	Carried out the orders of the NPC. Established and administered a network of regional peace committees (RPCs), one in each of the eleven regions in the country.[a] Staffed by six people from the NPC and one person from the Department of Justice. Made decisions by consensus.
Commission of Inquiry Regarding the Prevention of Public Violence and Intimidation (known as the Goldstone Commission)	Investigated the nature and causes of violence, identifying those responsible and recommending action to the state president. (Violence and intimidation declined when they were investigated and when the background and reasons for them were exposed and given media attention.)[b] A permanent commission composed of a judge (Richard Goldstone), a senior advocate, and three other legally qualified persons.
Police Board	Established to promote more effective policing and police-community relations. It included police officers and civilians in equal numbers and advised the minister of law and order on policy issues.

Regional Level

Regional peace committees (RPCs)	Worked to prevent and control violence in each region in a number of ways, including mediating conflicts, tackling the specific issues that were a source of violent conflict, and establishing and supervising local peace committees. Composed of representatives of political organizations, community-based organizations, business, the church, trade unions, tribal authorities, nongovernmental organizations, and the security forces.

Socio-Economic Reconstruction and Development (SERD)	Established to broker development projects that would help stop the violence. Poverty among black South Africans was universally acknowledged to be a root cause of violence, so the SERD committees attached to each RPC were to work closely with grassroots communities on local development projects that addressed needs that were a source of violent conflict.[c]
Police reporting officers (PROs)	Investigated allegations of police misconduct. PROs were nominated by the Bar Association and appointed by the minister of law and order. The PRO supervised a Complaints Investigation Unit composed of police officers who actually carried out the investigations. There was much skepticism that the police could investigate themselves impartially.

Local Level

Local peace committees (LPCs)	Addressed local violence and other community issues. LPC members also mediated conflicts. Each LPC reflected the composition of its immediate community. In a rural area, in addition to the political parties and community organizations, the farmer's union was usually included, whereas an urban LPC typically brought in squatter organizations and township civic groups. Each LPC was accountable to its regional peace committee.
Special criminal courts	Proposed by the Peace Accord to expedite the dispensation of justice in unrest-related cases but never established.

[a] South Africa has since been reorganized into nine regions.

[b] The Goldstone Commission investigated specific incidents of violence such as the ferocious massacre at Boipatong in the southern Transvaal that made world headlines in June 1992; sustained conflicts such as the internecine battles in Bruntville, Natal, where township youth and hostel dwellers coexisted on a near-warlike footing amid allegations that the police were fanning the flames; and the endemic minibus-taxi wars that cost lives and disrupted communities all over the country. The commission exposed the role of Military Intelligence in destabilizing activities, vindicating those who claimed that the hand of this so-called third force was behind much of the violence, which seemed to be turned on and off like a tap with exquisite timing and control.

[c] For instance, providing water, recreational facilities for youth, or a pedestrian bridge over a motorway dividing a community. This was a good and logical idea that never really worked for a variety of reasons, including a shortage of funds, lack of community involvement in its implementation, and, many people thought, an obstructionist government wanting to control the development process.

through the peace committees (originally called dispute resolution committees), applied conflict resolution to a whole society.

The Peace Accord formed the underpinning for the national negotiations. It drew most of the country's peacemaking efforts into its orbit and became the major force for counteracting the violence. It provided a safety net for the inevitable fallout from the talks. When things were going badly in Kempton Park (the venue for the national negotiations), violence would escalate and the National Peace Committee would convene to try to find a way forward. But it was the regional and local peace committees that absorbed the impact at the level where most South Africans lived, dealing daily with conflict and violence, defusing explosive situations, working to heal torn communities, and, in many cases, literally standing between a fragile equilibrium and chaos. The peace committees did not stop the violence but did contain it enough to make free and fair elections possible. I shudder to think what would have happened if the peace structures around the country had not existed.

The National Peace Accord was enshrined in law at the end of 1992 as the Peace Accord Act. It generated a wave of peacemakers who mediated, monitored, educated, trained, and built bridges inside and outside the peace structures. It didn't matter where the will came from; what did matter was the hope, commitment, and passion that we all brought to our common goal of ending the violence.

WESTERN CAPE REGIONAL PEACE COMMITTEE

I lived in beautiful Cape Town, watched over by majestic Table Mountain. It is South Africa's legislative capital city and the nerve center of the Western Cape region, which stretched to the Namibian border in the north and halfway to Port Elizabeth in the east. It was a vast region, one of eleven, and, like all the others, was facing its own specific problems as the negotiations process unfolded.

The text of the Peace Accord was distributed in 1991. It was a working document, dry, academic, and legal in style. I read it carefully and wondered how it would be implemented, and by whom.

A year before, I had started a project at the Centre for Conflict Resolution (then known as the Centre for Intergroup Studies), focused on supporting, sustaining, and catalyzing efforts to stop the violence in the

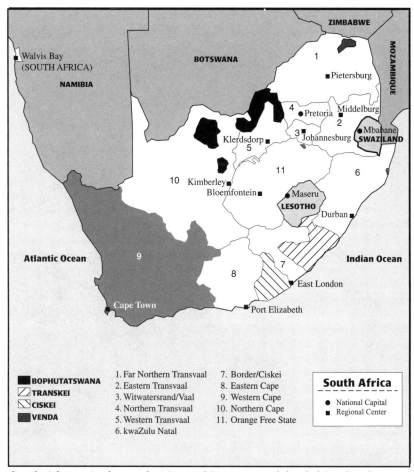

South Africa. As shown, the National Peace Accord divided South Africa into eleven regions. (The four "independent" states listed at bottom left have since been incorporated into South Africa.) Reprinted from Peter Gastrow, *Bargaining for Peace* (Washington, D.C.: United States Institute of Peace Press, 1995), 51.

Western Cape. One of my roles was to coordinate the Joint Forum on Policing, an alliance of civil and human rights nonprofit NGOs working on policing issues. When in January 1992 the National Peace Secretariat, the administrative body of the Peace Accord, announced a meeting in Cape Town to talk about the establishment of a regional peace committee (RPC),

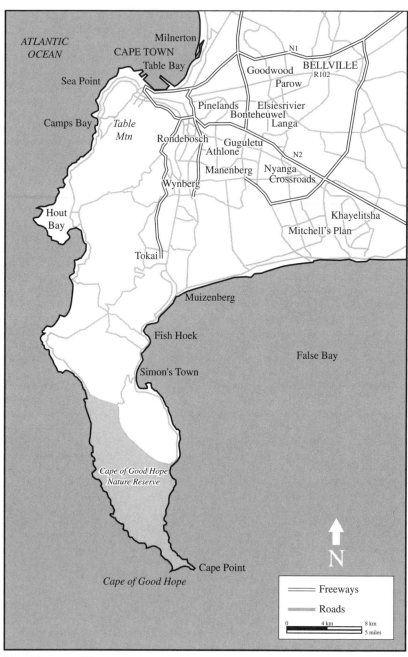

Cape Town and Environs

the Joint Forum agreed that two of us would attend the meeting to present our credentials and make a formal request for membership.

The meeting took place in the town hall of the Cape Town suburb Salt River. A large, low building with a car park that doubles as a vegetable market, it was chosen carefully for its position at the confluence of local railway lines from the Cape Flats, where many African and Coloured people live. It had easy access to the southern suburbs, which house the majority of progressive whites, and to the northern suburbs, which are largely white and conservative. Meeting places were a sensitive issue, posing both symbolic and practical problems that were difficult to resolve. Meetings in white suburbs presented transport problems for Africans and Coloureds; meetings in black townships presented safety problems for whites and transport problems for Africans and Coloureds from other areas. Meetings during the day conflicted with working hours; meetings at night presented transport and safety problems all round.

But this was Sunday and the meeting was at two o'clock in the afternoon. The hall filled up with many new faces, new not only to me but to one another: members of the ANC, National Party, Democratic Party, Communist Party, and Labour Party, of the police and the military, of the Muslim, Jewish, and Catholic and other Christian faiths; representatives from Black Sash and the newly formed Women's Alliance, from community organizations, the trade unions, and the black and white business sectors. Everyone sat together at the plain wooden trestles arranged in a square. A deep sense of expectation rippled through the room. Something was beginning that we did not fully comprehend, and we certainly hadn't the faintest idea what it would become.

At that meeting, the participants established the foundations for the Western Cape Regional Peace Committee, agreeing on such basic issues as the composition of the executive committee, the frequency of meetings, the housing and staffing of the secretariat, and the priority of tasks. Within six months, the secretariat had expanded from two people to ten, and then twenty, and by the election it numbered nearly fifty, including nine fieldworkers, each dedicated to a rural area, town, or suburb. It became a complex organization, fraught with its own conflicts, but knitted together by a determination to do everything possible to stem the violence. Watching over this growing institution, the executive committee met every two weeks without fail, with numerous meetings of subcommittees and crisis

Figure 1.3. Organizational Structure of the Western Cape Regional Peace Committee

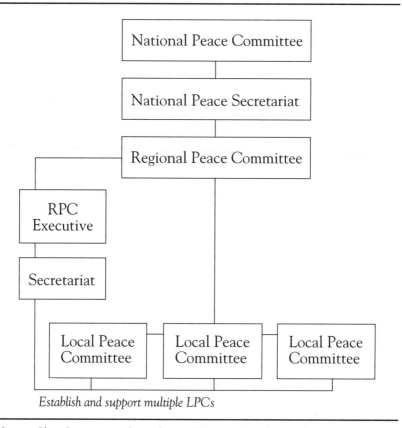

Establish and support multiple LPCs

Source: Chris Spies, regional coordinator, Western Cape Regional Peace Committee.

meetings in between; bimonthly meetings were convened for the full RPC. The phones started ringing from day one with calls for help with conflicts and crises, and they didn't stop until the Peace Accord was closed down three years later.

The effectiveness of the Peace Accord around the country was uneven. In some places, such as Natal, the province where the violence spiraled to unprecedented and terrible levels, the Peace Accord could hardly be implemented because the level of violence was too high, the level of trust too low, and the cycle of violence too entrenched. Yet even under such adverse conditions, there were some astonishing triumphs. In the Estcourt-Wembezi area in western Natal, a low-intensity war had been raging for years, and initially the existence of the Peace Accord was ignored by all the local leaders. Forming a peace committee seemed out of the question. Yet in early 1993, a local peace committee (LPC) was formed, transforming this violent community and the lives of all its people.[2]

In regions such as the Western Cape, the peace committees achieved much. It quickly became normal procedure for the political parties and organizations, the security forces, community leaders, and government to call on the peace committees in times of conflict and crisis. We set up and facilitated multiparty forums, and for the first time issues such as the taxi wars, police-community relations, and local government conflicts were addressed jointly by the people who were directly affected. Calls for intervention of every kind came from the entire region.

The Western Cape is sociopolitically unique in the South African context for three historical reasons. First, it is the spiritual home of the Coloured people, the mixed-race people who inhabit the twilight world between Africans and whites, a minority among minorities, fearful of the Afrikaners, with whom they share a language, and of the African majority that many Coloureds believe threatens to overwhelm them. Torn, the preponderance of Coloureds traditionally opted to support the apartheid government as the lesser of two evils, as was evidenced in the April 1994 election, when the National Party took the Western Cape region. The National Party also won because of the second reason for the Western Cape's uniqueness: the number of Africans living in the region historically has been limited by apartheid legislation. In its obsession with dividing the races, as it defined them, the apartheid government did its best to keep Africans and Coloureds apart too.

Third, the IFP is barely represented in the Western Cape, and the number of Zulus living in this predominantly Xhosa area is negligible. The devastating level of violence that was mobilized between these two groups in Natal and the area around Johannesburg was absent in the Western Cape. Relatively speaking, despite the existence of some fiercely radical groups among the youth in particular, the context within which the Western Cape Regional Peace Committee operated was far more conservative and much less violent than in these other two regions.

Consequently, this peace committee worked more effectively. The range of stories that can communicate a sense of the everyday life of the peace committees in the region is as broad as the region was vast. For example, when Operation Barcelona, the violent youth protest that culminated in the death of the American Fulbright student Amy Biehl in Guguletu township on August 25, 1993, created a so-called no-go area for whites in several other Cape Town townships as well, the peace committee was able to help the affected communities arrange safe passage to the local clinic for essential white medical personnel.

Another example concerns the town of Pofadder in the remote Northern Cape, where the eruption of a crisis provided the opportunity to establish a peace committee.[3]

One quiet weekend in the middle of 1993, three Coloured people were killed by whites in Pofadder. Two of them were shot in broad daylight in the middle of town by a member of the Afrikaner Weerstandsbeweging (AWB), the extreme right-wing Afrikaner Resistance Movement, in front of the Pofadder Hotel. The third was shot on a farm. The Coloured community, led by the local ANC branch, erupted in a wave of strikes, boycotts of services and rents, and protest marches, spilling out into the sun-blistered streets their accumulated anger about breaches of agreement by the white town council, a massive hike in rates (local taxes) for housing and services, and poor civic facilities. Things got so bad that both the town clerk and the ANC Youth League spontaneously sought outside help, calling the regional peace committee in far-off Cape Town. Chris Spies,[4] the regional coordinator, and two colleagues chartered a small plane to fly them into the bleached heat of Boesmansland (Bushmansland) just south of the Namibian border.

That afternoon, Chris and his team met with the town council. The councilors committed themselves to a joint negotiating session with the ANC the next morning. That night, the ANC convened a mass meeting for their mostly Coloured supporters, with Chris in the chair. Seven hundred people came and, during the course of the evening, told their stories, articulated their grievances, and agreed upon a process for dealing with them. They also agreed to attend the meeting with the council the following day.

The joint meeting turned into a marathon. Right at the start, a white councilor shouted, "You are wasting your time with these communists." Chris said, "What is it that makes you so angry?" A strange silence hung in the room, and Chris knew that how it was broken would set the tone for this small town's immediate future. The councilor needed to speak his mind, but would he say what he really thought in front of his antagonists, the ANC, and these outsiders from the peace committee? Looking out of the window at his beleaguered community, he made his decision. "We have tried so hard with these people, but you can't trust them, they do not negotiate in good faith," he said, nodding toward the ANC delegation. He spoke of events and incidents that had, in his perception, broken trust. He felt hopeless. "This is all a waste of the taxpayers' money," he growled. The meeting listened quietly. No one interrupted him, and he sat down into a long silence. But in a strange way, his speech had acted as a catharsis not only for him but also for the entire meeting. The anger and frustration were out. He had articulated his needs, however savagely, opening the way for the ANC to do so too, and the meeting was able to proceed. That day, the depth of communication between these historically bitter opponents was unprecedented. Six hours later, they had hammered out an agreement that included mechanisms for improved communication and feedback between the Coloured community and the council, the upgrading of services to the Coloured sectors, and agreement to establish an LPC.[5]

One other thing happened at that meeting. It is the custom that everyone at such a meeting introduces himself or herself at the start; usually the agenda lists the item as "Introductions." It is a courteous gesture, and it is important to know who is in the room. That morning, a police officer said, "I am the police representative on the peace committee in the Northern Cape," as he gave his name. The peace committee fieldworker who had accompanied Chris said, "I know you. You tortured me in Worcester in 1986." They looked at each other across the room and the years, remembering. The fieldworker had risked his life fighting against apartheid as an activist during the eighties. The policeman had worked with meticulous tenacity to fend off the so-called terrorist threat against the state, using the sweeping powers granted under emergency regulations to harass, detain, and interrogate suspects. He had also crossed that porous line into the murky underworld of torture, knowing that, despite the illegality of torture, his actions would be tacitly condoned by the state and his superiors.

Now the peace structures had brought together these former enemies to address a common problem and to cooperate in its resolution. The inconceivable was happening in this very room, and in rooms like this all over the country, as more and more people came together across the deep divides that characterized our land and made it a pariah in the world community. Under the auspices of the Peace Accord, the decades, the centuries, of rupture and split were beginning to come to an end. The healing process had begun.

The Peace Accord included everyone as equals, even the government and its servants such as the police. In many cases, the government became just another player, not a referee or a participant with extra powers.[6] One international observer could barely contain his amazement when, for the first time, he watched local, regional, and national government officials take their seats alongside community, trade union, ANC, and Communist Party representatives at a Transport Forum meeting on the taxi and bus war (see chapter 6, "Forums"). He was astonished at the government's readiness to be equal partners at the table, and went home shaking his head over the achievements that we took for granted.

We were learning as we went along, what we could and couldn't do, what worked, what didn't, and why. We discovered that if peacemakers are available, they are likely to be used. A peacemaker's worth depends on community recognition of that role more than on peacemaking skills per se. In Pofadder, Chris Spies found that crisis often provides the opportunity for establishing a peace structure, if peace workers grasp the moment. Another story, from Plettenberg Bay in the Southern Cape, taught us that, by its mere existence, a peace committee or similar structure can itself become the mechanism for conflict resolution, because it provides a safe, neutral, and legitimate place for former enemies to meet, build relationships of trust, discard divisive stereotypes, and approach conflicts as common problems to be solved in common.

Plettenberg Bay, located east of Cape Town, is a dream vacation resort. In the summer, blue and white waves sweep onto beaches of fine, golden sand, curved in the palm of a great natural bay. Dolphins play among the boats moored in the swell just beyond the breakers, and exotic seashells wash into the shallows. White people have always come from Johannesburg and Port Elizabeth and hot inland towns to play. They did not notice that behind its holiday facade, this sunny town was simmering.

The break point came when the revered ANC leader Chris Hani was killed in April 1993 by a white man. All over the country, black communities boiled over, releasing the pent-up rage of their oppression under apartheid rule. In Plettenberg Bay, the black community went on the march, toyi-toyiing (dancing the war dance that became a symbol of protest) and chanting their way through the placid streets. During the protest, two factories were burned to the ground. The next day, no one went to work, and the relationship between the workers and the industrialists hardened into a tense standoff. Both sides waited for something to happen, pressuring the municipality to find a solution. A sense of helplessness pervaded the town; no one knew what to do. The Southern Cape Peace Committee was asked to intervene.

Two peace committee fieldworkers got to work immediately. With a UN observer from Belarus in tow,[7] they met with the community leadership, the industrialists, and the town councilors. After hours of consultation and shuttle diplomacy, everyone agreed to come to a meeting to talk about establishing an LPC.

The meeting was held in the Arthes Hotel, neatly positioned on the road between the black township of Bossiesgif ("bush poison") and the white part of town. Forty people attended, and as soon as they had settled in the plastic chairs, the industrialists asked the ANC representatives, Why did you do it? Why did you burn down the factories that give your members work? The ANC replied, We didn't do it, we don't know who did it, we were marching at the time, we are just as unhappy about it as you are. And so they began to talk, a local peace committee was formed, and within three or four weeks, the town was back to normal.

One year later, the police shot a young boy dead as he was breaking into a factory. It turned out that the boy was the brother of the local ANC Youth League leader. That Friday night, a factory was burned down. On Saturday, the LPC convened an emergency meeting of its crisis committee. By late Saturday afternoon, the situation was under control. It had taken less than twenty-four hours.[8]

The local peace committee was key to the resolution of this potentially disastrous situation. Because of its existence, and the incipient trust that it nurtured, Plettenberg Bay was able to stabilize far more quickly after the second crisis than the first, preventing further violence, destruction, and possibly even death.

REGIONAL EXECUTIVE COMMITTEE MEETING

The regional executive committee decided what action to take on the ground. The following account of a typical executive committee meeting gives the flavor of decision making, personal interaction, and the kinds of topics that were regularly addressed. The committee met every two weeks.

Western Cape Regional Peace Committee
Executive Committee Meeting, October 13, 1993

I count twenty-eight people in the room, including representatives of the ANC, the National and Democratic Parties, the SACP, the police, the church, the black squatter community (Western Cape United Squatters Association, WECUSA), the provincial administration, business, and NGOs. International observers from the UN and the European Community (EC) missions and peace committee staff crowd into spare seats around the walls. Motlatsi Motoasele is a new UN observer from Botswana. We have mixed experience with international observers. We stare at Motoasele, wondering if he will be with us in the streets or if he will surface only at safe meetings like this one.

Professor Jaap Durand chairs the meeting, as usual.[9] He maneuvers through this minefield of disparate and opinionated people with the same aplomb with which he doggedly plays tennis in rain or sun throughout the year. Today's agenda includes a national candlelight vigil for peace, a conflict about housing that has so far killed seventy people, the taxi war, and police-community relations.

AGENDA ITEM 1: NATIONAL CANDLELIGHT VIGIL. "Commitment to Peace" is a national consciousness-raising campaign planned for November 2. "All the political leaders will light a candle for peace, but the idea is that the whole country should participate," peace committee manager Retief Olivier explains.[10] When the peace committee was established, Retief was lent to manage it by the Consultative Business Movement, a progressive business association that was providing the secretariat for the multiparty negotiations. He is grateful to be able to immerse himself every day in his passion for peace and call it a job.

These symbolic peace gestures work, so we welcome this new idea for a candlelight vigil. The last time, Friday, September 2, the entire country came to a standstill for five minutes of silence at midday. Everyone had a story to tell about that day:

- Cars stopped on the motorway shoulder and their occupants got out and hugged one another.

- Boardroom meetings were halted in midsession.

- A white woman stopped her car in the middle of town, got out, and held hands with an old African man who happened to be walking by.

- Schoolchildren stood in circles imagining peace.

- People stopped walking in city streets and looked into one another's eyes.

- Cars that could not stop flashed their lights.

Interrupting a meeting at the Centre for Conflict Resolution, twelve of us had stood on the verandah, intuitively adopting an attitude of prayer or meditation. When we continued the meeting, we noticed a new sense of kinship and common purpose.

AGENDA ITEM 2: HOUSING CONFLICT. Malibongwe Sopangisa, manager and fieldworker for the LPC that serves the African townships of Nyanga and neighboring Crossroads, updates us on Crossroads, where a long-standing conflict fueled by years of state manipulation has erupted yet again. Malibongwe says that rightful ownership of houses is still a problem, and the Residents' Association has asked for a joint meeting with the ANC and the Pan-Africanist Congress (PAC) regional executive to sort this out.

The disputed houses were once family homes, but the owners fled to escape the violence. Some moved to temporary accommodation nearby, while others left the area for good. Gradually, homeless families moved into the abandoned houses, but now some of the original owners want to move back. The ANC started a register of those who currently live in the houses and those who claim to have lived there before. The PAC-aligned Residents' Association reacted to what seemed like ANC control of this process. Concerned that the records were being stored in the office of the town clerk, Tollie Thorpe, whom they suspected of having ANC sympathies, the PAC Residents' Association staged a sit-in in Thorpe's office. They demanded that the records and register be kept at the LPC office. The ANC and Thorpe agreed, and the registration certificates were duly counted, tied with string, sealed in the presence of representatives of both groups, and stored in safekeeping in the LPC office in Nyanga. The LPC was available, and it was used.

Malibongwe is always so matter-of-fact and reassuring when he talks. His quiet voice never betrays his intense commitment to peace at all costs.

Most people don't know that he wears a bulletproof vest when out in the field because an assassin tracks him. Malibongwe looks expectantly at Vincent Diba, a member of the ANC Regional Executive, who nods. Yes, Vincent will try to arrange the ANC-PAC meeting.

AGENDA ITEM 3: REPORT ON LPCs. Chris Spies introduces a seven-page report on LPCs in forty towns, hamlets, townships, and suburbs scattered across the Western Cape region. We hear about many conflicts, the most troublesome coming from the Strand-Lwandle area. Earlier this year, violence there peaked with the killing of three white people.

For some time, tensions had been running high in Lwandle, an African township that sits in true apartheid fashion beside but separated from the white, mainly Afrikaans, beach town of the Strand in the cusp of False Bay. The provincial administration threatened to move the Waterkloof squatter camp from its mountain site to land right next to Lwandle, and the people of Lwandle were dead set against the idea. The Lwandle township supported the South African National Civic Organization, SANCO; the Waterkloof squatters supported the squatter organization WECUSA.[11] SANCO's urban progressives and WECUSA's rural traditionalists directly competed for power, and conflict continually flared between them. The settled Lwandle township folk distrusted the Waterkloof nomadic squatters, fearing increased crime and decreased living standards. Distrust, anger, and fear hung heavy in the Lwandle night air when three young white men wandered into a Lwandle *shebeen* (an illegal drinking house) looking for some action. Suspicion that they might be provincial administration officials erupted in one crazy instant into murderous rage, and the three were killed as spies.

Many months have passed since the murders, and Chris reports that although the trouble is not yet over, the area is stabilizing after the horror of the killings. An RPC fieldworker is working hard to establish an LPC for Strand-Lwandle.

AGENDA ITEM 4: TRANSPORTATION CONFLICT. The transport subcommittee, which I chair, has been intervening in crises and facilitating numerous regular meetings around various aspects of the taxi wars that continue to spawn violence, killings, and the destruction of vehicles and property. But today I am feeling glum about a project that could really make a difference.

For nearly a year I have been convening community members, the bus company, taxi industry representatives, and the local town council in a development committee for a new bus and taxi terminus in Nyanga.[12] Much of the taxi-related violence and killing has been concentrated at the terminus and the area surrounding it. Everyone involved is convinced that a new terminus will help defuse the violence, even if it does not stop it completely. The source of my bleak mood is that the Regional Services Council (RSC), which, along with its other responsibilities, controls the allocation of regional transport resources, has promised to consider providing funding for the new terminus but keeps putting off a decision. The development committee is despondent, and the uncertainty is sapping its unity and strength. A year's work could unravel in the face of such bureaucratic indecision. Please, will the chairperson put pressure on the RSC to address the matter urgently? I make a note to draft a letter for him the next day, while an RSC representative to the peace committee undertakes to follow this up immediately with the RSC executive director.[13]

AGENDA ITEM 5: POLICE-COMMUNITY RELATIONS. The most recent police-community relations subcommittee meeting had taken place the previous Thursday in this same conference room. The police and the former riot police, now known as the Internal Stability Division (ISD), were there in force, as were the human and civil rights NGO community and a few peace committee fieldworkers. As usual, it was a difficult meeting, spiked with anger and accusation from the NGOs and resistance and defiance from the police. Both sides always seemed to bring out the worst in each other. This particular meeting started on a different and surprising note. Advocate (lawyer) Neil Rossouw, a former attorney general and now vice chair of the Goldstone Commission, spoke to us. His willingness to criticize police behavior surprised us all.

"There is huge mistrust of the police by the community," he said. "The police learned aggression and arrogance during the apartheid era, and the community firmly believes that the police take part in the ongoing violence. It is up to the police to prove it if this is untrue, because the perception that the police take part in the violence is a cause of further violence."[14]

Rossouw continued in this vein for a full ten minutes, concluding that "the only way we can change mistrust to trust is by showing results, and by giving equal weight to violence on blacks as well as whites." He proposed that the police and community both practice introspection, that the police make every effort to resolve high-profile cases, and that we find new ideas for the new justice system.

It was a stirring speech from a man who just two years earlier, in the wake of his appointment to the Goldstone Commission, had come to the Centre for Conflict Resolution looking nonplussed. "Do you know what causes the violence?" he had asked. "Can you advise me about this new job?" he had asked the director, Professor H. W. van der Merwe. I remember sitting quietly in the meeting, silenced by his powerful Establishment presence. Now here he was, championing the need for radical change in the police force that had been ally and friend to the government that had appointed him. His investigations into the violence over the past two years appeared to have opened him to the wrongs of our land in a way that the judicial system could not, and to his enormous credit he had in many ways reinvented himself in the light of his findings.

I reminded myself about the courage it takes to go public with perceptions and attitudes that contradict the ideology of your own people, in this case the Afrikaners. Afrikanerdom is not just a language and a culture. It is a sociopolitical way of being with historical roots deeply embedded in the Afrikaner psyche, including Neil Rossouw's.

The relationship between the police and the community was only newly opened in South Africa and was probably one of the most contentious issues at that time. The subcommittee had engaged in some tough discussion about the framework for civilian detainee visits. The human rights NGOs wanted twenty-four-hour access, the police wanted some hours circumscribed for shift changes; the NGOs wanted access to all prisoners, the police wanted to restrict access to certain categories; the NGOs wanted access to every corner of the police station, the police wanted to limit it to the cells. We drafted proposals for cooperative investigations between the police and civilians and sensitivity training for the police in their dealings with the public.

Breaking down front doors during nighttime raids ranked as one of the thorniest and most long-standing problems with the ISD. Tipped off about illegal arms, drugs, or the whereabouts of a criminal, the ISD would descend on a community in the early hours of the morning, sweeping through the narrow streets with speed and precision, kicking down the doors of houses suspected of sheltering wanted men and women. The police said it was the only time that they had any chance of catching the wanted people, and the element of surprise offered them some protection from being shot at through the thin walls of shacks built from plastic sheeting, cardboard, or corrugated iron.

These raids left those householders who were mistakenly invaded angry and distraught. Tamara Ngcuka, the fieldworker for Khayelitsha township, had reported on the latest raid, saying that she had spoken to Gerrit Nieuwoudt, as police representative on the peace committee executive, about remuneration for the damage done and, indeed, had been assured that there were funds available to make good the doors. "But," she had said in her restrained way, "the damage forms are in Afrikaans and English, so the people often don't understand what they are signing. They also want to know how the police are arriving at their estimates for the damage." Her large dark eyes had swept the room, looking for answers. "People are left with broken doors in the middle of the night, which is dangerous," Malibongwe added, "and they don't have the money to repair the damage."

The regional commander of the ISD, Colonel Fanie Bouwer, was at the meeting. He nodded and agreed to try to find a solution. "We're considering taking carpenters with us so that the damaged doors can be repaired immediately," he said without irony.

Now at the RPC executive committee meetings, Vincent Diba wants to add to the police report. "I have to tell this meeting that a particular car has been coming to my house. Often. The people in it wear balaclavas and take photographs of the house. Now the police have raided another house in Bellville in the early hours of the morning, saying that they have information about arms caches and that I was allegedly hiding there.

"The police know very well that I am not involved in these kinds of activities," he continues evenly. "In my view this is just plain harassment, and it ought to stop."

Malibongwe has his own police story to tell. "The ISD keeps raiding KTC [a neighborhood in Nyanga], and the civic organizations now want to withdraw from the LPC unless the raids stop." He invites the executive to a police-community meeting in Nyanga the next morning to discuss the problem. I mark the time and venue in my diary. I will be there.

The afternoon light changes as the sun tracks down toward Table Mountain. We review training workshops for mediators, discuss media and marketing campaigns, attend to administrative matters and personnel. When we finally get up from our seats, we yawn and stretch. We have been sitting down for three-and-a-half hours, it is 6:30 P.M., and it is time to go to another meeting, or perhaps even home. We say our farewells, glad that we have dealt thoroughly with such a full agenda but keenly aware of how much work there is to do if we are to fulfill the mission of the Peace Accord and help keep enough peace for our country to hold its first democratic election six months from now.

2
PEACE WORKERS

Peace Is a Group Effort

In the face of overwhelming violence, the Peace Accord showed South Africans the way to sidestep that violence. Hundreds of South African peace workers quietly made the blueprint work on the ground. They made the transition to democracy possible, sometimes at mortal risk. Who were these peace workers? Where did they come from? Why did they come forward at this crisis in our history?

Consider the stories of six unsung heroes of the birth of democracy, the stories of peace workers Chris Spies, Sakkie Pretorius, Malibongwe Sopangisa, Val Rose Christie, Vincent Diba, and Gerrit Nieuwoudt.[1] Consider how hundreds of other peace workers like them made peace work.

SIX PEACEMAKERS

Chris Spies, White Afrikaner Clergyman

> *A white Afrikaner clergyman stepped through the looking glass of apartheid and found himself in the world of Colouredness and blackness that, in South Africa, was unknown to whites.*

In the Dutch Reformed Church, a fledgling *dominee* (Afrikaans: clergyman)[2] is not dispatched by the bishop to some distant parish to earn his stripes but is called by a congregation to come and serve them. So when at last Chris Spies finished his seventh year of theological training, he was delighted to be called immediately to the affluent Eastern Cape town of Somerset East. Set in the starkly beautiful dry-bush landscape of aloes and thorn that supports game farms and wealthy farmers, it was a plum post. Chris, newly married and eager to start a family, imagined the gifts of meat and produce that congregants tend to heap upon their pastors. He would be working with a good friend there, and he knew they would make an exceptional team. His father was excited too; all was well in the world of his son.

One hour later, that world was to change irrevocably. Chris was called again, this time by the Burgersdorp Mission Church, the Coloured church of the Dutch Reformed family. They had not had a resident pastor for six years, and there weren't any pastors at all in the local circuit. Chris phoned his father, who said, "But it's an obvious choice, isn't it?" Chris wasn't so sure. "I knew that Somerset East wouldn't struggle to get another minister if I declined their offer," says Chris. "They would get another one the next day. But the same could not be said of Burgersdorp, a small town, a poor community, no job opportunities, declining economy, lack of housing; whatever problems you can experience in rural areas were there. I accepted that one. It was the most important thing that happened in my life."

With that choice, Chris, a white Afrikaner, stepped through the looking glass of apartheid and found himself in the world of Colouredness and blackness that, in South Africa, was unknown to whites. "I realized that there was something fundamentally wrong with the way I understood South Africa, and understood myself in South Africa," he says. "My congregation was asking me questions that I had never been asked before. Before I got there, I was this well-trained bright young minister with all the answers." They asked him if he thought that it was God's will that they had been dumped in Eureka, the Coloured township, when the apartheid government had torn them from their homes so that Burgersdorp could be snow white. They asked him if it was right that they should use separate entrances and sections at the post office, the magistrate's office, and the bank. "How could I only tell them, 'Make sure you are converted and belong to God,' when they were hungry and exploited?" The church council decided to write letters to all the institutions in town that were segregated, asking politely that they remove the partitions. It was a tough mission in the political climate of 1982, when voicing any opposition to apartheid mores was considered treasonous, especially in conservative small-town communities.

The security police immediately began to harass Chris and his family, and the Burgersdorp white community shunned them. Strangely enough, the post office and the magistrate's office soon agreed to desegregate, but the bank, Volkskas (the Nation's Purse), refused. The bank said, "The majority of our clients don't want it." Chris said, "Have you asked them?" The bank responded with angry letters. At the 1986 Synod of the Dutch Reformed Mission Church in Cape Town, Chris stood up and said that this Broederbond bank (Volkskas), this bank that served the Synod delegates and marketed itself as being "on your side through thick and thin," this bank was still discriminating against people in rural areas. It was a bombshell. The story put Volkskas onto the front page of newspapers all over the country.

When Chris returned home from the Synod, the Burgersdorp white church held a special council meeting to condemn him. The Coloured Mission Church in Burgersdorp responded by inviting the white church to talk, but as one of the Broederbond members said to Chris, "You have touched the baby of the Afrikaners when you touch Volkskas. We can't forget that." White Afrikaners began intense harassment of Chris with twenty-four-hour surveillance, threatening late-night phone calls to his home, and harassment of members of his congregation. Chris knew that he could be killed "accidentally." It was a frightening and difficult time for Chris and his growing family.

In 1989, Chris called a meeting of his congregation and said, "I can't take it anymore," and the congregation stood up as one and said, "We want the security police in the church next Sunday." In the end, the police came. The security police brigadier also came up from Port Elizabeth, and when he heard the stories, he immediately removed the security policeman who had been conducting this reign of terror for five years.

Everything changed with the security police officer's departure. Suddenly the white people said, "We want to know who you are." Chris replied, "It's funny that after nine years you want to know who I am. I have been here for nine years, and we have not spoken a word to each other." Somehow, something else fell into place for Chris too. "I realized that what we needed was third-party intervention in Burgersdorp, somebody who could come in and say, 'Hey, what's happening here? Police, what's your story? Mission Church, why are you angry? White people, what sort of information do you get, and from where?' But there was nobody. We were caught in a spiral of conflict, and we couldn't find a way out. I could see how conflict prevented development initiatives to such an extent that people almost lost hope.

"I also saw how white people believed everything that was fed to them by the security police, and how they were totally thrown off balance when the security policeman left town. They started phoning me, saying, 'I want to confess, I was one of the people who told stories about you, but I now know that I was wrong.' As a family, we went into a kind of catharsis, and after a lot of prayer and meditation and reflection, I knew that the next step was to be that third party for other towns. That's when I moved over to conflict resolution."

In 1992, Chris joined the Western Cape Peace Committee as its regional coordinator. This meant working protracted hours intervening where there was violence, defusing potential or actual conflict, and supporting a growing team of fieldworkers across the region. It was the most exhausting time of his life, but it was thrilling. Chris smiles as he talks about how he experienced his acceptance into communities as a sacred thing. "To be in a position where people confide in you and really share stuff with you, that really gave me so much. I felt, I am responsible to help them get through this. And I saw the fruits of what we were doing. I can tell you lots of anecdotes about cases where there was simply no hope. People wouldn't talk to each other, as in Pofadder, where the ANC and the right-wing town council were at loggerheads,[3] and we would get them to the table and they would form an LPC or successfully take the lead and get on with it. This gave me a lot of energy."

But to be accepted, this tall, boyish thirty-seven-year-old Afrikaner had to build trust, and he found it on Christmas Eve as he stood among the (black) squatters in their camp near Grabouw watching everything go up in flames. At the next peace committee meeting, they recognized him as the person who had been there until late into the night when they had a fire. And he found it when the PAC marched after the St. James Church massacre, when black men had opened fire on a mostly white congregation and it was thought the attackers were members of the PAC.[4] The PAC were not signatories to the Peace Accord, so when Chris went up to their leaders, "these guys you saw only on television," and said, "I am from the peace committee, can I help?" They said, "No, not really, but you can join the march." Then Chris noticed that the chief marshal didn't have a megaphone, so Chris lent him his own. Chris used his walkie-talkie to communicate between the leaders at the front and the back of the procession and carried messages to and fro, and afterward, the PAC leaders said, "It was excellent that you were here; thank you very much for coming." He had let them know that they could feel safe when the peace committee was around.

"Besides building trust," Chris says, "the most important thing was that I wanted people to feel safe when I was present. I wanted to create a safe space where people could really sit down and talk about their problems."

The peace committee worked hard to defuse violence. Chris tells the story of going high into the mountains of the Western Cape one blazing hot day after ANC leader Chris Hani was murdered and the black community had erupted in violent protest all over the country.[5] There were two or three thousand Coloured people blocking the road to the tiny town of Prince Alfred Hamlet, throwing stones at any car or white person passing by. "I knew there was little chance of stabilizing the situation. It had to play itself out. You can talk to the leaders, but there is a point where the leaders lose control. They take the initiative to organize the event, but then you get an element of people who take over the energy, and long after the leaders have left for home, the youngsters and those who have nothing to do continue with that." Chris parked his car (not a peace committee vehicle, but his own) in a hail of stones and got out. "I said, 'If you want to throw, throw, but I am not going to leave,'" and he walked up to them, and they swore at him and threatened him, and he cracked jokes. "Hey," he said, "you throw pretty accurately." And they shouted back, *"Koes, jou boer! Koes!"* (Duck, farmer! Duck!) as they threw stones past his head to the cars on the other side of the road.

Afterward, when they were finally able to talk things over, this exchange was the source of keen amusement in the community. "That's when I learned that the anger that people show is sometimes only skin deep, and that it is difficult to ascertain whether it is the real anger of injustice or a nice event." That same evening he faced real anger in another hail of stones at the Coloured township of Touwsrivier. It was dark, so he couldn't identify himself; there were no phones, so he couldn't tell them he was coming. He knew he could be killed; he could hear the whir of the stones as they flew past his head.

But, he says, the peace committee work was fine; it was Burgersdorp that was the nightmare. At least the peace committee was able to get results. "We were able to get high-level politicians to listen to grassroots communities. To see a housewife meet with a government minister and talk about the problems in her particular community, I think that was a major success." Chris thinks for a moment. "The peace structures also succeeded in changing perceptions. I don't have words to describe the sort of change in paradigm that we were able to effect." He is thinking about the transformational stories from places like Nyanga, Pofadder, and Plettenberg Bay that you will encounter throughout this book.

Chris distilled some key lessons from his work on the peace committee:

- The overwhelming majority of people get fed up with violence and fighting and conflict. It takes only one or two angry people in a community to cause major conflict.

- Third-party intervention is crucial, but it must be structured. People locked into a fighting mood don't come out of it of their own free will and say, "Let's look for a solution."

- Good process is vital to ensure a good outcome. There are no quick fixes, and peacebuilding is a long and tedious business. There is no shortcut to the heart of the community.

- Never entrust politicians with the peace process. It was absolutely crazy how red tape and party political interests hampered the peace process.

In 1995, Chris joined the Centre for Conflict Resolution, where he helped rural communities resolve the inevitable conflict that comes with development. At this writing, he has established his own consultancy for third-party intervention.

Sakkie Pretorius, White Afrikaner National Party M.P.

> *He learned from his grandfather that politics had made him who he was, and when he was still young he also understood that politics was his destiny.*

Sakkie's forefathers settled in the Cape in 1669. It is a long heritage that in many ways defines who Sakkie Pretorius is. Sakkie still has the bandolier that belonged to his grandfather, who, as a British subject, was found guilty of high treason for fighting on the side of the Boers in the Anglo-Boer war. Sakkie's grandfather felt very strongly about the cause of the Afrikaners, but when he was dying, he said, "You know, you can be faithful to your own people, but you must try and be fair to other people as well." Sakkie, named after his grandfather, sees his grandfather as a patriot, and it was his influence that shaped Sakkie's politics and values. "After [defeat in the Boer War], the Afrikaner people were really down and out and had to fight for their survival and empower themselves. I think, in a sense, that history has never been written, about the empowerment and the influence [the war] had on Afrikaners, which in the end led to the policy of apartheid or separate development, which in the end caused unhappiness and misery to African and Coloured people.

"I would describe myself as a typical Afrikaans-speaking South African," he says. He grew up in the dust and shimmering heat of small towns in the Eastern Cape, as his father, a policeman, was posted from Elliot to Indwe to Bathurst to Lady Frere to Queenstown to Dordrecht. They often lived in the outposts of the district, where he learned the Xhosa language of the African children he played with. This is how it was, and probably to some degree still is, in rural South Africa. The children, African, Coloured, and white, played together until the white child went away to school. Then it all changed. The white children returned home with the ways of the outside world. They turned away from the joyful welcome of their former black friends, who, confused, dismayed, and humiliated, turned within and started to use the language of apartheid, to call their former friends *Baas* (Boss) and *Madam*. Apartheid was carved deep into the souls of children, black and white, and recycled through the generations with little change.

Through his grandfather, Sakkie understood that politics had made him who he was. When he was still young, he understood that politics was his destiny. He started when he was twenty-two, choosing the party that housed the collective spirit of the Afrikaner, the Nationalist Party (it changed its name to the National Party in the 1990s), first as an organizer, then as an administrator, a provincial representative, and finally, in 1989, a member of Parliament.

"I don't want to try and defend apartheid, but I think what we had in mind was that we thought we could make people free, give them freedom, but in the end it didn't work out that way," says Sakkie.

Sakkie's constituency was Tygervallei, a conservative, white, blue-collar neighborhood that basks under the distant gaze of Table Mountain. He had been their member of Parliament for barely five months when President de Klerk transfixed the nation with his speech on February 2, 1990, that unbanned the ANC and declared the start of a reform process toward democracy. "I regarded myself as a free-thinking man, as liberal-minded," Sakkie says thoughtfully, "and that is why the acceptance of Mr. de Klerk's speech wasn't for me personally such a great obstacle to overcome." But he knew that he would have a lot of convincing to do in his constituency. Within two weeks he held his first house meeting to discuss the implications of the speech. "I never made excuses for why Mr. de Klerk gave his speech," Sakkie says. "I said I believed it was the right thing to do; we've got no other choice."

Immediately, someone raised the question of the Group Areas Act, a key pillar of apartheid legislation separating blacks and whites where they lived, worked, and played. "Then the secretary of the branch said, 'Sakkie, before you answer that question about the Group Areas Act, I want to tell you that is one of the first acts that will go.' Then I realized that Mr. de Klerk's political judgment was 100 percent [sound]." A gasp rippled though the meeting, and someone said, "I wonder if that will happen?" And Sakkie said, "Well, I think it will happen, it will have to happen." And they accepted it, Sakkie says, and found that they were more adaptable than they thought.

Later, in July, he had a meeting in the hard right-wing suburb of Ruiterwacht. A colleague of his bumped into one of his constituents, who said, "We're going to give Sakkie Pretorius hell tonight." His wife wished him good luck as he went out the door. When he got to the meeting, Sakkie said, "Before we start, I want to tell you three things. Number one, the next state president will definitely not be white. Secondly, the next cabinet will have only a few white faces in it. And number three, the Group Areas Act [because that was very sensitive in that area] will be scrapped." He got home very late that night. Sakkie says, "In the end they said, 'All right, it is tough, but at least you are honest with us; we will think about it.' In the end I won them over. I kept their support."

These were difficult times for National Party politicians. Their constituents were understandably nervous. Their world was coming to an end, and they didn't know what would replace it. He remembered the headmaster of his school saying way back that a white skin was no longer a guarantee of survival. "He said, 'Well, we must find another way of dealing with racial problems of South Africa,'" Sakkie recalls, "I feel that somewhere we must find a peaceful way of talking to each other."

Sakkie's wish came true with the formation of the Peace Accord and his own appointment to the Western Cape Peace Committee as National Party representative. At first, he was not interested, but in September 1992, he found himself plunged into a conflict that proved to be a turning point in his personal life and his political outlook.

The conflict was about a school building. The formerly white Tafelberg School had been lying idle and empty for two years in the heart of the Cape Town suburb of Mowbray, and the pupils from the overcrowded, underresourced Thandakulu School in the African township of Khayelitsha wanted to take it over. Three times during August, black schoolchildren occupied the grounds. They needed this school.

Finally, one Friday afternoon at the end of August, over one thousand pupils and teachers gathered at Tafelberg for a massive protest while a delegation went to meet with the Cape Provincial Administration to plead their case. Then at about five in the afternoon, a message came through to the organizers that the minister had turned down the request for the school. They decided not to tell the pupils about the minister's decision until school on Monday. They feared their reaction.

The police heard the news too, and a squad of about ten formed a half circle in front of the two police vans. Now the crowd packed around the police, toyi-toyiing and singing, so close that they could have touched them. A group, including two teachers, waved sticks just inches in front of the police officers. Lu Harding, a Black Sash monitor, was amazed at police restraint in the face of this provocative and frightening behavior. Then, suddenly, it all stopped; the crowd responded to an order to move back, leaving a space in front of the police. The tension had broken.

The following Monday, Lu reported the events of the day to the peace committee. She wrote, "I am sure the anger will be enormous and I do not feel the school community will be prepared to accept the decision. . . . I feel extremely uneasy about the situation . . . in the light of probable further struggles to achieve permanent occupation of Tafelberg School. I think it is essential for the prevention of a serious incident that there should be far greater crowd control exercised at any future demonstrations at the school."[6]

The peace committee immediately met, and Sakkie quickly became a key player in the unfolding negotiations. He represented the government party on the peace committee, and he would provide access to the various education departments. Sakkie took the conflict straight to the ministerial level, and six days of mediation, lobbying, and intense negotiation later, the minister of education announced that Tafelberg School had been allocated to Thandakulu School.[7]

Sakkie says that the reason this was such a highlight for him was that it brought him into contact with the residents of Khayelitsha. He had long discussions with the headmaster of the school and with other residents. "I listened to the plight of the people," says Sakkie. He heard about lack of sewage, street lighting, and housing; people without jobs; people who, as he put it, needed protection. That changed him deeply. He was also deeply touched that although he was a member of the apartheid government, the people he met were never antagonistic or rude. He felt that they learned about one another and built "a strong sort of trust."

"That made me more confident to participate in the peace process," he says. "It also gave me more confidence whenever I spoke to my own constituents, to say, 'Do you realize how the areas look, what conditions these people are living in?' I brought this message to my traditional supporters." Sakkie was amazed at the reaction to the schools issue among dyed-in-the-wool conservatives. "They said, 'By Jove, man, give the school to the people, let them use it instead of it standing there with the wind and rain blowing over it and nobody using it.' There were other people who weren't happy, but when I talked to them, they said, 'Well, that's fair and reasonable.'"

Through the peace committee, Sakkie became convinced that it was possible to find peaceful ways of dealing with our problems. "A great amount of trust was built up amongst the members. With trust you can really speak to a man," he says. "You can say, 'Look man, we have got this problem, let's look at it and see how we can solve it,' instead of, as earlier, playing party politics. I know it is funny for a politician to say don't play politics, but personally I believe that if we could play less politics, it would be easier to solve problems.

"On the peace committee, we all tried to forget about politics for a while and concentrate on being proactive instead of waiting for a crisis and then trying to solve it." Sakkie thinks that the biggest asset of the peace committee was that it was able to act preemptively to defuse potentially violent situations. He says, "If a thing has exploded, to solve it is very difficult."

Sakkie learned that to be effective he had to learn to listen. "You couldn't just walk into a place, whether it was a township like Khayelitsha or a white Afrikaans area like Welgemoed, and think if you made a statement, they would accept it. So there was definitely a new style that was in a sense born there, and it grew like a little plant, it grew every day whenever we met each other, and you felt that maybe your approach yesterday wasn't the right one, maybe you must talk less and sometimes listen more. That was part of my style in many instances, I listened. And it was as if for the first time the residents of Khayelitsha and Langa and Guguletu and Crossroads felt that somebody was listening to them. I mean, that is very important in life.

"Sometimes I would just decide I was going to listen instead of keeping on arguing with people. I found that if you keep on trying to score a point every time the man asks you a question, and you try and impress him with a lot of figures and statistics, in the end he feels like a loser."

The peace structures provided Sakkie and thousands of others with their first opportunity to speak with other racial groups as equals. It didn't matter that he was a member of Parliament, he says, and that Mr. X was a resident of Khayelitsha. They had the same freedom to speak, and their problems carried the same weight. Sakkie says people really felt committed to finding a way around the problem and solving it. "Everyone was becoming tired of confrontation. They were all hoping we could rather find a settlement instead of having violence."

Sakkie says politics is changing. "People think you should consult them more. They say to us [politicians], 'But look, you voted for this and that bill, but we should have more consultation before decisions are made.' I think that we [politicians] must change our views to accommodate them."

Sakkie was reelected to the National Assembly in 1994 and 1999 representing the National Party.

Malibongwe Sopangisa, Black Fieldworker, Nyanga/Crossroads LPC

The peace process meant personal transformation from activist to bridge-builder.

Before Malibongwe Sopangisa was a peacemaker, he was an ANC and community activist. In 1976, many of his school friends were leaving South Africa to join Umkhonto we Sizwe (MK), the armed wing of the ANC, in the wake of massive black student protest against the system. Malibongwe left school to get a job because his family needed the money. It was during his standard nine (grade seven) year, and he never did complete his schooling. Instead, he found himself thrust into his first experience of negotiations when he was elected shop steward at the engineering factory where he worked for the next seven years. When he was retrenched (downsized), another chapter in his life opened up. He switched to community work, teaching literacy in the black community for another seven years.

Meanwhile, his involvement in the regional civic association and in his community was growing, so when the ANC was unbanned in 1990, he threw himself into that too, mobilizing people to join. It was hard work; people were still afraid of open membership; the organization had been banned for thirty years. His commitment paid off, and in 1993 he was elected chairperson of the Nyanga branch of the ANC. He was thirty years old.

❊   ❊   ❊

At the end of his curriculum vitae, right after "interests/hobbies: music, sport, and reading," Malibongwe writes that his goal is to empower people in solving their own problems. "Our people were not given the opportunity to solve things on their own," he says. "Most of the time, our people were told, if you want to do this, you must do it like that. People need to be trained; they are not sure enough of themselves to sort out their own problems." He says that when there is conflict in the community, what often happens is that the parties don't listen to one another, and issues escalate into violence and people getting killed. "I have learned that if the community leaders can be trained in how to facilitate discussions and how to mediate when there is a conflict, it could save us a lot of work."

He had been unemployed for two years, so when the peace committee advertised the job of fieldworker for the new LPC in Nyanga, Malibongwe applied and was appointed. He had known about the Peace Accord since its establishment in September 1991. "There was no one organization that would take responsibility for being the cause of the violence, which is why they all came together and said, okay, let's all sign this Peace Accord and try and make sure there is peace in South Africa." As a local ANC leader, he had tried to take part since the beginning, but, he says, it was difficult to promote peace because of the violence. "It is difficult to talk about peace when people are dying," he says. When the peace committee approached the Nyanga ANC branch, the Nyanga civic association, and other local structures to discuss the idea of forming a Nyanga-Crossroads LPC, it seemed like a good idea. The violence was escalating and the communities were at their wits' end as to how to deal with it.

The LPC office became the legitimate conduit into the community. "Whoever wanted to meet with community organizations went through us," Malibongwe explains. "For instance, the police first came to us and asked us to organize a meeting for them. We went to the communities and said, 'We know there is tension between ourselves and the police, but because of this process of maintaining peace, it is important for us to listen to what the police want to say to us so that we can also raise our concerns against them. If we are not going to listen to the police, then these things we are complaining about are going to continue.' We were used as a bridge by the police to the community. And," Malibongwe adds, "if the community wanted to get to the police, they went through us too. The police were forced to listen to us because they [the police] were part and parcel of the peace structure."

The LPC built the confidence of the communities as they went about the long, slow business of finding their voice and building some semblance of trust with the authorities, particularly the police. Malibongwe evolved from being an activist for the ANC and the community to being a peacemaker and bridge builder. "We were in a process of trying to win the hearts and minds of the communities to understand the behavior of the police, who were trained the way they were trained," he says, "and also to win the hearts of the police." Mistrust lay like dust over every encounter. There were times of cooperation, but it wasn't easy. Members of the community would come to the LPC and say, "The police have kicked our doors down, what are you doing about it?" And the police would come to the LPC and say, "People are throwing stones at us, what are you doing about it?" "As the LPC, we were not there to take sides," Malibongwe says. "If the communities were doing something wrong, we would tell them, 'No, this is not following the trend of peace in our area,' and we would do the same with the police." Malibongwe says that the skills he learned during this process helped him to deal with his own anger. "If you are dealing with these things, you mustn't be a person who angers quickly, you must know how to approach things." He took responsibility for demonstrating calm because, he says, if he expressed his anger, others would be free to express theirs, and another cycle of anger and violence would be set in motion.

There were criminal elements within the community who were dead set against peace of any sort. They thrived on the lawlessness of violence, and word spread that guns had been organized to assassinate Malibongwe. He began to wear a bulletproof vest. He was philosophical about it. "I know that one of these days I am going to die, and I know that what I am doing,

I am doing for the benefit of our people," he says. His calm belied the courage it takes to walk through unlit streets knowing that assassins could be lurking in every shadow. When the people of Crossroads called, saying, "We know you, Malibongwe, can you assist us here," he would take other people with him. "That way no one could just pull out a gun and shoot me because they didn't like what I was doing," he says, smiling wryly.

He learned that his safety also depended on his relationship with the community leaders. "If you don't keep the respect of the community leaders, it is easy for you to be threatened," he says. He also learned that to gain their respect, he had to give respect first. "Meet with the leaders first before you go to their constituency. Go through them so they can introduce you. Then you can tell the leaders the kind of work you are doing, and then you will be accepted," he advises.

There were two main threads to the violence: factional warfare in Crossroads and the minibus taxis. The minibus taxi violence had spilled over throughout the country. In Nyanga and Crossroads, rival taxi operators fought it out in the streets and alleyways daily, attacking their common rival, the buses, for good measure. The minibus taxi business is big business, and everyone wanted a big share. The conflict seeped into the very fabric of Nyanga society.

At the same time, Malibongwe was trying to cope with the violence in Crossroads. In the first half of 1993, the conflict escalated, the parties consistently refused to meet, and the death toll climbed relentlessly. Malibongwe soldiered on, but it was a losing battle. "I didn't know what to do in Crossroads when no one wanted to listen to me," he says quietly. In June, he asked the regional peace committee to convene a meeting for everyone involved in the crisis, including the warlords, the five factions in Crossroads, the police, the politicians, the provincial authority, and the independent monitors. After that, and the subsequent hearings on Crossroads by the Goldstone Commission, and the production of a video on Crossroads, the violence dropped dramatically, even though the conflict was not resolved.

Malibongwe says that he is a facilitator. "We are just there to see that the discussion is going in the right direction." His biggest challenge is to get the people involved in conflict and violence to come together to find a way out of it. Sometimes, it is just a matter of appealing to their common sense. Malibongwe recognized that it was essential to establish a working relationship with the PAC members in Nyanga. They said, "We didn't sign the Peace Accord, so we are not part of this LPC." Malibongwe responded, "'Yes, we know that, but if there is violence in this area, then your members are also going to be affected, so can we come together, even if you haven't signed, so that we can make sure there is peace in our area?' It was difficult, but not very difficult," he says. "People listened because what we were saying was true."

Malibongwe lives and works in Nyanga township, where his job is peacemaking. While the Peace Accord structures were in place, he was the fieldworker and manager of the Nyanga-Crossroads Local Peace Committee. Then, when the newly elected government closed down the Peace Accord at the end of 1994, the empty LPC office was reborn as Eluxolweni (the Place of Peace), and it has now merged with the Urban Monitoring Awareness Committee.

At this writing, Malibongwe continues his peace work through UMAC-Eluxolweni. He is the chairperson of the Nyanga Policing Forum, which brings together the police and the community to work on policing issues, with a particular emphasis on dealing with crime. His philosophy is, "Whoever serves our people, no matter if he or she is black or white, these are our people."

Val Rose Christie, White Black Sash Monitor

> *She cried all the way home from Bonteheuwel, not because she had been stoned, but because she had been called a liberal.*

Right through the 1980s, Val Rose Christie worked in Cape Town's townships, and the only time she ever felt threatened was one day in 1986 when she went to Bonteheuwel High School, a Coloured school out on the Cape Flats, during a sustained schools boycott. "There had been problems," she remembers. "The police were beating up the students with batons. In some incidents, rubber bullets and birdshot were also used. On this particular day, I had been speaking to the principal, teachers, and students about the problem, and as I was coming out of the school, some youngsters stoned me. They swore at me and shouted, 'Get out of here, you f——ing pink liberal.' I cried all the way down the N2 [motorway into the city], not because I had been stoned, but because I had been called a 'liberal' and I had never considered myself a 'liberal,' and I think that hurt more than the damned stones!" To the Coloured youngsters, a liberal is a rich, comfortable white person who plays at race politics. To Val, this casual epithet devastatingly questioned her commitment to justice and peace.

After 1990, conditions worsened, and there were times, Val says, when they got together at Black Sash and said, No, we're not going into the townships. In August 1993, the township of Guguletu was considered off-limits to whites because a critical mass of predominantly PAC youth were in the throes of Operation Barcelona, their violent protest against the education system. Val and her Black Sash colleague Anne Greenwell were trying to help with the crisis and were liaising closely with Maureen Hamse, who lived in Crossroads. They could visit her, avoiding Guguletu, but August 24, when they arrived at her small house, they found her distraught. Her husband had been murdered. "She wanted to go to his family in Guguletu," says Val, as though it were yesterday. "Anne looked at me and I looked at Anne. How could we refuse the woman? So we went right down NY1 [road] in Guguletu, just where the very next day Amy Biehl was murdered."

Val does not say that it could so easily have been her and Anne, but I remember that we white women who were working in the townships felt somehow that we had escaped, or been spared, and even though many of us did not know Amy, we relived over and over again how she died. It was as though she had died for all of us, that because of her dying, we would go on living. We mourned her as though she had been a close friend.

Val's journey through the townships started at the end of the 1970s, when, by helping out a friend who was running a welfare project in Nyanga, she got to know the area and a lot of people living there. She had already made her mark as a staunch activist for Black Sash and for the Progressive Federal Party (PFP), which, much later, joined the coalition that became the Democratic Party. Then, as the 1980s unfolded, and the struggle against apartheid intensified, the government of the day responded with massive force. "The streets of the townships were absolute war zones," Val recalls. "Children were beaten, elderly people and babies were teargassed, even in their homes." Calls for help came in to the PFP. In response, the PFP formed the Urban Monitoring Awareness Committee (UMAC) and, knowing that Val had worked in the townships, asked her to coordinate it.

Oppression, resistance, more oppression; the state was throwing its might at the people who opposed it. Val's job was to take the calls and send someone, usually a PFP provincial councilor. Later, as the PFP gained seats, Val would send a member of Parliament to the scene, which was inevitably a confrontation between the police and some sector of the black community. But when the Provincial Council was in session, her team was unavailable, so she started to go out herself and do what she could.

She tried to mediate police and community confrontations. She observed what was happening and recorded it; she took statements from victims of police assault and torture and gathered eyewitness accounts of events she missed. She channeled statements through Parliament to the minister of law and order. "As a political party, there was a way in those bad old days that we could play a good role," she says. She was arrested, thrown into vans, and fingerprinted three times. She always demanded the right to make a phone call from the police station. Once, she phoned the then-leader of the PFP, Van Zyl Slabbert, in Parliament, and he raised her arrest on the floor of the House. Within a short time, the minister ordered her release.

Soon Val was monitoring confrontations full-time, alone or with one of the PFP luminaries whom she credits with teaching her much of how to do it. *Grand dames* of the PFP demonstrated how to deal with a patriarchal and chauvinistic police force that tended to discount women. They would have none of it. "They gave me the strength to stand up to the police," Val says.

She learned about balance, "not to go overboard and see only one side." She found that the police were more cooperative when you spoke to them. Val says the youth in particular used funerals to express their pent-up rage, and they aggravated the police. That's when she got to know, by their behavior in the face of intense provocation, that there were also some good, professional policemen. "You could work with them and reason with them," she says. "You could appeal to their better judgment."

"We worked seven days a week," she recalls. "Nearly every weekend there were political funerals, because they were killing people, and we would go to ensure as best we could that the police kept within bounds. It was a confrontational time. You had to confront those police head on; there were some nasty bits of work out there, and you had to be strong."

※   ※   ※

Training workshops in conflict resolution and mediation helped with handling the police. Increasingly, policing became her focus, and she was roundly criticized for it, particularly by the United Democratic Front, an umbrella organization formed in 1983 as a stand-in for the ANC. From the standpoint

of the United Democratic Front, the only acceptable approach to the police through the 1980s was hostility. Val understood. "We had some really
bad policemen out there. The diabolical things we saw, the sacking of Crossroads and KTC, will live with me forever." But she also knew the value of
what she was doing, and despite the criticism, she kept going.

"I put myself in quite a difficult position," she says. "Members of the
community would say the police must get out of the townships, and I would
say you can't say we don't want a police force, because that isn't realistic.
Every country in the world needs policemen. What we've got to have is
decent, caring, professional policemen."

Val's courage, and her commitment to doing what she thought was right,
had deep roots. "I remember as a young child having great arguments with
my parents, whom I considered racist," she says. "Those were the years
when African people were often called *Kaffirs* [a derogatory word like *niggers*
in the United States]. Then, when I started to work in the townships and
saw the terrible, abject poverty and the conditions of repression that they
were living under, it got to me. It still gets to me."

In 1990, Val left UMAC and began to work with Black Sash as a volun-
teer monitor. It was a pivotal year for antiapartheid activists. The commitment of de Klerk and Mandela to negotiate a common future threw a curve
ball into the familiar battle between the state and its adversaries, changing
the rules overnight. For decades, opponents of apartheid had fought against
what they did not want. They knew how to do it and what to expect. Now
they could build what they did want, and for many it was an extraordinarily
difficult challenge. They did not have the tools. They did not know how to
bridge the gap between the past and the future. They did not know where
to begin.

None of us did. Within two years, the Peace Accord would provide the
needed framework, but at the start, individuals had to find their own way.
And despite Val's prior willingness to find the individual good cops and
work with them, the switch to working alongside the security forces as a
whole was "quite a change," Val says, smiling at her own understatement.
"But when the ANC was unbanned, and other organizations were unbanned,
and Mandela was released, immediately there was a different feel to things."

At first the change was gradual, but the violence that erupted in the
middle of 1990 and deepened into 1991 quickened the pace. The Joint
Forum on Policing was established at the end of 1991, primarily to monitor

police conduct as laid out in the Peace Accord. Black Sash and Val took an active role. This represented a major shift, because now, in addition to protesting police misbehavior, which she had been doing for most of the 1980s, with some individual relationship building thrown in, Val worked with the police. It was a delicate merging of the old activist ways and the new culture of conflict resolution. The Joint Forum gathered evidence of police misconduct for presentation to a special Police Complaints Investigation Unit. At the same time, its members worked closely with that unit to facilitate these same investigations. The irony was not lost on any of us.

At the beginning of 1992, Val was appointed Black Sash representative to the peace committee. Later she would say that through the Peace Accord structures and the Network of Independent Monitors (NIM)[8] she had had to learn a different way of working that involved reaching out to the enemy. She would also say that it was not easy.

※   ※   ※

Val was appointed to the NIM executive in the Western Cape. As the date for the 1994 election approached, a plethora of meetings, demonstrations, rallies, crises, and protests blurred into one another. The peace workers were barely able to keep up. Val was in the NIM office one morning in early 1994 when word came through on the radio pagers that the police were raiding the ANC regional headquarters in Woodstock, the neighboring suburb. The news took their breath away; within three months it was a sure bet that the ANC would be in the government.

Val and a number of other monitors arrived in Woodstock in three minutes. "We certainly put our conflict resolution skills to the test that day," Val says. "The police said that they were looking for a murderer and they had heard that he was seeking refuge in the ANC offices. They kicked the staff out of the building while they raided it. People were very angry, and a large crowd was collecting in the street. It could have turned nasty, as some staff members were armed.

"We tried to hold the staff back. We said it won't do you any good to get involved in there. Stay out of it, and it will only serve to make you look better in the eyes of your constituents." We linked hands to keep them out of the building.

"It was very tricky," says Val, referring to her unabashed sympathies with the ANC, as they expressed their outrage at this intrusion by the police.

"But something that we had learned from the Peace Accord structures was impartiality. There was no way we could be seen to be taking sides. Whatever we felt, we couldn't reflect it. And certainly as an NIM monitor that was very important. We were, after all, independent monitors by name, and that we had to be."

As with most of us, Val's role as an impartial peacemaker collided at least once with her personal sympathies for the oppressed. Toward the end of 1993, she slipped into a deep depression after a colonel from police intelligence interrogated her about bail that she had paid for three young men from Nyanga who had been arrested and charged with murder. It was her personal money and, in Val's view, a trumped-up charge. "I was trying to work with the police, trying to assist them in all kinds of ways, even battling to try and get a Community Policing Forum going in Crossroads," Val says. She felt abused by the police, and betrayed. It was a low point in her life as a peace worker, but, she says, we had a job to do, so she just kept on going.

Much later, after the election, Val felt vindicated when the Cape Town evening newspaper, *The Argus*, named her "Peacemaker of the Week." Archbishop Desmond Tutu presented the award, a medal. The award and Desmond Tutu made up for a lot.

At this writing, Val has retired but still receives calls for help. "Sad to say," she writes, "with this heart complaint I've developed, my activities are very limited. I do, however, try to keep abreast of what is going on, either by contact with my friends who are still doing regular work in the wider community or by going in (to the townships) occasionally to see all my old contacts and friends."[9] She serves on the board of directors of UMAC.

Vincent Diba, Former Robben Island Prisoner and ANC Regional Executive Member

> **When released from prison, he understood that in order to achieve a permanent peace, there should be no feeling of revenge. "We should forgive, but not forget."**

Vincent Diba says he is not bitter about the eight years he spent imprisoned on Robben Island; he does not regret them. "I knew," he says, "that

we could come through to what we have achieved today." He says he learned
a lot in prison. Apart from using his time to complete a B.A. degree in
industrial relations and political science, he attended the daily political
classes organized by the ANC prison leadership to keep all the ANC prisoners informed of the general trends in the country. He also rubbed shoulders with men of the caliber of Govan Mbeki, Harry Gwala (both of whom
have since died), and members of the present ANC National Executive.
"We younger men were hotheaded," he says, grinning, "and they played a
very important role in shaping our political outlook. When I went to prison,
I was bitter, and I wanted revenge. We had been involved in underground
political activities, politicizing people, but I was framed unfairly for something that I didn't do. I was never at the scene of the crime. That's what
made me bitter. But through these people, I began to change, to shed that
bitterness.

"We felt that we were fighting for the freedom of our people in South
Africa. We realized that if we wanted permanent peace, there should be no
feeling of revenge; we should forgive, but not forget. If we didn't forgive,"
he continues, "we would live in perpetual violence that would ravage the
country, like Mozambique, like Angola, and our people would live in poverty and hunger."

Vincent was a student at Fort Hare, a black university in the Eastern
Cape, when he was detained on charges of terrorism and murder and sentenced to fifteen years in prison. It was 1980, and he was twenty-one years
old. His political outlook was quite clear: he was an ANC supporter, even
though three years earlier, while he was still at Langa High School, he had
joined the Black People's Convention (BPC), an organization founded by
Steven Biko. "I wanted to contribute to the process of change," he says. At
the end of 1977, when the BPC was banned, he worked underground, dis-
tributing pamphlets. At Fort Hare, he registered for a B.A. with the inten-
tion of becoming a teacher. He was arrested, detained, and in 1983, ferried
across the seven miles of icy water that so effectively isolates Robben Island. Eight years later, on April 27, 1991, he boarded the ferry for the
second time and chugged back to a South Africa that was busy negotiating
its way out of the past that he had fought against and into a future that he
was determined to help build.

He went to the Cape Town township of Nyanga, his birthplace, and found
a community devastated by the full-blown crisis in neighboring Crossroads

and staggering under the violent onslaught of the minibus taxi war. He began working within these conflicts, trying to navigate their complexity and broker solutions. Later that year, he was elected to the Regional Executive of the ANC and appointed to head the newly established Peace Desk.

When the regional peace committee was formed, he joined as an ANC representative. A couple of months later, twenty members of the executive (including the author) went to the neighboring town of Stellenbosch for a two-day workshop on conflict resolution. It was a breakthrough in human relations. "We socialized together," Vincent remembers, "and started to question each other: Who are you? What do you stand for? What is your perception of the things that have happened? At the end of the workshop, the Defense Force representative said, 'We thought you [the ANC] were animals, now I realize that you are real human beings, just like myself.' That was the indoctrination that was taking place in the police colleges, in the army, that we were animals. In fact," he continues, "we were enemies, but this whole concept of each other as enemies had to be done away with to bring a new sense of understanding between us."

Vincent says the workshop, and others like it, played the very important role of bonding together these former enemies into a team that could, together, respond to crises. "In a very short time, the police, political parties, community organizations, and ourselves managed to come together on the peace committee and realize the necessity to work together to bring about peace. But," he adds, "there were problems with the police." He tells the story of the time he and an ANC comrade responded to a call to intervene in KTC (a neighborhood of Nyanga), where the people were marching in protest at the torching of some of their shacks, allegedly by the police. The police at the scene weren't wearing nametags, which was one of the requirements of the Peace Accord. "When reports of this got to the press, the police denied their accuracy. Fortunately, we had taken photographs of the policemen with no nametags on, and the *Cape Times* published them. Then the police changed their story. They said, when it is hot, the nametags melt!" Vincent chuckles at the memory. "What I am trying to say," he continues, "is that there were those people among the police who were not committed to the peace process, who were not interested in a change to democracy."

Vincent understood their fears. He says that in addition to the fear of losing their jobs and ranks under an ANC government, the police who had been involved in illicit activities to undermine or eliminate political opponents feared retribution. Vincent was a target and, he says, has survived seven assassination attempts. His home was under surveillance and continuously photographed. One Thursday at the beginning of 1992, balaclava-clad figures came looking for him. He wasn't home. "They called out that I should be the one who opened the door. Fortunately, nobody opened the door, but my family looked through the lace curtains and saw that they were armed. That is when I began to live a very unstable life, moving from place to place." Then one dark night in the winter of 1993, the police raided one of those places. Vincent is still outraged as he describes what happened. "They woke up the household, including old people, and searched the house, looking for an arms cache. The police knew that I had never undergone military training. There was not even a single incident where I was involved in a military operation. They knew that; they had a very, very effective intelligence system. It was so stupid. I sensed that it was caused by some elements within the police who wanted to stall the whole process of bringing about peace. I told the ANC, and they said, 'You've been coming to us saying we should negotiate with the police, and they are doing this to you! Maybe we should withdraw support for the whole Peace Accord.'"

But Vincent realized that South Africa needed a transformed police force. He had a lot of meetings with the police, and they began to identify "good cops." "At those meetings, some of the police would say, 'We don't agree with the brigadier but we can't say so because we will be persecuted. Please organize more of these kinds of meetings. They shed light on us. They are changing us.' That is how I gradually began to understand that there were some good police, but they were suppressed. I realized that we had to change the culture of the police."

In 1991, the Joint Forum on Policing was formed, and Vincent and some other ANC members took an active part. "We were more than anything else a pressure group on the police to have them change," Vincent explains, "to change their perceptions, to change the way they were doing their work. It was our task as the Joint Forum to try and bring about good working relations between the police and the community so that they could work together to bring about peace. I think we managed to do that in some areas." Vincent thinks that the monitoring work of the Joint Forum also had notable impact. "The police would say one thing, the community another." The monitors provided an independent view, although this was not always accepted by the police, who viewed many of the monitors as biased.

In 1992, Vincent was included in a mixed ANC-police-NGO group invited to Denmark to attend a training course on community policing. "We came back and tried to introduce these ideas, but they were shot down by the top brass of the regional police structure" (although later that year community policing was adopted as the new national strategy). Vincent saw his task as trying to infuse the culture of community policing into the police. He discovered that changing the institutions of the police is a long process.

But there were some personal triumphs. There was trouble with a white station commander in one area. "He was very, very negative," Vincent says. He could see it the first time he met the man. Soon the community was up in arms, marching and demonstrating against him. "I thought, 'Well, maybe this chap doesn't understand, because of the culture of apartheid. We should give him a chance.'" Vincent visited him. "We clashed, we looked at each other, we talked, we had good, constructive discussions, and I can tell you he changed completely. It wasn't politics that I ever discussed with him, but he came to see what community policing really was."

Working on changing the police has changed Vincent's perceptions radically. Now he feels that he really understands the police. He says he has learned four things in particular:

- He used to think that all the police were the same, but he discovered there are those who want to change and those who do not.

- He learned the importance of negotiations, of sitting down when people have problems. "Sitting down is the most important thing I have learned."

- People should understand one another and the factors that drive each person. By exchanging views you learn, even from the negative aspects of the other side.

- In order to understand your future, you must understand your past and present, because the future is the product of the past and present.

In 1994, Vincent was elected to the Western Cape Provincial Legislature and appointed shadow minister of safety and security for the region. He says he realizes that violence can never be the responsibility of the police alone; they need the cooperation of the community. At the same time, they need to be accountable to the community. "The communities have never before had negotiations with the police, and the opportunity to understand the real work of the police and the real role that they can play in partnership with the police in order for us to have stability." He says there are still problems within the police service, and racism, and sexism, but he is very hopeful about its future.

Gerrit Nieuwoudt, White Afrikaner Police Officer, Formerly of the Security Police

> *"The only way any policeman or policewoman can change is to decide that the things of the past were not right. I did this on a religious basis, but it could be done on humanitarian grounds as well."*

Gerrit Nieuwoudt says that, strange as it may seem, the shift from security police policing to community policing and the peace process was not that hard for him. In a way, he feels that his training equipped him especially well because, just as in the security police, where his job was to deal with opponents of the government, on the peace committee he was confronted with the very same people, though now their relationship was framed as collaborative rather than combative. "Police in the security police didn't deal with ordinary criminals," he explains. "We dealt with politically minded people, so we were in the best position to liaise with political people. In those days, whenever I had to deal with people who were regarded as opponents, I always tried to reason with them. Through the peace committee, we had the opportunity to listen to each other. It was just a different mind-set. We were no longer talking to a guy to find out what he had been doing but to reach a resolution of a specific problem."

Gerrit held the rank of police captain when he was appointed to represent the Western Cape police on the regional peace committee. He was very quiet for the first few meetings. It was part of his police training. "I just used to listen and try to sum up the people that I had to work with," he says with a smile. "That is something we learned through years of experience as policemen, to be able to judge people." Within a couple of months he was participating fully in the fortnightly executive meetings. It was the start of a process that would catapult him into the surprising role of police reformer, or even transformer.

The signposts to this unexpected future were visible two years earlier when Gerrit was selected to be one of the police liaison officers between the government and ANC in compliance with the Groote Schuur Minute, the prenegotiations platform that was cemented in Cape Town on May 4, 1990. On that day, the ANC effectively renounced the armed struggle, and the government made concessions on the release of political prisoners, the return of exiles, and the lifting of the state of emergency. In addition, point 5 of the minute provided for the establishment of efficient channels of communication between the ANC and the government. The government decided that the security branch should fulfill this task, and Gerrit was appointed.

He met Vincent Diba in 1991 at his first meeting with the ANC. Their collective assignment was to resolve conflicts that might arise between the ANC and the government at ground level. There was a lot of conflict in those early days. "The ANC and other political organizations were not always prepared to ask permission to hold their marches and demonstrations, which was against the law, and the police often overreacted and wanted to arrest the people," says Gerrit. "We had a lot of difficulty in trying to ease out the conflict and the differences of opinion in the different groupings."

Gerrit says that he is a policeman in his soul. His father had been a policeman before him, and even though Gerrit had tried to break the mold and study pharmacy, within two years he had abandoned his degree at Potchefstroom University and joined the police force. He transferred to the security branch and in 1984 moved to Worcester, a small town in the mountains of the Western Cape, as branch commander.

The security branch was established as a police political intelligence agency for dealing with enemies of the apartheid state. It was established under the law, but many of its agents acted above the law. It earned notoriety both at home and abroad for its harassment, torture, and ruthless pursuit of antiapartheid activists and was believed to be responsible for the deaths of many opponents of the state.

Gerrit says, "There was a law that made it an offense to be a member of the ANC, and I was a policeman put in a position to enforce that specific law, which I did to the best of my ability." He is unrepentant about his job at that time. He explains that he and his fellow officers saw the total onslaught of the *Rooi Gevaar* (Red Danger), or communism, as a threat to Christianity. This, in his view as a deeply Christian man, justified the government's actions to fight it. He also is clear that he never acted above the law. "I always tried to be professional in the way I handled people," he says of those years in the security branch. "I was always honest, and I respected the people I had to deal with."

His religion, the Reformed Church, which he says is more biblical than the Dutch Reformed Church, underpins every aspect of his life. "I treat people the way I expect to be treated," he says, as he talks about how he automatically measured the changes proposed by the politicians and the police against the Bible. His church had decided back in 1964 that people of color could be accepted. That was not the issue, but communism was.

The turning point came when the ANC and the South African Communist Party were unbanned, and nothing devastating happened. After six months, then a year, still nothing had happened. At the same time, Nelson Mandela had emerged from twenty-seven years in jail at the hand of whites and had unreservedly offered his forgiveness. This had a huge impact. "I couldn't believe he could be so accommodating," Gerrit says, shaking his head in wonder. Slowly the fear unraveled.

As the political certainties of the past crashed around his ears, Gerrit's personal journey into the new reality began. It was to be an accelerated passage, because first through his liaison work and later through the peace committee, he was exposed to former enemies in a spirit of reconciliation and, instead of monsters, he found human beings. He learned to listen to their points of view and to understand their perspectives. He learned that people must be given the opportunity to speak what is on their minds, to air their grievances, and that he should listen carefully and patiently. "It makes them feel better," he says. "They won't be able to think of solutions before they have had the opportunity to say what their problems are." He learned that it is possible to jointly resolve problems, even where there is a difference of political opinion.

Training workshops in conflict resolution helped, teaching him how to understand the process of negotiations, the process of talking to others and of reaching joint decisions. Together with the practical experience of dealing with conflict every day, Gerrit found himself personally enriched in his dealings with community and political conflict and with people generally. The peace committee played a pivotal role, providing a structure in which communication across former political barriers was expected and encouraged, and he began, tentatively, to build relationships of trust. He says that the only way he knew how to do this was by being honest, both with the other members of the peace committee and with the police. "When I had a problem with the police and the way they acted, I told them so." He says that he always tried to do everything in his power to rectify the problems with the police that were raised by others, and that in this way people would realize that he did not have a hidden agenda. "That is where mistrust develops," he says, "when people think you are really after something else."

Much of the discussion at the peace committee was about policing. He found it enormously frustrating that many of the accusations against the police were, in his view, inaccurate, untrue, or only reflected half the facts. At the same time, he was frustrated with the slow rate of change within the police, many of whom were still policing in the old way, "which was not acceptable, and I was expected to defend their actions at the peace committee. I didn't defend actions which I thought were wrong. It was a very frustrating, difficult time."

At the end of 1992, the police implemented a Community Relations Division and transferred Gerrit and other security police policemen to it, with the responsibility for implementing community policing as the new style of policing. Part of their strategy was to expose as many of the police as possible to the thinking of the community, the NGOs, and the peace committee to try to change the way they operated. Sometimes it backfired, as in the meeting about Kraaifontein. "The community and the police were at loggerheads," says Gerrit, recounting the meeting between the district commissioner and the squatter community.[10] "It turned out to be a very unsuccessful meeting. The district commissioner said this is the way we are operating and I am not going to tolerate the community telling me how to do my work, and stuff like that. But at least we then knew that that was his attitude, and we could work on it."

By now, Gerrit's official job was to act as change agent within the police. Resistance was tremendous. "It was extremely difficult for me to experience the slow way in which the police as an organization reacted to this new set of rules. Even today," he says, as we talked in 1995, "there are people who want to use the old ways of policing. That was one of the most difficult trials I had to face in the whole peace process, trying to change the police and not being able to do so effectively enough. It was a constant effort."

Gerrit's religious beliefs were a great help during this time. "Everything I do, I put in the hands of the Lord, and I also believe that the Lord gives you the strength to deal with any difficult situation you may find yourself in, so that made it easier for me," he says. "Every morning and every evening I thank the Lord for the knowledge and the confidence that he has given me to deal with these situations."

Gerrit says that the peace committee and NGOs played a major role in helping the police to change and become more acceptable to the community. He singles out Malibongwe Sopangisa for his work with the Nyanga LPC. "He had a lot of meetings with the police. That helped to change the ways in which policemen acted and reacted on the ground." But, he says, although the peace committee really did help to change the police, in the end, it is up to each individual to change within. "The only way any policeman or policewoman can change," he says, "is to decide that the things of the past were not right. I did this on a religious basis, but it could be done on humanitarian grounds as well." Gerrit says he would like to share his experience with as many policemen and policewomen as possible.

Toward the end of 1995 the Community Relations Division of the South African Police Service (SAPS) was disbanded as community policing became official policy. The members attached to this division were given the opportunity to apply for other positions. Gerrit was appointed commander of Proactive Policing at Khayelitsha with the rank of senior superintendent in March 1996. He says, "I applied for this specific position because I wanted to continue working with the communities antagonistic to the police. I felt that I could use my knowledge of the way these communities think, which I gained during my participation on the Peace Committee, to help the SAPS and the community to move closer to each other."

HOW WE WORKED

Thousands of peace workers across South Africa placed their minds, hearts, and bodies between chaos and a fragile equilibrium. Through them and the peace committees they represented, the Peace Accord took shape in the streets. The regional and local peace committees absorbed the real impact of the transition to democracy, dealing daily with the conflict and violence it generated and working to heal broken communities.

We peacemakers were not a homogeneous group. We included academics, clergy, conflict resolution practitioners, human rights lawyers, NGO fieldworkers, politicians, community organizers, peace desk officers from political and civic organizations, peace educators, psychologists, researchers, social workers, and members of the international community. We worked with the Peace Accord in a number of different ways.

The secretariat of the regional peace committee employed staff such as Chris Spies who worked full-time as fieldworkers, managers, or administrators. As local peace committees were formed, they too employed full-time staff, such as Malibongwe Sopangisa. In both cases, their salaries and expenses were paid by the Peace Accord, which received most of its funds from the government. A few European governments donated comparatively small amounts of money, but the signatories agreed that the government should pay for the lion's share.

The NGO community on the whole threw its weight behind the Peace Accord, and many of us worked under the auspices of our respective organizations and institutions, which in essence contributed our services. I was employed full-time by the Centre for Conflict Resolution, which paid my salary, but worked most of my time with the peace structures. Members of NIM such as Val Rose Christie worked cooperatively with the peace committees.[11] Similarly, a number of academics devoted varying degrees of their time and effort to the peace committee.

As the peace process took hold, increasing numbers of professional mediators, facilitators, and trainers began to work for the peace committees on an ad hoc basis. The Peace Accord made provision for their payment as consultants, but the daily rate was disproportionately high compared with the salaries of the full-time staff on the secretariat, and in the Western Cape we initially resisted calling on such expensive services. Eventually, when it was clear that more hands were needed, we negotiated reasonable rates, and a number of professionals were called in to help with the ever-escalating caseload.

A few businesses seconded (lent) staff for a year or even two to help out. And then there were those people who just came to help because they passionately believed in the peace process. Members of the peace committees, regional and local, politicians such as Vincent Diba and Sakkie Pretorius, local government officials, and business executives also became involved in mediating or monitoring. Later, our number included a small but growing band of police officers, such as Gerrit Nieuwoudt, who were dedicated to rebuilding the relationship between the police and the community.

❊   ❊   ❊

It was all new, and we had to create new roles. The Peace Accord was
untried and untested; the peace process as a whole unprecedented; and the
national negotiations, whereby the Nationalist government had agreed to
negotiate itself out of power, extraordinary. The roles we played—crisis
intervenor, facilitator, mediator, monitor, trainer, and observer—felt new
in the context of the times. Our work was to translate the words and intentions of the Peace Accord into actions that focused on confronting, containing, defusing, or resolving the conflicts that simmered or exploded into
violence every day around the country. We knew we couldn't stop all the
violence, but it was imperative that we try. We had to keep the violence
level down to some unknown threshold so that the country could, some
day soon, hold democratic elections.

Monitors became a catchall word for most peace workers, especially on
marches, at demonstrations, or in crises. When we were called out to monitor
a mass demonstration and ended up mediating, when our presence was
enough to prevent violence, whether we were called mediators, observers,
or monitors did not matter. We were too busy doing it to think about what
we should call ourselves.

"Monitoring" worked. People behaved differently in the presence of cred-
ible outsiders. The political organizations and the security forces in particular responded to the presence of monitors with astonishing changes in
behavior, moderating what they did and how they did it. When an agreement was reached, monitors could ensure its implementation. For instance,
the police committed themselves to wearing nametags and using marked
vehicles, small items with enormous consequences: individual police officers could no longer commit faceless acts using brute force. By consistently
reporting offenders to the Police Complaints Investigation Unit or the police
reporting officer—established by the Peace Accord to help clean up the
police force—however unsatisfactory the results, the police were held accountable for their actions for the first time in decades.

The peace workers took conflict resolution and peacemaking beyond their
known frontiers, forging new tools, techniques, and skills as we went along.
We found ourselves facing life-and-death situations for which there were no
textbook answers; we learned to think on our feet under enormous pressure;
we discovered the anger and despair that generate violence and the fear and

numb passivity that fuel it. We were the people in the front line of the peace process who somehow managed to keep it going against enormous odds.

We did not always succeed in quelling violence and dealing with the conflict. The statistics, the media coverage, and our own reports tell that story. We also needed to learn a lot about making peace among ourselves. There were power struggles, turf battles, and personality clashes. Some sought mediation or therapy to resolve these problems and, healed, were once more able to contribute. Slowly we learned that peace has to start with each one of us, that the only way to be a peacemaker in this troubled world is to be the peacemaker within, working to resolve the turmoil of our hearts and souls, and our personal conflicts with others. This does not mean that we can be peacemakers only if we are fully at peace, a condition that would eliminate most of us from the role. It does mean that resolving our inner and outer conflict should be our priority. As peacemakers, we cannot ask people in conflict in the world to enter the process of making peace if we are not willing to do the same in our own lives.

The other big hurdles were overextension and exhaustion. There were just too few of us facing too much violence, day in and day out. We were stretched to breaking point. But because for most of us our work fulfilled a deep personal need to give service and to make the world a better place, and because we felt privileged to do this work, we lost sight of the need to take care of ourselves.

It was a mistake. We would have been better able to serve if we had

- listened to one another's stories, and told our own, as a form of catharsis;
- set up mutual support systems to catch the pain of witnessing death and violence, the trauma of not being able to stop it, and the guilt of surviving;
- gotten more sleep;
- learned to say no.

We needed to find ways to keep our balance and our perspective, but in the intensity of the times we focused on keeping on keeping on.

We also needed to understand our role. A poster taped to a wall facing me for the three hours of a political funeral in St. Francis Church in the township of Langa said, "If you have come to help me, you are wasting your time. But if you have come because your liberation is bound up with mine, then let us work together."

This was key. Apartheid had damaged all of us, oppressor and oppressed. We all needed liberation and healing.

The international observers played a critical role. They came from the United Nations, the European Community, the Organization of African Unity, the Commonwealth, and various church groups. The presence of these outsiders gave an increased sense of security to the communities in which they operated, confirming that the eyes of the world were focused on their plight. It also provided some real security as the police and the army behaved with restraint in their presence. Indeed, in general the security forces moderated their behavior somewhat because they were never sure when monitors or observers would arrive on the scene.

International observers were able to say things that local people could not for fear of repercussions. They could address deviant behavior within the security forces directly with the officers concerned or with their superiors. They could ask direct questions of political and civic leaders that might be considered offensive coming from local people and exacerbate tensions. They could ask questions that were interpreted as information gathering but were intended to draw attention to conflictual behavior.

Given that the police were a major focus of conflict, observers from the European Community were particularly effective because many were police officers. They were able to talk in familiar police terms with their South African counterparts; they understood the policing culture; and they shared much common ground in terms of ordinary policing activities, problems, and constraints. There was an instant bond of respect, and the international officers were able to influence the local officers to modify their behavior.

The international observers worked with the Peace Accord structures, independent monitors, and NGOs. They attended demonstrations, rallies, meetings, and public events. They were mandated to observe and report. Some read this in a restrictive way and distanced themselves from the action. Others pitched in, and were there, on call, wherever they felt their presence would make a difference. Later discussions about their mandate questioned their observer status.

Should they have been allowed to directly intervene in conflicts? My response is a loud *no*, for a number of reasons. They didn't have the local knowledge to engage effectively. Engagement would have undermined their effectiveness as the impartial eyes and ears of the international community. It would also have endangered them personally, making them acceptable targets. It would have removed the protective aura that they were able to bring to scenes of violent conflict, just by being there. It would have severely limited their freedom of movement, with parties to the conflicts challenging their presence instead of welcoming it. It could have put the entire peace process at risk, because one of the key tools at our disposal was the presence of outsiders.

As it was, they enshrined the world "out there," beyond the immediate confrontation or conflagration, reminding those with violence on their minds that they could no longer act unseen. They supported us, the local peace workers, in our daily rounds and gave us added legitimacy and clout. They made everyone feel safer.

Their presence didn't always avert violence, but it helped. I would look out for the familiar caps and colors in the crowd, because most of the international observers wore special jackets and hats and on occasion even carried flags to draw attention to their presence and to provide a measure of protection in crisis situations. Domestic monitors and peace workers also wore identification. Very quickly all the parties to the conflict and violence got used to the presence of this array of outsiders. They became an accepted part of the landscape, and as the peace process progressed, all the parties, including the security forces, began to request a monitoring presence to ensure that their activities were not misinterpreted or misrepresented.

This community of observers, monitors, peace workers, and operational members of the peace structures was accessible twenty-four hours a day through radio pagers. It became usual for international observers, domestic monitors, peace committee workers, and representatives of the press to arrive at the scene of a violent incident at the same time, all responding to the same page. The radio pagers became a part of us, attached to us, and we to them. We could not do our work without them. We could be contacted wherever we were, and if we could reach a phone, we could make contact with everyone else. The pagers were lifelines and probably the means of preventing violence and saving lives on many occasions. A message would loom shrilly on the tiny screen, "1,000 ANC marching on police station. Angry mood. Fear police will shoot." We could immediately respond, alerting

ANC leaders and other influential people to intervene with the marchers, calling on the police command to deal sensitively with the situation. We could send in monitors, both local and international, to act as a brake on extreme acts by both sides and to stand between them and mediators to uncover the root of the problem and start the process of trying to find a solution. Cellular phones were not available at the time; they would have been very effective in these conditions. There were few telephones in the black townships, and that limited the ability of residents to raise the alarm and of peace workers to respond.

This crisis intervention and monitoring of demonstrations, rallies, and marches was a consuming part of our work. At the same time, we were committed to working with conflicts before they erupted, and, increasingly, we were invited to intervene as black communities and the authorities sought an alternative to violence or force. We mediated or facilitated conflicts between town councils and township residents, the police and local ANC leadership, the military and black civic organizations, the provincial authorities and squatter warlords, youth and the education department, taxi organizations and commuters, and between competing political and civic organizations. We established peace committees in small towns and rural communities to provide a peacemaking presence, and we lobbied government ministers and senior government officials to change conditions that provoked violence. We ran training workshops in mediation, facilitation, and general conflict resolution skills. We introduced peace education into schools.

The peace workers came together with a common commitment to trying to end the violence that was killing thousands of our fellow South Africans, traumatizing tens of thousands, making life miserable for millions more, and threatening to derail the negotiations process completely. We appeared from unexpected places in the fabric of our divided society, and we entered into a joint venture. The significance and drama of this alliance of opposites should not be underestimated. Neither should its effectiveness.

3
PLANNED INTERVENTION

Standing in the Middle

CONFRONTATION IN THE STREETS OF CAPE TOWN

As peace workers, we tried to anticipate a crisis and plan for it, if possible. The national upheaval following the murder of the beloved black leader Chris Hani put our planning to the fiery test. In the aftermath of that crisis, peace workers and police together forged practical recommendations to avoid the mistakes we all made.

Saturday, April 10, 1993

Two o'clock SABC radio news:

> At approximately 10:25 this morning, Chris Hani, secretary-general of the South African Communist Party, was assassinated outside his Dawn Park home near Boksburg. Fifty-year-old Hani was returning from a trip to the store with his daughter when he was shot four times in the head and died immediately.

Chris Hani, a former ANC military commander who was idolized by the youth, was shot down by a white man. His prestige flowed from his image as a militant leader and his lifelong commitment to the struggle. I know that a great cry of anger and pain will surge through our land, with especially great force in the black community.

Monday, April 12

The peace committee calls an emergency meeting of the executive to plan how to deal with the upheaval sure to follow Chris Hani's murder. We troop into the meeting room to discuss the coming Wednesday, which has been declared a national day of mourning. It will be a time for the nation to acknowledge the pain of Chris Hani's killing, the anger, the loss. We hope that it will be a catharsis. We fear it will be a bloodbath and realize that the two outcomes are not mutually exclusive.

The peace committee chair, Jaap Durand, has met with the ANC regional executive and with the police. The ANC is organizing a march into the heart of Cape Town, to St. George's Cathedral, where a service will be conducted by Archbishop Desmond Tutu. Then there will be a rally on the Parade, Cape Town's central square; speeches will be made and songs sung. Plans are being drawn up, discussed, discarded, and reconfirmed at a feverish pace as the peace committee, the ANC, the security forces, and the city administration try to find the best course for containing the violence we fear will tear apart the city and the peace process.

The rest of the country is organizing too. The executive committee fields reports from the region as fieldworkers and local peace committees relay their plans and ask for direction and reinforcements. Tomorrow there will be marches in Villiersdorp, Lamberts Bay, Saldhana, and Springbok and, on Sunday, in Ceres. The Grabouw march is still to be confirmed. In George, Oudtshoorn, and Mossel Bay, peace committees have brokered agreements between the police and the ANC. Three vehicles were burned in Mfuleni today, and Bloekombos has exploded into violence. Whites should avoid Lwandle and some other PAC no-go areas. There will be a mass rally in Khayelitsha on Saturday at the stadium and a sit-in at the Elsiesriver police station all weekend.

Information is gathered, resources stretched, shared, and allocated, and roles agreed upon. Local monitors, international observers, volunteers, peace committee executive members, and staff divide up the areas and tasks. The precious radiotelephones, walkie-talkies, peace committee jackets, and car stickers are doled out. There are never enough. Plans for a joint operations communications center (JOCC) in Cape Town staffed by representatives of the peace committee, the ANC, and the police are consolidated. Phone numbers are handed out and beeper numbers exchanged.

JOCCs are multiparty coordination centers that include members of the security forces and that are set up to deal with specific crises, expected or unfolding, for the duration of the crisis. They can coordinate information on the crisis, develop strategy for critical events as they unfold, and respond. The participants represent decision-making powers of all parties to the crisis. They are in direct communication by radio or mobile phone with multiparty teams of monitors on the ground that report incidents as they occur, intervene in conflicts, and provide accurate information to the participating parties. Because of their multiparty composition, the teams are able to intervene effectively, control rumors, and reduce tension and mistrust on all sides.

This JOCC is the first in our region, and we are not sure how it will work, especially as there is so little time for preparation. This is nothing new. The National Peace Accord has no precedent, and much of what we do is untried and crisis driven. We learn as we go along.

Meanwhile, the Cape Town City Council, the ANC, and the police make their own plans. All worry about violence between marchers and security forces. The ANC will provide marshals, but it is impossible for there ever to be enough. Ten thousand people are expected to converge on Cape Town city center. More monitors are needed. The Network of Independent Monitors (NIM) will cover Khayelitsha, Nyanga, and Elsiesrivier and will as usual provide a presence in most other places too. Resources will be stretched all over the region, as there are not yet enough peace workers to meet the demands of these turbulent times. We can only do our best.

Wednesday, April 14

We peace workers will be on the front lines today between the police and the demonstrators. I dress in well-worn jeans, a plain T-shirt, and sneakers. I know it is going to be a long day, and it is important to be comfortable. I take off the gold chain that belonged to my mother and my habitual ring. I replace my watch with a Swatch. I carefully pack my belt bag with coins for the telephone, a ten Rand note for emergencies, tissues, chewing gum, pen and paper, cigarettes, and matches. I consider whether to drink a cup of tea. No, I dare not eat or drink more than absolutely necessary as there will not be any toilet facilities all day.

We all meet as prearranged at a parking lot about five minutes' walk from the Parade. The UN and EC observers are dressed in full uniform, crisp blue-and-white symbols familiar to the watching world. Police and demonstrators can easily recognize the NIM monitors in their plastic turquoise bibs and caps. But peace committee members will wear a jacket inexplicably emblazoned with the unknown insignia of the National Peace Secretariat instead of the familiar "Peace Committee." In the chaos and turmoil of mass confrontations, we wish we had a more readily recognizable symbol of our role.[1]

We head for the Parade. It is all things to all people—a parking lot, a minibus taxi terminus, a food and flower market, a target for demonstrations and protest, a meeting place—framed on four sides by the bus and train stations, military headquarters, City Hall, and street vendors. Three years ago, tens of thousands of us had stood here under a February sun waiting to greet Nelson Mandela on his release from prison. Today we are here to mourn his friend, "Chris" Martin Thembisile Hani, widely considered one of the few black leaders able to control a generation of so-called young lions within the ranks of the ANC. These were the militant, highly politicized black youths who had received little formal schooling because of nearly continuous protest, strikes, and disruption.

Now Chris Hani is dead, and the young lions roar their rage. We walk across the Parade into Adderley Street and find ourselves between a unit of the Internal Stability Division (ISD), as the infamous riot police are now called, and a chanting crowd that is daring itself to defy the authorities. Black youths pick up anything they can lay their hands on and fling stones, soda cans, and bits of wood at the heavily armed police, who stand facing them, guns at the ready.

Despite the protection of guns and of one another, there is fear in the eyes of the young, overwhelmingly white policemen from the ISD. They face the *Swart Gevaar* (the Black Danger) that the *Groot Krokodil* (the Great Crocodile), former South African president P. W. Botha, warned them lurked in the shadows and would one day come and get them; here it is. Security forces in most places around the world attract and recruit predominantly right-wing, conservative folk. As I watch these men, their knuckles stretched white around the barrels of their rifles, I imagine their fear of blacks, nurtured by generations of racism and taken in with their mother's milk, focused on this taunting crowd. One shot could spark terrible consequences.

Somehow the peace workers must try to prevent injury, damage, and death. We stand between the two sides, trying to look bigger than we are, trying to look reassuring. We back up against the police, hoping that in some way they will feel more secure and have less inclination to shoot. The two sides sway back and forth like the tide, and then the crowd changes its focus and heads for the Parade. The police unit slides around a corner, suddenly the crowd surges, and the police are backed up against a wall among the flower sellers, their guns pointing directly at the youthful crowd.

We run to fill the small gap between them. They are close enough to touch one another, but the tension eases as once again the crowd wheels away and dances onto the Parade.

The ISD establishes a blockade at the corners of Plein and Darling Streets. Police vehicles are strategically placed for communications and backup, and the colonel in charge spends a lot of time shouting into the radio, talking to his commander in the helicopter circling above and to the operations room back at headquarters. The noise of the day is deafening, and the register of his voice rises with the tension.

By now the anticipated ten thousand people has swelled to fifty thousand, mostly jammed onto the Parade. Emotions already running high are fanned by exasperation as the program for the day and the public address system break down under the strain of these unexpected numbers. While the ANC leadership mourns Chris Hani in the cathedral, all hell breaks loose on the Parade. Leaderless, frustrated, and spoiling for trouble, gangs of youths go on the rampage, stoning the stalls and nearby shops, breaking windows in preparation for looting, and setting fire to parked vehicles, pay-and-display machines, and refuse bins. Others are making mock attacks on the police position. Chanting "War, not peace," fists pummeling the air, two hundred or three hundred youth at a time charge toward the police, toyi-toyiing their challenge, only to disperse at the last minute and then regroup for another pass.

Standing tensely between them and the police, we watch them come toward us, feeling the policemen behind us stiffen. Each time, the tension builds, the danger point is reached, and then somehow it is over. The air is heavy with the strain of uncertainty, and we try to hide our worry that next time the crowd will not stop.

Great plumes of black smoke from the burning cars drift toward Table Mountain. The ANC marshals, reinforced by independent monitors and other peace workers, heroically try to contain the crowd. A marshal pushes his way toward me, sweat streaming down his face. He asks for help. I follow him to the intersection, where a line of marshals tightly holding hands is surging back and forth with the crowd. Behind them is a double line of police dog handlers standing impassively with their leashed German shepherds sitting at their feet. As the momentum of the crowd pushes the marshals back, the dogs bite the backsides of the marshals. I negotiate new lines for both the police and the marshals with sufficient neutral space between. Relieved marshals get back to the exhausting task at hand.

Some members of the clergy use their influence and stride purposefully in flowing robes to crisis points. Rob Robertson, a Methodist priest with a lifetime of commitment to the practice of nonviolent direct action, disarms some of the roving youth of their bricks, sticks, and stones. He says, "What are you going to do with that brick?" The response is invariably, "Nothing," to which the gentle but intrepid priest replies, "Well, in that case, let me have it so that you don't injure someone by mistake." He finds himself laden with bricks. His campaign is a success, a ray of light in this day fraught with danger.

A rumor reaches the ISD colonel that the post office is on fire. He decides to send a detachment to investigate. We fear that a group of police bristling with firearms pushing their way through the crowd will provoke a response and could spark a spiral of violence in the highly charged atmosphere. I offer to go and look on the colonel's behalf; it turns out that the rumor was false. Later, I play messenger again, seeking out the ANC leader Trevor Manuel, later minister of trade and industry in the new government, to deal with a crisis. My role is an improvised one, but anything that may prevent violence seems useful.

A fight suddenly develops between some of the crowd and the ISD police. We peace workers pile into the middle of it, squashed between pushing, shoving, panting bodies. Everyone is shouting at once, and it is impossible to discover what happened. Comrades and colleagues on either side intervene too, and the combatants are pulled back to safety. The day is made up of such small acts by numerous peace workers across the city and duplicated across the nation. Countrywide, the death count for the day is later calculated at twenty-five, remarkably low.

❋   ❋   ❋

The breaking point on the Parade comes at about two in the afternoon. The report next day in *The Argus*, Cape Town's main daily newspaper, was terse and to the point:

> There was a tense standoff as the policemen came to face an angry crowd.
> Peace monitors tried to intervene, but a policeman, apparently angry with a protester who had come too close or hurled a projectile at him,

leveled his gun and let off a round of what appeared to be bird or buck shot.

More policemen followed suit with multiple volleys. Protesters, monitors and journalists scrambled for cover. Some went down wounded and were dragged to safety.

The youth with neck and back wounds and blood pouring from his nose was taken to the mobile clinic where he was pronounced dead.

Clergy and monitors blocked the way as a few protesters, angry at the shooting, tried to get at police.

For the next twenty minutes, bursts of gunfire and the crash of breaking windows cut through the din of the crowd. At about 2:30 P.M., a hand grenade explodes at the historic castle that has served as military headquarters since it was built in the seventeenth century, slightly injuring ten police officers and one member of the public. *The Argus* reported:

> About the same time thousands of people scattered from the Parade as police fired many rounds of tear gas and bird and buckshot. . . . Sporadic shooting continued over a wide area, but marchers, encouraged by clergy, marshals and monitors, made their way to the station and left. Some shop windows at the station were smashed.

About 150 people are treated for bird and buckshot wounds. About 20 are taken to the hospital.

One is dead. He begins his dying at my feet. He is one of the ones who does not get up when the shooting has stopped. Everyone who had flung themselves on the ground for protection now runs for cover. Friends rush to the aid of the injured, running low in case of further shooting, and carry them away. Abandoned shoes are scattered across the streets. Later someone collects the shoes in a blanket and places them in a nearby doorway. No one steals them, and the shoes remain huddled together, a forlorn shrine.

On the other side of the battlefield a foreign journalist staggers to his feet, disbelief on his face as rivulets of blood pour from his head and stain his white shirt bright red. I become aware that I have been shot by a rubber bullet in the back of my right thigh. I am limping and my leg hurts.

After this, most of the people go home. A hard core remains, mainly youths, defiant to the last, burning rubbish bins, breaking open parking meters, and taunting the police. The Parade is mostly empty, and I start walking through the litter and glass and some pools of dried blood to join EC observer Kaj Jensen,[2] who is standing in front of the City Hall.

Suddenly bullets and tear gas come flying from the center of the Parade behind me. A tear gas canister lands in front of me; bullets are still coming at my back. I decide to run into the tear gas, and when I reach Kaj, we dive into the gutter, eyes and noses streaming, gasping for breath as the tear gas burns our lungs. Seasoned black marchers light scraps of paper and hold them near our faces to burn away the gas.

When the police stop shooting and we begin to see again, a young woman from Guguletu helps me to stagger upwind of the smoking tear gas canister. Rob Robertson appears magically with a jar of Vaseline, which we smear on our faces, pushing it up our noses and into our eyes. Tears dripping onto our clothes, the young woman and I hug each other with relief as the pain begins to ease. I make a mental note to add strips of paper and Vaseline to my crisis kit.

❊   ❊   ❊

We survey the wreckage of the Parade, the burned-out vendor stalls, cars, motorcycles, and rubbish bins still smoking and crackling amid a sea of litter. The next day, *The Argus* banner headline will scream out "Day of Shame" at the events of the day. In the frenzy of blaming, everyone will blame everyone else for the breakdown of organization and lack of crowd control. But now the last of the crowd has dispersed, always a tense but crucial phase in any public demonstration and one that needs careful attention and organization, such as trains and buses for transportation and megaphones to inform the crowd that it is time to go.

I drive with Kaj and others the six miles to the bustling white suburb of Rondebosch to eat something before going home. In Rondebosch, everything is normal, absurdly so, untouched by the events of the day, the people unaware of what has been happening in their city center. Their mostly white detachment from the mostly black protest gathering and march reflects the parallel realities that have marked South African society for decades.

I order bread, soup, and very hot tea.

Thursday, April 15

Time for a post mortem. The peace committee convenes a debriefing session with the police at 8:30 A.M. Peace workers, international observers, and monitors; ANC, National Party, and Democratic Party representatives; and uniformed police and ISD officers ranging from captain to general all cram into a conference room that is never quite big enough.

Residual fury and frustration from yesterday spill over from all sides, a necessary catharsis. After the venting and storytelling, we evaluate the preparation, actions, and reactions of yesterday. Hard words are said, points of agreement and disagreement are minuted (noted). Then we get down to the real task of sifting through what happened and did not happen, gathering the lessons and shaping them into some kind of blueprint for the future. Our meeting this April morning is a classic joint problem-solving exercise, although none of us frames it as such. At the time, it is simply the obvious thing to do. We have to try to make sure that the chaos and violence of yesterday are never again repeated. Next time we may not get away with just one death.

GUIDELINES

We agree on a number of concrete recommendations "for the prevention of uncontrollable situations during mass protest gatherings."[3] These focus on the organization of the event, the police, and other forms of control.

> All role players should be involved in the setting up and operation of a JOCC for the duration of the entire event. These role players include the organizers, other participants, monitoring organizations (including international monitors), the peace committee, the police, the military, business sectors, emergency services and local authorities. Further, Peace Accord officials and key marshals should be equipped with radios or radio telephones.

The JOCC did not work very well this first time round, in many ways becoming yet another casualty of the general breakdown in organization as the hastily prepared plans for the day unraveled bit by bit. Contact between the peace workers in the field and the JOCC were hampered by radiotelephones that worked only intermittently or that were useless because the peace workers just could not hear above the din of the crowd. The political representatives on the JOCC did not turn up. The police and the city council ran their own crisis centers. In the end, even peace committee members abandoned their posts. But we could see the plan's potential for future events. JOCCs that were convened for the election and the inauguration of President Mandela were effective.

The organizers of marches should provide written proof of the number of and deployment strategy of marshals, what training the marshals have undergone and details about the communication mechanisms between marshals, organizers and the JOCC.

Two hundred ANC marshals struggled valiantly to maintain order among fifty thousand people, an impossible task. Even though other peace workers joined in, linking arms to form long, fragile human barriers, they were hopelessly outnumbered and unable to do more than contain the crowd at a few strategic points. They did well under the circumstances, and it was clear that, sufficiently reinforced, they could play a critical role in future crises.

The leaders should be in contact with the people participating. Organizers should inform the public about the strategy to deploy leaders at strategic points.

It had been a mess from the start when the anticipated ten-thousand-strong crowd had quickly swollen to fifty thousand, and the organizers had made the decision to shepherd the crowd onto the Parade while the regional ANC leadership continued with the service in the cathedral. Leaderless, frustrated, bewildered, the bulk of the crowd had behaved with remarkable restraint. But the two hundred marshals had fought a losing battle to control the unruly fringe, which grew to thousands as the focus of the day got lost in the breakdown of planning and communications.

There should always be a back-up public address system since it is almost impossible to control a crowd when the PA system fails. Megaphones should be organized for both marshals and police.

The public address system had broken down early on, and without a contingency plan for addressing the crowd, or for the day as a whole, crowd control went downhill before it had even started. It was an object lesson in the power of the microphone.

After the shooting, when the marshals were trying to clear the Parade and get everyone to go home, I had asked for and been lent a megaphone by the police for a young ANC official who wanted to help. Later, as promised, he brought the equipment back to me, and I gave it to the relieved sergeant who had requisitioned it for me two hours earlier. Nothing much was said, but it was a significant transaction of trust all round. This kind of cooperation between security forces and civilians was still new and relatively untried, and every time it worked, something was built, just as every time it didn't, the trust that had been built was disproportionately broken down. The big picture that was unfolding day by day was colored and shaped by these little incidents. They were as critical to our future as the major events because they allowed individual people to explore new forms of relationship, to cross old divides and to experience change in their hearts and souls in parallel with the distant process of political negotiation. The one needed the other if this great experiment was to succeed.

> As a matter of principle, marches should be convened at stadiums and not in overcrowded city centers.

This recommendation was wishful thinking. For the decades of apartheid, black suffering had been confined to the townships, far from the eyes and ears of the white electorate who every five years reelected a government that would continue to protect them from having to know what was happening. The black community knows through bitter experience that the only way to have an effect on the white community is to bring the struggle into white streets and into white lives. And affect the white community they must if the new South Africa is to be born soon, born without civil war, or indeed born at all. These demonstrations are a continuation of the struggle in another form, and though it is true that they provide a platform to vent pent-up emotions, their more cogent role is to keep the power and will of the people sharply before the minds of whites, the politicians, and the world.

> The police should be equipped with fire extinguishers.

Yesterday I had watched raging gangs of young blacks torch the cars and vans that had been abandoned on the Parade. They used newspaper, cardboard, bits of wood, and pieces of cloth to light the fires inside the vehicles, and then stood around to make sure the fire took. The first time this happened, a man from Guguletu came running and, out of breath, asked me to intervene. "The children are burning the cars," he panted. "Please try and stop them." I understood his panic. He was afraid that the police would open fire on them. There was also the danger that the fuel tanks would explode in the densely packed crowd. I warned the children about the danger of the fuel tanks exploding and ran back to ask the police for a fire extinguisher. No, the police said, we don't have those, they are not part of our issue. I found it hard to believe that such an obvious tool could be missing from their crisis issue, but it was true.

> While the police are to be commended for the way they have tried to protect lives and property under very difficult circumstances, certain incidents where no warning shots were fired, and where people were wounded above waist level, need to receive urgent attention.

I express horror that the police fired into the crowd without warning. The police respond that they cannot fire shots overhead in the city center because of the danger of hitting people on balconies or in the buildings overlooking the crowd. I point out that there were no buildings in the line of fire when they opened fire around me. Kaj Jensen says that these police arguments against warning shots don't hold water. I ask why they shoot at the upper bodies and heads of the crowd. The police say that as soon as the firing starts, everyone drops to the ground. If they were to fire lower, they would hit the people lying on the ground. We argue back and forth.

> Some practical hints for the police, the organizers and the political parties are noted. These include suggestions that the police should minimize the pointing of guns at people, the organizers must have effective contingency plans which they should communicate to everyone involved, and vehicles should not be permitted to drive through the crowds.

Guns pointing at people had become a flash point. I had run to flank an ISD patrol of six that the colonel had sent into the crowd to try to stop the arson attacks. They had taken up position in the middle of the Parade, protecting one another's backs, guns at the ready, a tiny bristling island in a sea of angry black people. Demonstrators said to me, "Tell them to stop pointing their guns." I had seen fear and anxiety in their eyes as they tugged at my arm. The guns could so easily go off. When another police patrol had shouldered their way toward a fire and found themselves pinned against a building, reckless youths, showing off, had dared one another to try and push the pointed guns skyward. "Tell them to stop pointing their guns," they too had chanted. But the young policemen had known no other way to make themselves feel safe. The paradox was that the act of pointing their guns so unsettled the crowd that it made the police less safe.

※　　　※　　　※

An odd apparition: visiting world heavyweight boxing champion Muhammad Ali and his entourage had arrived in the midst of all of this and then scurried into the City Hall for safety. I had glimpsed his gaily bannered luxury bus as it inched its way through the dense crowd but had been too busy at the time to wonder what on earth this alien craft was doing in the middle of the demonstration. In retrospect, it seemed to me that the celebrity bus had added an inappropriate note of carnival to this tragic day.

Odd behavior: other vehicles had also forced their way through the crowds, carrying the regional ANC leadership between the cathedral and City Hall. I was astonished when I saw famous faces peering out of car windows. Why weren't they out front controlling the crowd? Why were they signaling their separateness to a crowd that was mourning the assassination of a leader and desperately needing solidarity with its surviving leadership? Why were they creating a dangerous precedent by driving their vehicles through the packed crowd, especially when they would have made faster progress on foot? None of it made sense in the critical course of a day that above all needed the calming, reassuring presence of familiar leadership figures.

A week later, the Cape Town City Council produced its own nine-page report, which included similar recommendations. The lessons are clear: organization is critical, and joint control by the organizers, the police, and others involved is essential. It all hinges on communication with the crowd.

ANC VERSUS AFRIKANER RESISTANCE MOVEMENT

As the election looms, a new kind of political conflict emerges in some communities as self-styled gatekeepers jealously guard political access to the constituency they represent. Democratic Party officials are beaten up while holding a meeting in Khayelitsha, allegedly by local ANC members. PAC and ANC supporters skirmish in Langa. ANC students at the University of the Western Cape drive the Democratic Party from the campus. The ANC decides it is time to break new ground too, and the regional executive announces that it will hold a meeting in Parow on Thursday night, May 13, 1993.

Parow is right-wing. It is also completely white: the conservative, Afrikaner heartland of the Cape Peninsula, a bastion of the National Party and the Dutch Reformed Church. It is a middle-class and blue-collar municipality gathered alongside highway R102 as it curves east out of Cape Town toward the Hottentot Holland Mountains, which loom over the expanse of the Cape flats. Its member of Parliament is none other than the minister of law and order. I picture busloads of ANC supporters singing and toyi-toyiing their way into the cool shadows of the civic center set back in quiet dignity from the traffic of Voortrekker Road. The street name itself is ominous in this context. *Voortrekkers* were Afrikaner pioneers who set out in the last century with their oxcarts, courage, and guns to tame and claim the wild interior. Now, their descendants are the core of the Afrikaner Establishment. This is their stamping ground. It is also home to a hard core of the neofascist Afrikaner Weerstandsbeweging (AWB, the Afrikaner Resistance Movement). They will not take kindly to enemy invasion of their territory. The peace committee calls an emergency executive meeting to discuss how we can prevent serious trouble.

The peace committee chair, Jaap Durand, opens the meeting with a situation report. "The AWB has called the ANC, threatening to disrupt the meeting, blow up the building, and kill people. The ANC executive has met with the police, and they are discussing joint monitoring of the event. You need to know that the bar in the hotel opposite the hall is frequented by the AWB. The peace committee should be available to mediate if necessary."[4]

I groan quietly and curse the ANC for choosing this particular hall in this particular neighborhood for its first foray into the land of the white right. Jasper Walsh, Democratic Party M.P. and regional party chair, seems to hear my thoughts and responds, "This meeting is important because freedom of speech as a principle is at stake." It was his meeting that was so violently disrupted in Khayelitsha a month before. He says, "We need to establish a climate in which political parties can operate as political parties; therefore, all the political parties must be visibly seen to be supporting this meeting, sending representatives, making statements encouraging the meeting and discouraging disruption, and providing monitors."

Sakkie Pretorius, as a National Party M.P., says he has spoken to the minister of law and order about the meeting: "Meetings have been held with the AWB to give the message that they must not interfere. I propose that all the political parties take a resolution not to interfere in each other's meetings through to the election."

The ANC's Allan Boesak says, "I agree. ANC members must act tolerantly and take action against their own members who don't. But there is a difference between making another party angry and inflaming the situation. In the political arena, you can't promise not to make speeches that are angry, but you can try to be responsible."

The conversation becomes practical. We agree that the other major political parties will be present and identified, that political leaders will issue statements through the peace committee to encourage tolerance, and that the peace committee will issue a statement about freedom of speech. We will arrange extensive outside presence, including the international monitors, NIM, and the peace committee. Sakkie, Jasper, Jaap, and I will represent the executive committee. Someone proposes a meeting between now and Thursday night with the AWB and the Conservative Party, the official government opposition party that broke away from the National Party, which it viewed as too liberal. "No," Sakkie replies firmly, "we mustn't give the AWB the recognition of a public meeting with them."

We decide to establish a JOCC here at the peace committee offices and are heartened to hear that the AWB has agreed to maintain radio contact throughout the meeting on Thursday night. The police agree to provide metal detectors at the door to the hall, and as the right of admission will be reserved by the ANC, the police will be within their rights to remove any weapons. We ponder the more difficult question of the armed right-wingers who will gather outside. Can the police act, will they prevent armed groups from forming? We make detailed plans for the event that is still two days ahead and try to predict what will happen and how best to respond.

Soon after 6:00 P.M. on Thursday, wearing our peace committee jackets, the peace workers gather. The peace committee gives us shortwave radios, and we wander around, getting a sense of the building, the parking lot where the buses will deliver the ANC participants, and the vulnerable bathroom window at the back of the hall. The police are already in place, a phalanx of officers standing in a solid line across the access road facing the hall, the deputy district commissioner himself in command. ANC VIPs and their guests begin to arrive for cocktails in an inner room. Crowded buses carrying ANC supporters from Guguletu and Langa fill the car park, and by seven o'clock, the hall is filled to capacity and overflowing. ANC security staff operating the metal detectors at the entrance close the double doors and lean against them in a determined effort to keep out the growing crowd.

The doors of the bar across Voortrekker Road are flung open, and the first AWB members stride purposefully toward the hall. They are big men, armed to the teeth, with handguns in holsters and rifles or batons in their hands. Some have knives stuck in their heavy boots. Many are bearded in an Old Testament style that conjures up fiery prophets and thundering fundamentalist faith. They mean to intimidate and they do. They gather facing the hall, with the police at their backs. Soon their numbers have grown to about eighty. We peace workers number eight.

About two hundred ANC supporters mill around outside the hall, toyi-toyiing their bravado behind a fragile line of marshals. We peace workers stand between the two groups, ANC and AWB, occupying the small space that divides them and trying to keep it safe from incursion by either side. The AWB men glower at us and refuse to be confined. A pair of fledgling AWB teenagers, in great coats that flap open to reveal handguns, walk into the ANC crowd. I follow three paces behind and stand facing them when they stop. They walk purposefully toward the back of the building and gaze up at the lone bathroom window. I stand beside them. They walk to the other side of the building, back up the steps to the hall entrance, finally returning to their comrades. I peel off and am returning to no-man's-land when I am suddenly surrounded by the AWB. One of them stands in front of me. "Why are you following those boys?" he demands. He is clearly a leader. "Because," I reply, "they are very young to be armed and I think they are dangerous." I try to look him calmly in the eye as I speak. "They are not dangerous, they work for me," he snaps, pushing his face close to mine. He is angry and threatening, but the police are across the road and I remind myself that these men who are so enormous that they could snap me like a stick will not hurt me. "They have the right to walk wherever they want, you can't stop them." He is shouting out his pent-up rage at me, a viscious concoction of fear, bewilderment, betrayal, and isolation. I attempt a conversation about freedom of speech.

"Do you know something?" I begin. I wait for his eyes to focus again. "I would protect your right to hold a meeting anywhere you wanted to, provided you were not inciting people to violence or racial hatred or the derailing of negotiations. If you wanted to hold a meeting to tell people what you truly believe in, I would protect your right to hold it." I repeat myself, wanting to make the point. I am not sure that it is true, because I can't imagine the AWB holding a meeting that would meet these criteria. I believe in the principle, but I doubt it can be translated into practice. But at that moment, I want to believe that it could be so: that the rage and negativity that define the AWB in their resistance to negotiations with the ANC, and their futile determination to stop the clock and turn it back to the old apartheid times, can be defused by the simple act of recognizing that they have a right to be heard.

The man is silent. The AWB crowd that has gathered around us starts to shift its feet and splinter. I imagine that I see his face soften, and then the boundaries snap back into place and, if it was there at all, the moment is gone. He shakes my hand with the formal courtesy of the Afrikaner and turns on his heel. The crowd turns away. I stand alone in an empty island in the middle of the AWB group, which parts for me as I make my way to my position in no-man's-land.

The biggest AWB man of all is busy developing a pattern that he will follow throughout the evening. He too is determined to exercise his right to walk unhindered wherever he wishes. Without warning, he suddenly thrusts his huge bulk through no-man's-land into the ANC crowd, up the steps along the walkway, down the steps on the other side, back through no-man's-land, and into what has become AWB space. We peace workers too develop a standard reaction. We rush toward him, scurrying around him in an untidy escort, shouting at the marshals to clear the crowd in front of us as he grandly sails through the sea of upturned faces. I suspect he is enjoying himself hugely, and after a while even some of the ANC supporters start to laugh, although tensely, at the spectacle we present. It is pure theater, but at the time we cannot be certain that it will continue as a set piece. The tension thickens. We know from experience that violence is lurking in its shadows. Anything could happen.

As the evening turns into night, two other AWB members, who have somehow hoodwinked security into believing that they are ANC supporters, are thrown out of the hall. Otherwise, the hours pass without major incident. Yet every peace worker there will have his or her story to tell of an encounter or a conversation or a small act that changed things. It is these human connections that will one day deliver us in all our diversity as one people.

❊   ❊   ❊

Around 10:30, we hear the scrape of chairs and sustained applause signaling the end of what appears to have been a successful political rally, and we brace ourselves for the last hurdle, the dispersal of the crowd. The ANC will walk straight out the door into the arms of the AWB unless we can divert their flow, which we do by linking arms with the marshals and forming a safe channel to the buses. As they come out of the door, the ANC meeting participants immediately understand the situation and walk quietly between the human chains and board the buses. Their euphoria from the meeting is instantly subdued, but they are safe, violence has been averted, and for once the police have not had to lift a finger to ensure the law and order that they are dedicated to.

Nearly everyone is gone: the buses, the police, the organizers. The peace workers are handing in their radios, a tight knot of AWB men has gathered in the parking lot around their pickup trucks, preparing to leave. A press photographer finishes packing away his gear and ambles toward his car.

Suddenly the AWB group swings into action. With surprising swiftness, it attacks the African journalist, venting the frustration that has been simmering for the last five hours of inaction. The ANC has violated their turf, and they have not been able to do anything about it. The police have stood by, allowing and even condoning this incursion. The police have always been on the side of the white right in the past, making the events of this evening even more confusing and frustrating for the AWB.

Probably the one thing that has incited the AWB bile beyond endurance has been the toyi-toyiing, the symbol of black defiance that is a legacy of the African war dance. Toyi-toyiing in the townships is one thing. Toyi-toyiing in Parow, on the steps of the civic center, is another. For the two hundred ANC supporters excluded from the meeting and trapped outside the hall, it has been a way of keeping their spirits up, a unifying activity, an act of bravado in the face of the threatening AWB and police presence. For the AWB, perhaps it previews an unthinkable future when the black hordes take over the country and desecrate the dignity of the Afrikaner by, among other things, showing noisy disrespect in the quiet repose of Afrikaner neighborhoods.

We rush to the journalist's aid, and soon the scuffle is over. The journalist is safe except for a few bruises and a fit of the shakes. The AWB men leave in a squeal of tires. A group of peace workers repairs to a late-night restaurant to chew over the events of the night.

❋   ❋   ❋

We review the last few days, the joint planning, the contact with the right wing, the security arrangements, and the role of the police, and we conclude that this time we got it more or less right. We note that this is the first time that the police have just stood by while we, the peace workers, have in essence kept the peace. It is an interesting dynamic. The police presence deters violent behavior while the presence of the peace workers prevents the opposing parties from entering into conflicts in the first place, by keeping an eye on them and keeping them apart.

We talk about the AWB. Despite high-level communications giving assurance to the contrary, they still came with violent intent. We learn from this that the AWB is fragmented, the command structure is weak, control is sketchy. We should not be lulled into any sense of security by assurances from the top of the AWB that their people at the bottom will not act. Clearly they are as independently minded as their ancestors who ventured into the great unknown to find freedom rather than live under the yoke of the English oppressor. It is an insight that probably has implications for our dealings with other political organizations too.

We discuss the organization of the event and wonder how the ANC could have so underestimated attendance at the meeting. They could have hired the bigger of the two halls in the Parow civic center. We commend the marshals who once more behaved impeccably in a difficult situation. It is no easy thing to keep two hundred spirited but nervous young people under control in a confined space for four or five hours, especially when the tension level is so high.

We tell snatches of stories to one another about what we heard and saw and did, but it is past midnight, and rain is beginning to fall. We feel a bit flat, but this is the roller-coaster life of the peace worker, the adrenaline highs alternating with exhausted lows, and we are used to it.

A few years later, in Washington, D.C., an African-American woman would tell me, "It's just what we did in the civil rights movement." "I didn't know," I say, but I am not surprised. Whether we are talking about the AWB and the ANC, or the Ku Klux Klan and the Freedom Riders, the same fears, antagonisms, and power dynamics apply and can be met by similar reactive or proactive responses. It underlines the logic of our peace-making plans and actions and confirms for me once again that the principles we followed during South Africa's peace process could make sense almost anywhere.

4
CRISIS RESPONSE

Doing What Works

Often, we had no time to plan. We had to respond in the moment to one crisis after another, as each boiled over.

THE CRISIS CALL

Thursday, April 15, 1993

After the mass grieving and mob violence on the Parade yesterday, Chris Hani's memorial day, and the mopping up today, I am deep in an exhausted sleep when my phone rings at eleven at night. It is the white town clerk of Khayelitsha, the biggest African township in the area. "The civics [black township civic organizations] are demanding the resignation of the town councilors," he says, talking fast. "They are going to march tomorrow without permission, which means that the police will have to use force to stop the march, and who knows what will happen. The township is in flames. It's Chris Hani's murder and yesterday, the memorial service. They're burning cars and trucks all over the place and the warning's gone out that it's a no-go area for whites." His voice trails off; it is all too difficult. He says that the leader of the civic association wants me to call him. I hang up and dial the civic leader's home. "We need you to come out to the township for a meeting immediately," he says, a question mark hanging in his voice.[1]

"I can't come," I say. Eleven o'clock at night is too late, too dark, too dangerous, but I will meet him at the start of the march the next morning. He understands, and we talk about what we should do. "The youth are out of control. Emotions are running high. I don't want any more lives to be lost," he says, remembering the killing of the boy yesterday afternoon at the Parade.

I have no time to prepare myself with the issues. Perhaps the civics have demanded the removal of the councilors at this unstable moment to score political points in their community, or perhaps it is a matter of attacking the system when it is under maximum stress. The town clerk has assured me that he and the civic leader are "brothers" and that he negotiated with a township delegation on this very issue two weeks previously. Although the town councilors finally broke up the meeting with guns, the meeting went well. Why then, if he is as relaxed as he purports to be, does he need peace committee intervention this time? The councilors are armed and dangerous; the police are stretched thin and stressed; yesterday's violence at the Parade could be repeated in Khayelitsha. The simmering tension in the township is clearly explosive.

I start telephoning, first confirming with the town clerk that I have acted on his call. We estimate what time he expects the march to reach the council offices, and he assures me he will be ready and waiting. Next I negotiate with the police, and they agree to refrain from stopping the march, despite its illegality. The police will stand at the council offices, which they fear the marchers will attack. In return for being allowed to march, the crowd must halt fifty meters in front of the perimeter fence, out of hand grenade range. The police fear a grenade attack like the one yesterday on military headquarters during the violence on Cape Town's central Parade. I page Kaj Jensen; he calls me back from a downtown pay phone and agrees to accompany me. I wake up the coordinator of NIM; he finds two monitors for the march. I tell Chris Spies what is happening. When I check in with the local police station commander, he offers a police escort into the township. Feeling uncomfortable acknowledging my vulnerability, for the first and only time during those turbulent years, I accept.

Friday, April 16

Up early, I gingerly inspect the massive bruise from the rubber bullet two days before when I had been caught in the crossfire between the police and the crowd. It is black and covers the entire back of my thigh except for a perfect circle of white where the impact expelled the blood from an area about four inches in diameter.

I make a few last calls before the day spins into action and try to contact various members of the ANC regional executive to alert them to the imminent confrontation between the community and the councilors and ask for their help. I get referred from person to person. No one will take responsibility. Suddenly it is time to go.

Kaj and I use the official EC car festooned with as many official stickers as we can muster. Given the troubled mood in the township, it is important that we are seen as a benevolent presence. The monitors, Val Rose Christie and Rob Jenkins, similarly decorate their car with NIM identification stickers, and we meet up on the motorway bridge into the township. Looking back, I see Table Mountain, tranquil in the morning sunlight, solid and unmoved by the events unfolding in its shadow. I look across the bridge to the teeming shacks stretching as far as I can see. We drive into their midst, and with our police escort following at a discreet two hundred meters, we make our way to the stadium where the marchers are to convene later that morning.

I am glad that Val and Rob have volunteered to monitor the march today. Val is one of the most experienced monitors in the region. Rob, who has recently arrived from America, has thrown himself into monitoring work with astonishing commitment to a country and a cause that are not his own. Already I have found that I can count on him to be there when needed. He has courage too. Once when he and I were the only outside presence at a demonstration in the pouring rain in the center of Cape Town, a fight developed between ANC and PAC youth and one of the rocks that was raining down around us as we stood the middle ground between them hit him on the head. Despite copious bleeding, he stayed on until reinforcements arrived so that I would not be left alone.

As we pass the smoking hulls of burned-out vehicles that line the road, we practice what we have learned, driving slowly and carefully, concentrating on looking relaxed and making friendly eye contact with pedestrians as often as possible. The less threatening we appear to be, the less likely we are to be attacked. The police escort peels off before we turn the corner to the stadium.

We mix with the crowd that slowly gathers. By lunchtime about a thousand people are milling around, laughing and talking, singing and dancing. I meet some women who were at the Chris Hani memorial demonstration in the city center on Wednesday and show them my bruise from the bullet. There is a festive air, but in a corner of the field a knot of people collect, talking quietly, and it is clear from their gestures that they are not discussing a picnic. They are the civic and political leadership who will lead the march, and spotting the civic leader who had asked me to come, I walk across and join them.

I raise my hand, and when I am invited to speak, I tell them about my midnight conversations with the police. I explain that the police will allow the march even though no permission has been requested or granted and give the reason for the fifty-meter standoff at the council buildings. They listen politely and then continue with their conversation. Even though it is in Xhosa, it is clear that I am being ignored. I am bewildered; I am here at their request. The agreement with the police is crucial to prevent violence. I try again and once again meet a wall of unresponsive courtesy. I am not sure what to do. What I do know is that I have to find a way to make these men, and the handful of women on the edge of the circle, listen. So much is at stake. If they breach the fifty-meter limit, the police will shoot. In desperation, I make a quick decision and take a deep breath.

Once more I put up my hand and keep it up insistently until I am again invited to speak. I speak very loudly. "You have asked me to come to help, and yet now that I am here, you ignore me. I was on the Parade on Wednesday, you saw me there, and I have shown some of these women the rubber bullet wound I got trying to help stop the terrible violence of that day. I am here to try and help stop the terrible violence that might occur today. The police have agreed not to stop your march. For reasons that I have explained, they have set a fifty-meter limit. I need to know that you accept this condition in the interests of preventing violence and possibly death." I am as stunned by my words and my vehemence as they are. I walk away from the circle and wait. My entire body is shaking. I have broken almost every rule in the mediator's handbook. I have no idea what the result will be.

After what seems like forever, they call me back and agree to stop the march fifty meters before the fence. I nearly cry with relief, but instead we discuss the logistics of the march and the presentation of their petition, the route and the timing. We all snap into action. The marchers form some semblance of a procession and, singing loudly, set off into the narrow streets, escorted by Val and Rob. Kaj and I watch them round the first corner, and as their voices fade into the distance, we drive slowly to the council offices.

I wonder what was going on in that tight circle of men and assume that the gender issue was at the heart of their problem with my presence. In the traditional tribal setting, it has always been the men that gather to discuss weighty matters, and it is the men who have the dominant voices, especially in public. These are progressive, urban civic leaders, but the subservience and secondary role of women is so entrenched in both black and white South African culture that it is often cited just after racism in the long list of problems to be resolved.

Or perhaps the civic leader who asked me to come and help had not consulted with his comrades. Perhaps the leadership have changed their minds and now wish to be seen to control the events of this day without outside intervention from the peace committee. Perhaps it is a complicated combination of all of the above. One thing I am convinced of is that my rubber bullet bruise this day is a badge of honor and that the women who have seen it and can tell of it, some of whom were in that circle, have tipped the balance of legitimacy in my favor.

I also wonder how I could have avoided that desperate confrontation. I feel that I should have been able to find a better way of dealing with the situation. Later I conclude that I should somehow have found the civic leader who had invited me to be there and discussed the police plans with him so that it was he who presented them to his colleagues. I wonder why I did not do that and decide that it was probably a mixture of the tension of the day, the difficulty in locating the man, and, I have to admit to myself, ego. I become uncomfortably aware that there was a part of me that wanted acknowledgment for having been able to negotiate a midnight deal that could well save the day. After a few minutes of contemplating my own inadequacy and sense of failure, I remind myself of my immediate mediating job.

The conflict resolution literature is clear. The mediator does the following:

- ensures that credit for agreements resides with the parties concerned;
- takes the blame when things go wrong so that the parties don't have to blame one another;
- empowers the parties to find their own solutions; and
- comes to the fore when needed and then fades into the background.

Somehow, mediators have to find a healthy balance: they must have sufficient ego to believe that they can make a difference but not so much that they cast a long personal shadow over the process. It is a paradox that I will encounter throughout the afternoon that lies ahead, as the drama of the people's march against the councilors unfolds in Khayelitsha.

※   ※   ※

The council offices are an unprepossessing series of long, low buildings set on a rise opposite the police station. New security gates are being installed in the high perimeter fence for added protection. Once inside the gates, entrance is through a security room staffed by policemen. The council chamber and staff offices lie behind great steel doors operated by armed personnel. It is a telling picture, and a puzzling one to most citizens of the West, who view their local council as an infuriatingly bureaucratic but benign entity charged by the community to act in the local best interest.

In South Africa, local black councils were regarded as illegitimate by the majority of the communities that they were meant to serve. The seeds of this discontent were sown in October 1988 when the government-sponsored elections for black town councilors were boycotted by blacks throughout the country. The United Democratic Front (UDF), the umbrella organization formed to oppose the government's proposed constitutional reforms in the early 1980s, declared the boycott to highlight what it perceived as yet another attempt by the apartheid government to be seen to give power to blacks when, in fact, it intended nothing of the sort. The UDF was determined not to accept half measures and certainly was not willing to support government efforts to present an acceptable face to the world. The UDF argued that government policy, despite talk of reform, was not to change the apartheid system, but to try to make it presentable. Notwithstanding a national average turnout of just 11 percent of the eligible electorate, the elections were declared valid and the councilors installed as the duly elected representatives of their communities. The UDF promptly rejected any claims by the councils, and councilors, to legitimacy. This stance set the scene for dire consequences, including the murder of councilors, the burning of their homes, and attacks on their families, that still reverberate five years later, putting fire in the bellies of the players acting out today's drama in Khayelitsha.

Politics underpins everything in South Africa. That men and occasionally women choose to serve as councilors in the face of such solid and uncompromising opposition by their constituents is a measure of the longing for power, money, and position that apartheid and prior governments had denied to blacks. Inevitably, those long years of deprivation produced people prepared to face the contempt of their communities and even mortal danger in order to taste relative plenty. The bitter political act of harassing, killing, and burning apartheid-created puppets is in the end a Pyrrhic victory. Sadly, it is common.

Today, the councilors of Khayelitsha barricade themselves in their heavily defended council chamber. They are armed and sit glumly around the big table in the smoke-filled room, waiting for the arrival of the delegation that will bring with it the memorandum demanding their resignation. In a nearby office, the town clerk is outwardly calm, assuring me once again that he has handled negotiations with the community before and can do it again. Outside, the police, including the ISD, and the military have taken up defensive positions around the entire compound. Kaj and I meet with the police officer in charge. We confirm the community's agreement to the fifty-meter standoff, and he walks us along his defensive line, explaining the deployment plan. We remind him of the events of Wednesday and exhort him to act with restraint. He nods grimly. With icy calm, he watches for the march to arrive.

We can hear the distant voices of the march cutting through the stillness of the early afternoon. Kaj and I squat on the earth in front of the gates. There is nothing more for us to do except wait.

Suddenly the chanting procession is in front of us, and the marshals are running to stop it on the imaginary fifty-meter line. We walk toward the crowd to greet them, holding our breath. This is the first test. More than a thousand people are milling around. Some youth begin to toyi-toyi, and others shout slogans with raised fists, but the line holds and people begin to settle down, sitting on stones or the curb, calling to friends to join them. The marshals patrol, shouting into megaphones. Kaj and I wait at the gate. All eyes are on the protester delegation as it gathers around us, and we feel the crowd watching us as we disappear into the cool, dark interior of the council buildings.

We lead the twenty-five men representing the local branches of the civics and the ANC, and a handful of journalists that they have invited, through the steel doors into the inner courtyard. The local station commander and some members of the ISD stand guard. I move toward the council chamber, but the delegation changes tack and announces that it will meet with the town clerk, not the councilors, and they quickly cram into his office, the few seats reserved for the senior leaders, who sit in a solemn row in front of his desk.

The delegation gets right down to business. Their bottom line is the removal of the town councilors, and they are going to stay right where they are until their demand is met. The town clerk explains that he does not have the power to do what they ask. They insist. He huddles in his chair, at a loss for what to do next. Perhaps the provincial administrator can help. Sweat is forming in small drops on his face. He telephones the administrator, who relays his regret that he too is powerless to remove the councilors. It is a matter of the law. The delegation responds that they don't care about the law; it is the white man's law, not theirs, and their demand stands. They repeat that the councilors must go, and they will stay here for as long as it takes to get rid of them. Plumes of black smoke rise into the clear sky above the courtyard as the increasingly restless crowd outside begins to burn tires.

Kaj whispers in my ear that the councilors are threatening to use their guns to break up the meeting. This is no idle threat. I remember the town clerk telling me that two weeks before they had stormed into a similar meeting brandishing their guns and assaulting people and had thrown everyone out by force. I ask the police to ensure our safety, and we continue with the meeting.

The town clerk leaves the room, and, when after some minutes he has still not returned, it dawns on me that he has fled. I slide into his seat and telephone the provincial administrator in Cape Town. For the next two hours, I channel a conversation between him and the delegation. Gradually some openings for negotiation emerge, and with the smell of burning tires and the rising tide of strident voices drifting over the high walls from the crowd outside, a three-part agreement is hammered out. The administrator will consult with his executive committee on Monday and discuss with them the affidavit that the delegation will fax him now, spelling out their grievances. He will meet with the delegation the following week to discuss their demands. With the permission of the town clerk, the town council will be closed forthwith, in effect, preventing the councilors from functioning as councilors. We fax back and forth until everyone is satisfied with the wording, and three hours after their arrival, waving the agreement above their heads like a victory flag, the delegation jubilantly sings their way out of the council gates toward the impatient crowd.

The crowd surges forward to surround its leaders, and I anxiously swing round to watch the police. It is clearly not a threatening gesture, and they stand impassive. I had previously discussed this moment with the civic leaders, and they had understood that the immediate dispersal of the crowd is critical to a happy ending. They had agreed to return to the stadium where this all began six hours earlier for the report back. Now the entire gathering, which has grown to about two thousand, toyi-toyis away, glad for some activity after their long wait. The dust settles back onto the sandy earth. Trembling with relief that this potentially disastrous day has ended peacefully, Kaj and I go back indoors.

The town clerk reappears and turns on me in rage, blaming me for his humiliation. The town councilors emerge from their chamber and do the same. I remind myself that this is part of the job, but it hurts. There is nothing more to be done until tomorrow. We must just get home safely. The police escort us to the edge of the township, and we drive away from the angry township toward the picture-postcard evening star rising through the sunset above calm, dependable Table Mountain.

Saturday, April 17

The *Cape Times* reports yesterday's confrontation at Khayelitsha with twelve column inches on the front page. I note that once again the central role of the peace committee goes unreported or, more likely, has been edited out.

Ramotena Mabote, an African reporter who had witnessed the events in the council offices, writes of his fear that he would not get out of there alive. Reading his report, it hits me how dangerous yesterday had been.

> "Am I going to see the light of day," is the question that goes through my mind as I stand in the [Khayelitsha] Town Council offices while the tough negotiations progress and the toyi-toyiing 2000-strong crowd outside becomes increasingly angry and restless.
>
> My heart pounding, my fears deepen as I recall the sight of the still-smoking shells of torched cars in Khayelitsha when photographer Benny Gool—now standing nervously next to me—and I drove into the township along the infamous Zola Budd Drive.
>
> And when the meeting deadlocks at one stage and I notice black smoke outside the offices, I nearly collapse—or maybe I do, but no one cares to tell me.
>
> I realize that if Wednesday's march was anything to go by anything, including myself, could go up in flames.
>
> And well, when I (or part of me) finally squeeze through the crowd shouting "Amandla!" [Power!] to their victorious leaders, I realize with relief that although I am quivering, I am at least still intact.[2]

I dial the home number of the provincial administrator. We discuss the events of the previous afternoon and what needs to be done next. We will meet on Monday at his executive committee meeting. Meanwhile I suggest that I research what has happened in similar situations in other parts of the country. I spend most of that day gathering information from the Transvaal and Eastern Cape, where militant communities have succeeded in ousting unpopular councilors. I also call one of the Goldstone Commission lawyers, Max Hales, at home. Could he review the Black Local Authorities Act with a fine-tooth comb and let me know if there is anything I should know that could be useful in this situation? We have never discussed fees, even though this is clearly not Goldstone Commission work and will be done on his and his staff's own time. But all he says is, yes, he will do it.

I had blustered into his office at two hours' notice one day some months before to ask for help with a conflict over allegations of corruption in another black town council, and he has been available to me ever since, becoming part of the indispensable support network that makes my work possible. True to form, his report is delivered by hand to the Provincial Council offices in time for the meeting with the administrator on Monday morning. I feel a surge of gratitude for the camaraderie that binds so many of us as we work for peace in our land.

Events unfold predictably over the next four days, facilitated by the peace committee. It is clear that the councilors will have to go. It's just a matter of how and when. On Thursday, April 22, Jaap Durand chairs the meeting between the civics and the provincial administration to fulfill the agreement struck in the town clerk's office in Khayelitsha. During the following week, a deal is done, and the councilors are bought off with handsome golden handshakes.

For me, the best moment comes at the end of the Thursday meeting. It is all over, people are getting up from their seats, talking loudly as they make their way toward the door. Suddenly through the crowd I see the provincial administrator sitting in his city three-piece suit at the corner of the table talking animatedly to a casually dressed young African civic leader. This white man and this African man who inhabit the completely different realities of most white and black lives in South Africa are exchanging home phone numbers. I remember why I choose this work. The rewards are priceless.

VARIOUS RESPONSES

Calls for crisis intervention come in from the ANC, civic associations, community leaders, the police, the taxi organizations, other NGOs, and sometimes from all sides of the conflict: "Please help." They usually come to more than one of us; in a meeting of peace workers, a chorus of radio pagers may interrupt the proceedings.

Typical scenarios:

- Members of the ANC and the local civic associations are blockading the police station in Khayelitsha to demand the removal of the station commander, and shots are being fired into the crowd from an unmarked car.

- Armed black minibus taxi drivers are blockading the streets of Cape Town to protest the traffic fines imposed for a previous blockade, bringing the entire city to a standstill; the traffic police, supported by the ISD, are moving in.

- Coloured high school teachers from all over the region descend on Cape Town and march to Parliament to present the minister of education and training with a letter protesting the meanness of proposed salary increases and teaching conditions generally. The minister refuses to meet with them and the three-thousand-strong crowd pressed against the high parliamentary fence is getting restless and angry.

- The ANC has planned a march in a conservative white Cape Peninsula town starting at ten o'clock the next morning, and at five o'clock the evening before, the town clerk refuses permission for the march.

- The regional chair of the civic association phones to say that houses are burning in Crossroads and that he has been told that the police are responsible.

- The chair of a branch civic association phones to say that a member of his executive has been arrested and beaten up and is being held incommunicado.

I discover that one of my next most potent tools for crisis response after the beeper is the telephone, and some of my most effective resources are the power brokers.

The Power Brokers

Politicians; government officials such as mayors, provincial and city administrators, and town clerks; community leaders; leading businesspeople; and opinion formers of all kinds can be formidable allies or opponents. Their power lies in the influence that they wield as decision makers within their constituencies and how that influence can be brought to bear in a conflict or crisis situation. It is helpful not only to have them on our side in principle, but also to have them actively participating in the conflict resolution processes that we practice daily.

The secrets are involvement and inclusivity. Sakkie Pretorius, M.P., was involved throughout the peace committee intervention into the Tafelberg School crisis and played an increasingly active part in the negotiations with his own government's education department. He was present when the message confirming the transfer of the school came through. He heard the young black community leader, tears of joy streaming down his face, say, "Now I know there is another way of doing things," as for the first time he experienced achieving an objective involving collision with the state through third-party intervention and negotiation instead of demonstration and the threat of violence. It was a turning point for that young man and Sakkie, and neither of them ever looked back.

When the call comes in, I usually start with the phone, even when my instinct is to go to the crisis location. But this is before the advent of cellular phones and there are things that must be done first from wherever I am when the alarm is raised: home, the office, or even the checkout desk at a supermarket.

The calls and their order depend on the situation, so here I describe a generic response. I call the police, perhaps the peace committee police representative Gerrit Nieuwoudt, perhaps the local station commander, perhaps the regional commander of the ISD, Colonel Fanie Bouwer, perhaps the general responsible for police-community relations, or the regional commissioner himself. I have all their office phone numbers, their direct lines, their beeper numbers, and their home numbers. I alert them to the situation, ask for information, and request their presence at the scene of the crisis or that they act to restrain the junior officers who, it is alleged, are using unnecessary force. Just by my calling, something will happen, because now the police will be aware that the spotlight of the peace committee and others is on them. The call will restrain police excesses. A senior officer will almost certainly be dispatched immediately to ensure proper conduct. Wheels will be set in motion with the astonishing efficiency that is both the best and the worst characteristic of the police force.

I call the regional executive of the ANC or the civic organization or both. It is probably their constituents who are involved, in trouble, or at risk. I call the mayor of Cape Town, or the attorney general, or a human rights lawyer. I call the international observers and NIM, who are probably already on the case. I call members of Parliament, church leaders, any person I can think of who can bring influence to bear for a quick, bloodless resolution of the crisis. I call them at work or at home, even at their weekend or vacation numbers.

It is a powerful network, so much so that it may on occasion work all by itself. The police may restrain the officers involved in the incident, or in the interests of public safety agree to allow the march, even though it is illegal. The ANC leadership may negotiate with its own people to withdraw from their protest and join ongoing discussions on the issue. The attorney general may agree to meet with the taxi organizations to discuss their traffic fines. The local member of Parliament may decide to pursue the possibility of allocating the empty white school to the overcrowded black school, obviating the need for further protest.

Telephone Mediation

Telephone calls to the conflicting parties themselves may also work. I speak to the town clerk of a conservative white Western Cape town who is refusing to give a permit for an ANC march tomorrow morning. He faxes me a copy of the municipal rules and regulations governing marches, but I am not convinced that he is blocking the march just because of some bureaucratic technicality. He sounds genuinely worried. "About what?" I ask. "Well," he finally says, "they want to end the march in front of the town hall and make speeches. What will happen to all those people who have been fired up by political rhetoric?" He fears that they will run wild, and he is worried for the safety of his town. He is also unsure of himself, this is all so new, there haven't been ANC marches in his town before. I hear him blustering his way into a corner where he has said no once too often to be able to change his mind and still keep his dignity. My job is also to provide a face-saving formula for his inevitable agreement.

Our conversation goes on into the night, as I mediate by telephone between the ANC regional executive and this man whom I will never meet,
first while we are all still in our offices, then as we go to our separate homes
and evening lives. In the end he reverses his decision when he is given
certain assurances about the time frame for the speeches and the dispersal
of the crowd when it is all over. I sense that he is as relieved as I am.

Mostly, though, the telephone calls are just a start, the first line of approach to situations that could lead either to a defusing of the anger, an
agreement to negotiate, a catharsis completed—or to violence, destruction, and death. Often there is not really an outcome at all, because the
crisis is just a blip in the ongoing, low-intensity violence that simmers beneath the surface and periodically erupts.

Monitoring

We go toward the crisis, racing in our cars with their identification mark-
ings, wearing our identifying bibs, jackets, hats, or armbands, to see what
can be done. Sometimes just our presence will tip the balance.

The power of bearing witness cannot be overstated. A beleaguered community feels supported and safer because it is no longer isolated in its anguish. The security forces modify their behavior and act with unaccus-
tomed restraint. Politically violent and criminal elements tend to melt into
the shadows in our presence, bringing temporary relief. The houses already
torched burn noisily to the ground, but the torching around them usually
stops.

The monitors from NIM take statements from witnesses, and, transformed into affidavits, these become the basis for further police investigation. The allegations generally focus on police misconduct, and few trust
the police to investigate themselves. But the monitors are taking statements from witnesses and are themselves witnesses. This has a profound
effect on the dynamics of daily conflict, particularly between the police
and the black community. Later, when the police have begun to implement community policing and are really trying to transform, they request
the presence of monitors at conflicts to be sure that their actions are not
misreported or misconstrued.

On-the-Spot Mediation

Sometimes we can find a solution immediately. Remember the three thousand teachers who marched to Parliament only to be refused access to the

minister of education and training? The ANC regional chair Allan Boesak presses their demands for a better deal and, confronted by the locked gates and baleful stares of parliamentary security officers, he calls for the peace committee over his megaphone. I agree to see what can be done. Invoking the National Peace Accord and escorted by the police major in charge of security and one of his officers, I meet with the minister in his inner sanctum. I explain that he may have violence on his hands, that the crowd is at that stage of frustration where anything could happen. The major nods in agreement. But the minister is afraid. Can we guarantee his personal safety?

We hammer out a deal that the crowd will step back ten paces, making a space for him, and a delegation will bring the petition to him. I run back to Allan, and we try to get the ten paces, but it is impossible, the weight of the crowd is too heavy and their forward momentum too strong. I suggest that we open the huge, heavy gate, which hinges inward, creating new space, and finally, after what seems like endless delay, the gate opens. The minister's security officers surround him so tightly that he can barely be seen, but the teachers are able to hand over their petition and address the crowd, which then disperses peacefully. Another crisis has been averted.

Mediation and Facilitation

As my work takes me into more and more conflict situations, I find myself losing touch with the theoretical distinctions between mediation and facilitation. At the Centre for Conflict Resolution, we talk about mediation as intervention in a conflict by a mutually acceptable third party with the aim of achieving a mutually acceptable outcome. Facilitation of communication aims primarily at improving communication and the relationship between the parties.

The definitions no longer fit. Each time we work it is different. Sometimes we are more proactive than either mediation or facilitation; at other times all we hope for is to keep people talking instead of acting violently. The certainty of theory is giving way to the uncertainty of practice.

The model that begins to emerge is a spectrum. It has facilitation on one end and mediation on the other. The overarching rubric is third-party intervention. Each intervention ranges across the spectrum, sometimes changing by the day.

Chris Spies, Vincent Diba, and I are working on a conflict between township residents and hostel dwellers around a scarce and sought-after resource, housing. Hostels were designed to house single African men, enticed from rural villages to work as contract laborers for white industry. For some years now, the rules have been relaxed, and the men have brought their families to the city and moved in permanently. They are soulless, run-down places, but at least they provide a place to stay, and the families jealously guard their tenancies, passing them on to relatives and friends.

This has incensed the township youth, who, like young people everywhere, are desperate for a place of their own away from their parents. They see these strangers from the countryside taking accommodation that they believe is rightfully theirs because it belongs to their township. They allege corruption in the town council that administers the hostels, and in the last year they have decided to fight for their rights. They storm selected rooms in the middle of the night and evict existing tenants, belongings and all, onto the street, or they steal into rooms during the day when the tenants are out at work and take over. Now the tenants are fighting back, and the battle may become a war. Though it is a pale shadow of the hostel conflicts outside Johannesburg, it causes enough havoc in the Langa community to worry us. Chris, Vincent, and I are determined to prevent it from developing into a full-blown war.

The conflict goes around in circles. Both parties insist that they have the legal and moral right to live in the hostels. What can we do? How can we help people break out of their positions? They seem like stuck records, repeating the same things day in, day out. Yet it is our job to help them get unstuck.

It slowly becomes clear that one party does not want the conflict to end. That party is using the conflict to secure a power base for itself within the community. It doesn't matter what Chris and Vincent and I do, we cannot be effective if one (or both) of the parties is unwilling to settle.

We also begin to see that real reconciliation between the parties at this moment in South Africa's history is improbable. The housing conflict is an expression of the apartheid legacy, and the intricate web of structural inequities and power dynamics will not be adequately addressed until the dawn of a democratic government and a new constitution. We can't change the system. Meantime, it limits what we can achieve.

At the same time, as third-party intervenors, we expect to help conflicting parties find solutions. We long to stop the violent fallout of the conflict. We hold out beacons of hope for its peaceful resolution. When we are at our most effective, we work from our hearts, and sometimes our role is just that—to bring the heart back into the relationship between the conflicting parties. We are driven to do this work from a deep sense of vocation.

Now I realize with painful clarity that we must give up this notion of a *solution* and concentrate on turning the *process of conflict* into the *process of peace*. Sometimes, we have to give up being able to make things better. Instead, we must focus our energies on keeping open a safe space that conflicting parties can enter if and when they wish. It is in this space that the process toward peace can begin.

Imagine a fight in any community anywhere: wounding words, irrevocable deeds, violent intentions, righteous rage, the source of the conflict lost in the cycle of tit for tat. Then comes escalation, maybe, or as is more likely in this case, exhaustion, boredom, and resistance by affected bystanders to support what is increasingly looking like a lose-lose situation. The community has polarized around the conflicting parties; relationships and promises have been broken; irretrievable words have been said. What then?

If the safe space exists, the parties can retreat into it. If trusted intermediaries from within or outside the community have been able to maintain contact with all sides, now they can provide the face-saving devices that can kick-start negotiations out of the mutually dug hole. The mediators can encourage the leaders of the conflicting parties to choose the "high road," and support their sound good sense, their altruism, and their leadership qualities, as they finally choose to seek settlement. They can reach out in understanding, knowing that the leaders were driven by their own and their communities' demons. They can suggest appropriate symbols to signal the long, slow walk toward agreement. They can help think of ways for a mutually satisfying end to the conflict. The healing can begin.

The space can be widened as more and more individuals and groups of opposing constituencies choose to end their part in the conflict. Finally, the space expands to encompass most of the whole, ending the conflict temporarily. But you can maintain the space only at the price of constant vigilance. The conflicts of the future are already simmering beneath the surface.

Over the next weeks and months, we are not able to hold the space in Langa. One of the parties is still unwilling to settle for anything less than absolute victory and is stoking the conflict. I feel that our team is being manipulated, and in the end I retreat, sad, bruised, and feeling guilty that I haven't been able to do better for this community. Chris and Vincent also extract themselves. Perhaps we have helped prevent a full-blown war, although we will never know what would have happened without our intervention.

What I do know is that this work demands that we are willing every day to learn how to do it better.[3]

MORE LESSONS

As our peace work experience broadened and deepened, we discovered some fundamental principles.

Building Trust

All the parties to the conflict must trust the mediator. But what is trust? How is it created? Can it be acquired, transferred, or cloned?[4]

You build trust brick by brick on the foundations of integrity, consistency, and action. Monitors, observers, mediators, trainers, fieldworkers—all of us build trust by being ourselves, by being there, by keeping our commitments, by caring, by talking and listening, and by doing.

Sean Tait is a committed visionary for peace and justice, an excellent organizer, and a conscientious peace worker. He was the peace committee fieldworker for the Cape Peninsula and Cape Town urban metropole when he first heard rumors of Operation Barcelona in March 1993. His information was that the youth, both ANC- and PAC-aligned student organizations, had entered into a unity agreement to address the education crisis.

Student and teacher protests had been going on for some time. The issues were pay, conditions, access to resources, safety in schools, size of classes—everything in the second-rate Bantu Education system designed for Africans under the apartheid system. Now anger and frustration around this infamous system were compounded by proposed salary increases that were considered insulting. There was a sense of hopelessness about the imbalance between the high standards of white education and abysmal African education and whether it would ever be righted. But the issue that sparked off the violent protests and brought the townships to a grinding halt was school fees. Blacks had to pay school fees that, on apartheid regulated wages, they just couldn't afford. The youth argued that education was a right, not a privilege, and that all black school fees should be abolished forthwith.

Sean describes what he remembers happening when Operation Barcelona, as the violent campaign was called, started:

> All hell soon broke loose. Cars were being stoned and set alight along the N2 motorway [which runs east out of Cape Town past many black townships]. Student marches were disintegrating into chaos. And, of course, as the central aim of Barcelona, Department of Education and Training officials responsible for African education were being driven from the schools, their motor cars left burning behind them. Everyone was getting a bit jumpy. While it was always, to a certain extent, dangerous traveling in conflict areas in the townships, Barcelona made it more so. A morning might be quiet, the afternoon might be littered with burnt-out cars.

How did Sean build trust with the youth?

> By being me, I suppose. They used to say that I was one of the few people who was not arrogant, someone they could communicate with who wouldn't respond to them as children.
>
> The other thing, of course, was being seen out in the field sticking my neck out in a dangerous situation and they in a sense being responsible for my safety.
>
> The rest was just common sense. I didn't pressurize them into stopping the action. Rather, I exposed them to another way of achieving results they said they were after, that is, through negotiation.
>
> Lastly, they probably sussed [checked] me out in the work I'd been doing with the local peace committees.[5]

Integrity, consistency, action. Sean built trust instinctively, and the youth instinctively trusted him. More than anything, Sean was himself.

Recognizing Pitfalls

CONFLICTING PARTIES' COMMITMENT TO A SOLUTION. If the parties do not really want a solution, there is nothing the mediator can do. The story about the Langa hostel conflict shows that parties may ask for third-party intervention, but the conflict may have to play itself out for a while longer before intervention can be effective. Timing is all-important. Sometimes no amount of surfacing of interests, fractionating of issues, or venting of emotions will move the process forward. Then, all you can do is to work hard at creating a window, the safe space in which the parties can choose whether or not to resolve their differences peacefully. If the parties choose to continue the conflict using violence, mediators need to guard against the sense of failure that settles in the pit of the stomach. Often there is nothing that we could have done better.

MANIPULATION OF THE MEDIATION PROCESS BY CONFLICTING PARTIES. Beware of being used. As the culture of conflict resolution took root and gained credibility, parties realized that it was often useful to be seen to be trying to resolve their differences. Sometimes they would come to the mediating table by day and continue their violent strategies by night. They would, of course, deny their duplicity. Mediators would earnestly continue the process and wonder why the usual methodology wasn't working. With experience, we could usually (but not always) spot when we were being used, and at times we chose to continue anyway. Mediation is extraordinarily powerful and, by continuing, we could extend the agreement to suspend much of the violence and even, perhaps, persuade the parties that this is a better way of solving their differences.

Using Mediation Teams

Mediators work best in teams of two or more. The team can reflect the composition of the parties. This is a confidence- and trust-building measure. The parties feel more comfortable if the mediator has some natural affinity with them of gender, age, or race. In a conflict between predominantly white senior members of the security forces and a black community, the team would ideally have a black and a white person, each of whom had the trust of at least one of the parties. In an intraorganizational conflict involving men and women, the team should be balanced for gender, and for race and age if possible. Political and ideological preferences could also be matched, but the mediators would need a profound commitment to the mediation process, not to their political party.

Team members can offer each other practical and moral support and someone to talk to. It is difficult to recapture the nuances of a mediation successfully enough to discuss it sensibly with a colleague who was not present. A team of two (or more) can support each other during the mediation process and debrief each other, offer advice, and strategize the next steps. A team of mediators offers continuity if one or the other is not available.

Teamwork provides an excellent training opportunity. At the beginning of 1993, overwhelmed with requests to help in conflicts that we couldn't possibly meet, but lacking the funds to dramatically increase our staff, the Centre for Conflict Resolution established what it called a Mediation and Training Team. The goal was to increase the mediation and training capacity of the Centre and the region to respond to conflicts. A dozen diverse men and women from all walks of life volunteered to be trained as mediators and trainers. They participated in our training courses, attended monthly meetings, and teamed up with our staff mediators and trainers for on-the-job experience. The concept was successful to the point that within three months we found funding for it, within six months a number of the trainees had progressed to the point where they could intervene in a conflict with a fellow teammate with minimal supervision, and within a year many were able to operate as full-fledged trainers and mediators. The team continues to operate, now with a full-time coordinator, and aims to train about twelve people a year.

PROCESS ADVOCACY

Conflict resolution literature talks a lot about the need for the mediator to be neutral when intervening in a conflict. I do not believe that it is possible for any human being to be neutral about anything. Each of us operates from a position that makes our individual view of the universe unique and subjective. Whether we like it or not, we are saddled with the baggage of the beliefs and experience that shape our perceptions. It is not a matter of choice, even for someone who chooses to be a mediator. And even if neutrality were an option, I believe with my colleague Ron Kraybill, then director of training at the Centre, that it would not be desirable.

Toward the end of 1992, Ron wrote an article in which he says that he would like to remove the word *neutrality* from the English language because of the damage that it does to peace workers.[6] He says, "It confuses many mediators with a false understanding of their task; it blocks many sincere leaders from acting on their own deeply held principles of justice; it damages the credibility of the entire enterprise of peacemaking." He observes that mediators often try to be neutral because they think there are no alternatives. Ron says that, rather than hiding our values, peacemakers can be explicit about them.

People in a society riddled with injustice are often critical of the mediator role because they see it as value-free or as evading values. Many feel that the only way to express values is to be an advocate for one side or the other. I believe that people who choose to be mediators do so from the same base of values as those who are fighting injustice as advocates. We have just chosen a different way to help effect social and political change.

Ron argues that, whether we like it or not, we are all advocates at heart, that "we are advocates of something all the time, whether we are conscious of it or not. The question is not if we are advocates, but rather of what." He suggests that we become passionate about the process of third-party intervention and the principles it supports, that we commit ourselves to process advocacy and to a set of principles that apply to the interventions we conduct.

These principles include demanding respect for dignity and equality among all participants, trying to balance their relative power and access to information, making genuine attempts at problem solving, and encouraging accountability between the parties and the parties and their constituencies.

Ron is good at crystallizing the ideas that we often discuss, reconfiguring them into a framework that makes sense of the often bewildering disparity between the theory and the practice of conflict resolution. His article bears out my beliefs, and I feel pleased with myself. I now have the experience to truly practice *process advocacy*. The term rolls off my tongue.

Four days after Ron's article is published in the journal *Track Two*, I take the tumble that my hubris has set me up for. On the evening of Thursday, November 5, 1992, I respond to a crisis call to the peace committee for someone to go out to a squatter camp thirty kilometers (almost twenty miles) north of Cape Town first thing the next morning. The regional authority that owns the land has demolished twenty-one shacks and the squatter community is in an uproar. The squatters are angry and afraid, and when I arrive there with the ever-faithful NIM monitor Rob Jenkins at nine o'clock that Friday morning, I feel my own anger rising.

Land has always been a source of conflict in this vast country of ours, and terrible things have been done in its name. But now that the winds of change are blowing hard across the veld, an unofficial moratorium on removals has been implemented until the future becomes clearer and new land policies emerge. The National Peace Committee has brokered an agreement that shacks should not be demolished and squatters should not be evicted, whatever past policies may have dictated. These demolitions are therefore a direct contravention of that agreement.

The squatters live on a tract of sandy veld peppered with trees surrounding a rubbish dump and toxic-waste tip. Some of them have lived there for as long as fifteen years, improving and expanding their plastic and wood dwellings over time. The building method is simple. Cut down trees, build a frame, cover it with plastic sheeting. Then embroider with tin or wood or whatever building materials the dump yields. It isn't much, but it is home to sixty-six families who have nowhere else to go.

Africans and Coloureds live together, in this case the bond of poverty stronger than the divisions of race. Few of them have jobs away from the site, as the majority consider the dump their work. They work it in shifts, regulating their days around the arrival of the trucks from the suburbs of Cape Town. They have to walk two kilometers to collect water from the only tap available, but one of their number has started a shop right in the middle of the settlement that has made this harsh life that little bit easier.

When the site manager arrives, he says that two months ago he warned these people that the houses he considers illegal would be demolished because they fell outside the quota of sixty-six. Yesterday, he brought in a demolition crew, and with armed security guards standing by they demolished twenty-one houses. The houses were all empty of possessions at the time of demolition, he says. A man was arrested during the demolition and has been taken to jail. The manager will not say why. The dispossessed people will be moved to the de Noon serviced site in the municipality of Milnerton near Cape Town as soon as it is complete.[7] The manager plans to meet with the squatters on Monday at nine in the morning.

Three of the squatters, Flora, Nathan, and Deon, say that they were not warned of the demolitions, and there were possessions in the houses. The site manager came with three yellow police vans, three blue security vans, two white landowner vans, a white landowner car, and a dog. One squatter, named Pinky, was arrested for holding onto a sail (plastic sheet) when the demolition crew were knocking down his house. They do not know about the proposed move to de Noon and are unhappy at the news. They have lived here so long, their children have been born here, there is no crime, and how will they make a living without the dump?

Rob and I walk along paths that twist through the shadows of the sparse bush to view the demolished houses. We see poles that have been sawn through so that they are not reusable, wooden walls broken in half, plastic ripped with knives, clothes and broken pots beneath the wreckage. With Ivan, the son of the shopkeeper, we step across the broken wall of his house to see what can be salvaged. There is nothing. Nomakwande tries to pull the clothes out from under the broken poles that were her house. The clothes are ruined.

My role as the serene process advocate crumbles. I am feeling furious, not in the least bit impartial, and I am already scheming ways to help the squatters fight this tyrannical landlord. I find it hard to believe that even as notorious a landowner as this one could wreak such mindless damage in the lives of a few harmless, homeless people on a site miles from anywhere. I am outraged. We sit in the sand in front of Nathan's house and wonder what to do. Perhaps the site manager did warn a few individuals about the impending demolitions, but because the community is not organized, the word did not spread. We suggest that Flora, Nathan, and Deon call a community meeting over the weekend to elect a committee of five people who will represent the community in their dealings with the landowners. At least then they can negotiate with one voice. They like the idea, and we agree to meet again the following week.

That afternoon I track down Pinky at Malmesbury jail. The record shows that he has pleaded not guilty to the charge of trespass and that his case will come up for trial on Monday. I contact a human rights lawyer. I put a call through to the chief executive of the landowner, but he is not available. I call the site manager and tell him that Pinky will be represented by a lawyer on Monday and that I will be discussing the whole episode with his boss. He tells me that he believes in God and does not wish anyone harm and that he will request that Pinky receive no fine and be given a suspended sentence.

On Monday morning I manage to talk to someone senior in the landowner's office and inform him that the peace committee is now involved in this case. Midmorning the site manager calls to say that Pinky has been released with a suspended sentence and that he will be reinstating most of the twenty-one homes that were demolished. For the moment, the crisis is over, but I know it is only the end of one small battle in an ongoing war.

But what next? The disparity of power between the squatters and the landowner is enormous. What, if anything, can be done to bridge the gap?

I telephone a lawyer at the Legal Resources Centre (LRC). I know that land issues are complex, difficult, and the focus of unprecedented attention. We agree that it would be best for an NGO specializing in squatter issues to be brought into the picture. They would be able to navigate the intricacies of the law, and as activists, they would work to empower the squatters. In addition, this case can be brought under the umbrella of a major negotiation on land issues that is currently in process and that includes the de Noon site.

I have tried to restore some balance to the community by aiding the release of one of their number from jail and facilitating the reinstatement of the destroyed houses. I have also encouraged the community to organize and will be bringing in an activist NGO to support them. I have notified various agencies about the case both to elicit help (LRC) and to prevent further action against the community by the landowner. The landowner is less likely to take further action now that the spotlight is on the situation. In other words, I have acted as best I can to empower and protect the weaker party to the conflict. I play the party advocate, not mediator. It is clearly the right thing to do. Isn't it?

※　　※　　※

I still feel uneasy and ambivalent. I try to justify my actions at the squatter camp. The landowner, a government agency, was an integral part of the structural injustice that characterized the apartheid era, and until the old institutions were transformed, this kind of action would continue. I am reminded that, as mediators, we have to understand that there are some things that fall outside the scope of conflict resolution methodology to resolve, primary among them the structural injustices that only new legislation can change.

Why do I feel such a failure? I failed to hold onto the role of process advocate that is my passionate commitment, and that just days before entering the life of the squatter camp I had believed I could do with ease. I failed to remember that my job is to hold the middle ground, to reinforce and expand it. My actions would have only further alienated the beleaguered government landowner, pushing the agency further into its lonely corner, isolated, alone, and definitely disinclined to venture out into the middle space. I did not make it safe to do so. On the contrary, I contributed to the sense of danger, bringing to bear the wrath of the peace process backed by legislation when what I needed to do was to help loosen the position, get the parties unstuck. My actions may have brought some temporary relief this time, but they would only make it harder the next. And the next. Our main task is to hold the space open between the conflicting parties.

This story does not have a happy ending, or indeed any ending at all. When I return to meet with the squatters as arranged, I find that they have not held the community meeting, because everyone got drunk on Friday night and spent the rest of the weekend hungover. And when I bring the activist NGO group to meet with them, and we sit on overturned crates in a circle in the sand, the activist leader incites them to turn against the *Boer* (literally, "farmer," but the word also symbolizes the Afrikaner government) who is oppressing them. It is fighting talk for people who do not have the will, the wherewithal, or the cohesion to fight. Afterward I speak to him about it, but he is unresponsive. It is how he does things. I understand his perspective; I know his inner rage is fueled by exactly this kind of injustice and blind cruelty. He is what I would call hard left, and for him conflict resolution is too soft. He does not understand that peace is much more difficult than conflict.

I cannot continue this intervention. Squatter and land issues are a minefield requiring specialist knowledge and experience that I just do not have. I know that the hard young man will fight with passion for what he believes is right, not to solve the problem. And perhaps that is all that can be achieved right now. I have made the decision to let go, and I turn and walk away from that sandy site in the veld for the last time, from Flora, Nathan, and Deon and the other folk who live beside the rubbish dump.

5
TRAINING

Winning Hearts and Minds

Thirty-five rural community leaders are adamant that they do not want conflict resolution training. "We don't have the time. We don't have the energy to consult or negotiate," they say. "We just want the authorities to provide us with what we need."[1]

It is the first morning of a three-day training workshop in conflict resolution skills. The leaders have made the long trek from their communities to this place in Pretoria called Voeldrif, and the first session is scheduled to begin. The places they have left behind typify the lot of rural Africans in apartheid South Africa. Barred from seeking work in urban centers, relegated to barren lands that the whites did not want, most rural blacks have for decades been consigned to eke out a living in abject poverty from which there seems no escape. They have learned to live below the poverty line, building houses of available materials, of mud, stone, wood, plastic, or tin. They collect water from dams, streams, or a single tap and carry firewood over great distances. They have learned to live with broken families, as the men and the young in desperation have set out bravely for the big cities to find work, often never to return. They have learned to live with despair.

The training team, led by Craig Arendse,[2] has flown up from the Centre for Conflict Resolution in Cape Town with a workshop agenda, case studies, and role plays. They bring a plan for communicating the tried and tested tools and techniques of mediation, negotiation, problem solving, and principled bargaining. These are experienced trainers, so the paradox of a group of people gathered for training who declare that they do not wish to be trained is a challenging but not insurmountable problem.

The community leaders have come because they recognize the need to increase their skills base generally. The daily grind under the apartheid years has left millions of black South Africans undereducated and underdeveloped, and they know it. The trainers also know what a free weekend away from the shacks and the deprivation of their lives means. "The food was absolutely fantastic," Craig says, as he tells me this story some months later. "Imagine them, really grassroots people with an average educational level of standard six or seven (eighth or ninth grade in the American system), living in real, rural poverty. And here there is remote-controlled TV, a La-Z-Boy recliner, a shower, and fabulous food."

Craig is talking into my tape recorder as we sit one Sunday afternoon at his dining room table. His conversation is peppered with the raucous laugh that is his trademark. I play it back to him, and for the first time he hears the laugh. "Now I know why everybody laughs at my laugh," he says, exploding with amusement. "It really is very funny." When our laughter is worn out, he tells me what it was like to grow up as a so-called Coloured, a nonwhite person of mixed race but who spoke Afrikaans, the language of apartheid South Africa.

He used to love May 31, Republic Day, an annual public holiday that included pageantry and parades to celebrate South Africa's conversion to a republic in 1961. He loved the singing of the national anthem, "Die Stem" ("The Call"), and the flags. He always wanted to be in standard five (grade seven in America) and be a prefect so that he could walk with the red, white, and blue flag and hoist it up and be proud of it. Then when he was nine years old, his mother started to tell him and his siblings what it really meant. She said, "We are not real citizens of this country, we can't vote, 'The Call' is not really our call, and the flag is not really our flag." She discouraged him from participating in Republic Day celebrations. When he was twelve in 1976 and the students rose up and said a resounding, violent, and bloody no to the black educational system, his mother was one of the few teachers to stay home from school. She said it was the call of the people to stay at home. In high school, he and his brother became involved in political movements. He remembers going to meetings and sitting in someone's lounge on the floor with all the curtains drawn. His mother always supported them. The first time his brother was detained, he can still picture his mother standing in the doorway and saying to the police, "I wonder how you would feel if this was your child."

This mother of all mothers died in 1985, but not before she had witnessed events in Craig's life that changed him irrevocably. Wanting to be a priest, he completed a diploma in youth ministry and became a youth pastor in a circuit that included white congregations. A bitter young man, angry toward white people, he nevertheless started a youth group in the predominantly white suburb of Observatory. The children would run to him, jump up to hug him. "For them I was just another person," he marveled at the time. They saw him as a person, not a black person. That changed his life. So did an event at a youth camp where he was the only black person. "This one young kid, about ten years old, looked at me and asked, 'Are you white?' My friend who was white and standing next to me said, 'Yes, he is,' and in real confusion this kid said, 'You must have been on the beach for a very long time!'" The indoctrination of apartheid had taught his friend to defend him as white, and the little boy had learned that tanned was all right, black was not. "It was those little experiences that said to me, yes, we live in different worlds. It is unfortunate that these worlds, without our consultation, have been developed for us, and that the only way we can move beyond and move on is if we have an understanding and are exposed to the world of the other person, and try and understand what makes that person who she or he is."

Working closely with young white people, and hearing their stories, had such an impact on Craig that he involved himself in a number of cross-cultural programs. Training followed on from his activism. It gave substance to what he was doing. He was also influenced by Paolo Freire: "He says that reflection without action is mere pacifism, and action without reflection is mere activism." Craig sought the balance, and he found it in training.

And here he is in Voeldrif once again standing before a group of expectant workshop participants, except that this time the participants say they do not want to be trained. Craig does not miss a beat. He listens to the earnest voices of the community leaders describe the real problems of their lives.

The community leaders say they cannot learn conflict resolution because they have no water, no sewerage, abundant unemployment, and social evil. They do not want to talk to the councilors or the government or the police. Another side of the story will make no difference to their problems. These are the people who have abused them. These are people in powerful positions. The powerful must yield.

Underneath the words, an unspoken fear is also holding them back. Craig understands it instinctively. "If they go for joint problem solving, it looks as though they are being too soft, as if they are giving up their power, giving in. People find that scary because for so long all we had was our anger. All we had were our grievances."

Craig said, "It's your choice. It's your choice to do brainstorming with the authorities and raise options, or it is your choice to use pressure tactics, but let's evaluate it."

They role-play pressure tactics, observing how the other party responds, noting the delays in moving forward. In many cases, no progress is made and antagonism develops. Then they practice joint problem solving, looking at needs instead of positions, finding ways for people to work together, building sustainable relationships, and accelerating delivery dates. The parties find to their amazement that they can find mutually beneficial processes that are less threatening to both parties, and that they can resolve the problems. "That was empowerment," Craig says. "They suddenly saw another way of doing things. We didn't force it down their throats."

They role-play real issues. There are only ten water taps for five thousand people. The community wants fifty water taps. By role-playing the town councilor who has been told that his budget will stretch only to ten more taps, not fifty, they understand the reality of the other person's work, his orders, his budget constraints.

Craig explains that they will get the best results if they have the best process. This includes focusing on what information they need, what they want to do, who they need to speak to, how to keep the rest of the community involved, how to listen to the community, how to get a mandate and how to present it, and how and when to listen to the other side. If all the energy is directed into fighting for the fifty taps head-on, the space disappears for a win-win solution. The community, which has the conviction and the constituency, and the authorities, which have the power and resources, deadlock. "People think that if there is a conflict situation, the stronger they come across, and the louder, the better. They often forget that the other person can also be strong and loud. It then just becomes a [shouting] match, nobody wins, and everything is delayed," he says.

Craig sums up his training philosophy: "The kind of training that we do does not assume that we have the answers. We are saying that we can provide an opportunity, a space, for reflection. It is experience-based training. We take extracts from real life and reflect on them. I don't have the answers, but I do have the tools to help people think through the problem."

Craig believes passionately in the power and importance of the training he and his colleagues are doing. His words fall over one another. "Look at the number of black youth who still think that pressure politics is the only way to go, that boycott is still the way to do it, that looting is still the way to go. Where are the trainers? Why don't we go in and teach them nonviolent ways of protest? Why don't we teach them analysis so that they can identify the best avenues for their voices to be heard and their grievances to be placed on the table? Why don't we train them in negotiation skills so that when they meet a minister or a city councilor they can articulate and in a very dynamic way express what they need and also be able to understand where the other person is coming from? Why not teach them skills in conflict resolution so that they understand that violence is not the only way to achieve a particular end, that there are other ways to deal with someone you perceive as an opponent? Get them away from competition into the concept of collaboration."

SOUTH AFRICA ADOPTS AND ADAPTS

Professor H. W. van der Merwe pioneered training in conflict resolution skills in South Africa at the beginning of the 1980s. As director of the Centre for Intergroup Studies (now the Centre for Conflict Resolution), he convened mediation skills training workshops and brought in American and British trainers to run them. He and others built on the success of these initial workshops, and by 1990, trainers in mediation, negotiation, and facilitation skills came in large numbers from America and Europe, bringing the tools of nonviolent conflict resolution to the players who were bargaining the future at every level.

The South Africans learned quickly, and they soon offered training more adapted to South African culture. Organizations already working in the field expanded, and new ones emerged. Foreign trainers continued to come in. Generally, they were no longer so welcome. Suspicion grew that many of them were driven by personal agendas, that they were in it for what they could get out of it, not for what they could give. Training in South Africa, a conflict hot spot, gave credibility that enhanced their image elsewhere, we thought. Many of them would come into the country, give the training, and leave. We called it "parachuting," and the term was pejorative.

Training should empower trainees to be independent. Paradoxically, parachuting can be disempowering and create dependency because the trainees are unable, in the course of a single training, to gain enough confidence and skill to go it alone. Learning a new set of skills is a process that needs continuity. The formula that worked best was when foreign trainers who brought new skills worked as a team with their South African counterparts, who could support the trainees after the initial workshop, long after the foreigners had gone home. And there were a few trainers who came back again and again, willing to serve where they were needed, to meet the local agenda instead of their own.

This mix of South African and foreign trainers trained the political organizations' and parties' high-level negotiators, even providing one-on-one negotiation training to key people. Conflicting parties competed for the best trainers, determined not to be outdone in the quality of their training, afraid that the opposition might outmaneuver them with sharper skills. Others in political, civic, and religious organizations also demanded to be trained. Soon, town councilors, government bureaucrats, educators, community workers, youth, women, and the security forces had caught the bug, and available trainers were worked off their feet.

With each training event, the content subtly shifted, as the South African trainers searched for even more appropriate frameworks for the South African context. Three NGOs set up a joint project to explore indigenous forms of conflict resolution, and even though the reports were inconclusive, the experience brought new thinking into their training. The shifting context, the cumulative experience of the trainers, and the growing expertise of the trainees as the methodology took hold kept the field of conflict resolution training wide open to self-evaluation and constant adjustment.

So what was the bug? Why was every open workshop at the Centre booked up? What were these workshops giving that so many wanted to receive?

Hope. The context was overwhelming, seething violence. Now, for the first time in their lives, many people discovered a response to conflict other than violence. They learned that conflict does not have to be feared and avoided, that it is a necessary dynamic for change, that the conflicts around them were part of the transformation of the country to something better. They discovered that they could be powerful in conflict without using violence. But most of all, they discovered that conflict resolution skills worked. At the end of every workshop, most of the faces turned toward the trainer would be shining with delight at their newfound skills, and they would say, "I didn't know there was another way." "This has changed my life." "From now on, my life will be different."

Many lives became more than just different: they were transformed. Instead of fighting to win so as not to lose, people began to see conflicts as joint problems to be resolved by all the parties for mutual benefit. The shift to a win-win culture had begun in a wide sweep up and down the country, penetrating many sectors. When it was all over, when the election of April 1994 had been held and the new South Africa was at hand, the proof was there at a conference in February 1995, when one after another, the country's leaders—President Nelson Mandela, Vice President de Klerk, cabinet minister Roelf Meyer, provincial leader Tokyo Sexwale, leader of the right-wing Freedom Front General Constand Viljoen, and others—spoke of the need to build "a cooperative, inclusive society."[3]

But the story does not end there, because this is not a fairy tale. Later still, as new leaders emerged who had not been immersed in the experience of discovering joint problem solving as an effective negotiating tool, and with no Peace Accord to reinforce its teachings by demonstration on a daily basis (the Peace Accord was shut down by the new government in December 1994), the old ways began to reassert themselves to some extent in national and local politics. The politics of confrontation, of winners and losers, emerged again, especially in war-torn Natal, where old loyalties and new anxieties were manipulated for political gain at enormous cost in human lives and misery. In other incidents too, the politics of greed, revenge, shortsightedness, and ignorance overcame the hard-won wisdom that had brought about the negotiated solution.

Despite this erosion by circumstance and political expediency, the culture of conflict resolution that emerged during the peace process lives on in many ways. The new Land Act legislated mediation as the preferred means of resolving land claims. The specialist Labor Court employs conciliation to cut down on the number and intensity of disputes. In the latter half of 1994, the Centre initiated an evaluation program to test the effectiveness of its training workshops. Armed with a questionnaire, a researcher interviewed a cross-section of former participants. Invariably, the response was a torrent of enthusiasm for the effect of the training and for its effectiveness in their lives.

RIOT POLICE

Training in mediation and other conflict resolution skills takes the Centre trainers across the country and into the hearts of every kind of organization. They train Umkhonto we Sizwe cadres, police captains, teachers, students, clergy, government officials, and members of the ANC, PAC, Anzanian People's Organization (AZAPO), IFP, National Party, and Democratic Party. They train within Peace Accord structures, including the Western Cape Peace Committee, and as the elections loom, they write materials for training election monitors and conduct pilot workshops.

It is the beginning of July 1993. Ron Kraybill,[4] Craig, and a trainee trainer are honored guests at Verdrag (The Covenant), the advanced training base for that most feared part of the police, the Internal Stability Division (ISD). "A strange experience," writes Ron in his journal. "This has probably been the most unforgettable week of my life."[5] They are there to run a four-day training workshop in conflict resolution skills for twenty-eight sergeants in the ISD.

The ISD is the new face of the former Riot Police, notorious for their brutality and apparent impunity. The line of accountability runs parallel and separate from that of the uniformed police; local uniformed station commanders are not informed of ISD covert or overt actions. It is a self-defeating structure as the police now begin to shift from policing by force to using a community policing strategy. The station commander who may be building some relationship of trust with the local community can be undermined without warning or recourse by an ISD raid. This way of doing things is at odds with a peace process that includes the police at its heart. It is also one reason why this training is of such groundbreaking importance.

Verdrag is in the bush against a mountain in the remote emptiness of the far Northern Transvaal. Nevertheless, high fences, sentries, lights, and security dominate. Ron writes in his journal, "Everyone on the base wore standard ISD uniform, a camouflage suit, the whole time. They also wore their service revolvers the whole time, even the cook!

"When the next morning we approached the training classroom, an open pavilion set on a concrete slab, the sergeants were already sitting inside. Someone barked out an order and everyone stood at attention as we entered. Boy, this really is a different world, I thought!"

The members of the mainly white group are clearly stunned that Craig, a Coloured man, could possibly be there to train them. Craig laughs at the memory. "Here is this black man whom they perceive as not intelligent, and part of the enemy, coming to train these white males." The turning point comes on the first afternoon. Ron is working on listening skills with the group, and they just are not getting it. He is handicapped by language.

The language of preference during the workshop is Afrikaans; an American, Ron does not speak it. He is frustrated that he cannot demonstrate more effective use of paraphrasing in a confrontation situation. Then his training partner Craig demonstrates in Afrikaans. The group is impressed; they break through their own inhibitions about this new technique and find that it works, and they see Craig in a new light. Ron was deeply relieved. There is another reason: "Groups in the early phases of training can be quick to write off the skills themselves if they can't see effective use of them. Thus Craig became the linguistic linchpin for the course. But he became the emotional center of the week as well, connecting with great ease and confidence to the policemen."

That evening, they have a *braai* (barbecue) with some of their hosts. An officer, his tongue loosened with beer, says to Craig, "You know, when I saw you last night and realized you were one of the trainers, I was really surprised. But I'll hand it to you, you're very good. Anytime you want to bring your wife and family and spend a holiday here at the guest house, you just let me know."

Craig cements the connection on the second morning. "I sat down with them and told them who I am. I was very open, very frank. I told them my activist history, that I have for close to ten years been involved in the anti-apartheid movement, that I have been detained quite a number of times, but that by virtue of my experience, I can understand that people come from different backgrounds.

"I told them that when I got married, my best man was a young white man, Dominic, who was doing military training. They were astonished. I told them that my family couldn't understand it either. At the time, I was politically outspoken, and very against conscription, but I understood Dominic's fear and that gave me the openness to accept him."

Craig's story also gives the young sergeants the openness to tell him who they are, how they perceive South Africa and their role in it. They are honest. Some say they are motivated in their job by the power and control that their uniforms, guns, and batons give them, by the adrenaline high and the thrill of danger. Others are certain that demonstrators and protesters are a danger to the safety and security of the country. They are the enemy and must be crushed. "Everybody knows that the PAC is a wing of the ANC," asserts a sergeant called Micky, blissfully unaware of the astonishment his political ignorance generates.[6]

A comment from another sergeant immediately lifts the mood. He says, "When we heard you guys were coming from the University of Cape Town [UCT], we immediately assumed you were people from the left, because UCT is left-wing students and liberals and End Conscription Campaign [which supported war resisters], so we were very skeptical. But the fact that you came in and didn't try to force us to change our minds, that you accepted that we have our own perspectives, that you were prepared to interact and dialogue with us, that was very helpful."

❋   ❋   ❋

The trainers notice that whenever the conversation shifts away from an overt policing focus, participant interest wanes. For homework, the trainers ask the sergeants to think of a role play that demonstrates exemplary handling of a conflict situation or provides a scenario of what not to do. The resulting case studies reflect real day-to-day issues that police confront. The training team uses these throughout the next three days to provide the raw material for working through skills.

They role-play dealing with an angry, loud black person. They must find out why he is so angry, what happened, and what can be done about it. The sergeants struggle as their colleague playing the black person embellishes his role with all the rage he can muster. Finally Craig takes a turn. Craig says, "I gave the person the opportunity to vent, then I paraphrased him, saying, 'I can see that you are very angry and upset because this and this has happened, and you are feeling that the police are not very sensitive; you see them as animals.' I drew him out, and then I asked, 'What do you want to do? What do you want from the police? What would you give if the police give this or that?' They could see that the things we are teaching can actually be done."

They role-play the situation, and for the first time in their lives, some of the sergeants step into the experience of the downtrodden, the homeless, and the oppressed who have been baton-charged, shot at, and beaten whenever they have tried to protest.

"It gave them the opportunity to reflect on why the police have this painted image, why they are seen as brutal, with no humanity and no feelings for others. They could also begin to see how their actions contributed to the anger and increased the violence instead of reducing it." Craig thinks that role plays are more significant than theory because they show that there are two sides to every story, that people have different stories, and that their stories are influenced by their experience.

"The problem is," Craig says, "police training enforces a particular way of thinking, that is, to use the hard tools to reduce violence. It has also been an attitude problem, that black is bad, that unrest and protest are part of terrorism, that this has to be stamped out. Our training provides them with an opportunity to reflect on their role in creating peace in South Africa. I don't think the police as a whole are particularly aware of their role as peacemakers, that instead of acting the bully, they can become the facilitator.

"We need to come to the point where the police and the community together decide what policing is all about. You see, I think it is not just the responsibility of the police to ensure that we have a peaceful South Africa. It is also the responsibility of the community, who need to understand their own contribution to a peaceful society. I think joint police-community workshops would work; I am absolutely convinced of it."

Back at Verdrag, it is day three. The class decamps to a nearby dam and sits on picnic benches to evaluate the course so far. Ron's journal records that the group is highly affirmative. They like the relevance of the course, the way it is presented, and they think it will make a big difference in their handling of situations in the future. "It's the first time I've ever been at a [police] course where I didn't feel screamed at," says the one warrant officer. They unanimously agree that it should be run on a much broader basis. Several note the need for captains and colonels to have the training, because they are the ones that usually undertake intervention in the more ambitious long-term negotiations.

That evening, the training team is given a surprise. Ron records the event in his journal:

> Their big treat for us was a chance to fire the full arsenal of ISD weapons on the firing range. Over the course of an hour-and-a-half, the three of us each were patiently drilled in the mechanical aspects of a series of weapons and then allowed to shoot a magazine of rounds. "Allowed" puts it too mildly; my fascination with the mechanics of death left me in no need of encouragement. But for Craig the experience brought him too close, I think, to the darkness of apartheid, and he lost heart at a couple of points. Each time our instructor coaxed him into proceeding anyway despite his misgivings.

First it was rubber bullets, of two different types, fired from a shotgun. Then it was a shotgun, with birdshot and slugs. There were eight or ten rounds in the pump action magazine, and they insisted that we fire every one of them! I was worried I'd have a hopelessly sore shoulder! Next came an Uzi machine gun, wonderfully light, compact and maneuverable, elegant as a laptop computer, then an R4 and R5 rifle, which are machine guns of the same caliber as the American M16. Then ten rounds from a Beretta pistol. A recurring dream for years has been that I'm shooting an unknown invader with a pistol, and I wondered as I picked up this object of nighttime fantasy whether real-life experience would exorcise or further arouse this obsession!

It was an experience I will never forget. These are weapons which I've dedicated a lifetime to render unnecessary. Yet my love of technology and mechanical elegance made me irretrievably fascinated. At one level I felt like I was being invited to share someone else's wonderful toys, and the enthusiasm of our hosts made it clear that they were relishing sharing their delights. But at another level it felt like enjoying forbidden fruits.

On the fourth and last day, the ISD trainees role-play a realistic ANC-IFP confrontation and negotiation.

The class prepares for their final spectacular role play. They will intervene in a simulated confrontation between archrival black political parties, the ANC and the IFP. In the past, the ISD intervened with tear gas and rubber bullets. Now they will try something different. They will put into practice everything they have learned over the last three days.

The class divides into factions. ANC, IFP, and ISD role players are briefed on their perceptions of one another. The ANC will march past the IFP hostel, the IFP will attack, the ISD will intervene. It is a well-known scenario, and everyone knows exactly what to do.

Dressed appropriately, shouting slogans, toyi-toyiing as best they can, and throwing stones, the ANC delegation starts its march, banners aloft. More stones fly and the chanting gets louder as the march progresses across the soccer field to the IFP hostel. The IFP fires two shots at the ANC marchers, and in a rage the two sides charge toward each other, hurling rocks and insults. With split-second timing, the armored personnel carrier arrives on the scene before the two sides get to each other, and the ISD unit runs between them, stones raining on their helmets and riot equipment. The ANC have time to fire a few blanks at the IFP, but with speed and precision, the ISD section takes up its position, tear gas and rubber bullets at the ready. It is a realistic scene and frighteningly familiar.

But the ISD officers use words instead of bullets, and forty minutes later they have negotiated a mutual withdrawal.

Ron's journal notes, "Everyone had a blast, and it was thrilling to watch as an instructor. It was clear that the ISD negotiators had learned well. I was particularly pleased when the warrant officer in charge, Louie, said with pride on his face as we convened afterward, 'And we did it without firing a single shot!'"

"Afterward," Craig says, "the police said, 'We wouldn't have done it that way before. We wouldn't have identified the leaders, we wouldn't have asked one group to move fifty meters away so that there's a space in between them, we wouldn't have perceived our roles simply as coming in and ensuring that we are a buffer between the two groups.' For them that was so important. They couldn't believe the fact that dialogue worked. For them it was an eye-opener.

"But they were also very skeptical about it. They said it's easy to do within a training situation, to simulate experiences, but sometimes when it's really happening and a lot of things are going on, it's difficult. But I think that the fact that they now know what could be done, that is the difference."

The day finishes, the course is over, the training team packs up to go. Craig notes that most of the sergeants come to say good-bye and thank him. He smiles, remembering that only four days before they were wondering what this *Boesman,* this ignorant bushman (a derogatory term), was coming to do here. He has no illusions that the four days have changed them, but he hopes that they are set on a path of reflection that can lead to a different kind of action and reaction, that they will critically rethink their role.

❊   ❊   ❊

For many years, Craig has been a lay preacher. Sometimes he is invited by church groups and other denominations to take the pulpit. One Sunday in the 1980s, in the white Cape Town suburb of Sea Point, a little old lady commented on his sermon about the role of Christians in society. She said. "Why don't you pray for our boys on the border when you pray for those in detention?" She was referring to the young white men who were called up annually for compulsory military service in the battle zones between South Africa and then-hostile neighboring states. Craig was stopped in his tracks. "Suddenly I realized that this congregation is moms and dads who have sons who are on the border. What right do I have not to intercede on their behalf for the safety and security of their children?" He changed his prayers and began to pray for the safety and security of the boys on the border, not blessing what they were doing, but asking that God protect them and help them understand their role in contributing to a peaceful society.

Craig says, "It is these kinds of things that make me continue to reflect on what I am doing. Yes, I have my pain, anger, and hurt, but the other person whom I perceive as my enemy has their pain and hurt. If I want to work for a new society that works for the highest good for all, then I have to understand where that person is coming from, you see."

Craig Arendse has since trained peace workers in Australia, America, the Middle East, and Africa. He has established his own training consultancy. Ron Kraybill is Associate Professor in Conflict Transformation at Eastern Mennonite University. He has trained around the world, including countries in Africa, Asia, Europe, and the Americas.

6
FORUMS

Meeting on Common Ground

In the transition from apartheid to democracy in South Africa, relationships engineered by apartheid broke down and pent-up grievances suddenly released by the changing order led too often to violence. In horrified reaction, South Africans of all races desperately searched for ways to end the destruction and killing, and encouraged by the national climate of negotiations and the National Peace Accord, they spontaneously began to talk to one another in what came to be known as forums.

These forums emerged at all levels and took various forms. Alliances of service organizations and human rights groups formed to try and stop, or at least defuse, the violence. Another popular formula brought together diverse stakeholders and interest groups around a common problem. Forums were formed at national, regional, and local levels around health, taxi conflicts, youth, women's issues, security in a community, and land. The contentious issues of the day were brought into the open and discussed by the people who legislated them, administered them, worked in them, used them, benefited from them, and were in conflict over them.

In the Western Cape, concerned citizen organizations and frustrated community groups banded together to address the violence that was enveloping the black townships and threatening the peace process, and the regional peace committee sponsored a series of forums around the taxi wars.

SOURCES OF VIOLENCE

In 1991, only three years before the scheduled national elections, the Western Cape community of Nyanga finds itself caught in the crossfire of a bitter taxi war. Gun-toting taxi operators, one hand on the wheel and one holding a gun, shoot at each other as they weave their taxis wildly through dense traffic. Accidents are frequent and sometimes fatal; drive-by shootings become commonplace. Taxi operators intimidate passengers into using their taxis, mount midnight raids on their rivals, and burn their rivals' houses.

Many of these battles are fought over access to the Nyanga Bus and Taxi Terminal. Sometimes bullets fly through the windows of the neighboring Oscar Mpetha and John Pama Schools, closely followed by fleeing gunmen crashing through the classrooms. Or a panicked crowd surges into the nearby day hospital, pursued by gunmen sprinting down the corridors scattering patients. Or old men and women flee before the gunfire as they try to collect their pensions at the Zolani Centre across the road. And one day, a stray bullet cracks a small hole in the window of a neighboring house and enters the right temple of an innocent woman who lives there, killing her.

In March 1991, Michael Mapongwana, chairperson of the regional civic association, leads the black community in a boycott of all black taxis. He tells a local newspaper, "We have to show them that their money comes from the community and that they therefore must respect the community and not endanger the lives of passengers with their fighting."[1] Within four months, Mapongwana and his wife have been murdered.

❋   ❋   ❋

The minibus taxi business provides many jobs, and taxi wars have erupted throughout the country. Rival township taxi organizations fight over lucrative routes, ranks (taxi stands), and permits. But these are more than just commercial clashes. Like most conflicts in South Africa, their roots are deeply embedded in the apartheid system.

Over the years, apartheid legislation pushed the urban black population into satellite townships, often miles from city centers, creating a demand for commuter transport that the public transport system could not begin to meet. Alternative transport had to be found, and township taxi services burgeoned in response. But this too was circumscribed by apartheid legislation, which dictated who among black people could legally live and work in urban areas. Prized taxi permits were issued only to black applicants with the right stamp on their papers. In time, despite being harassed, imprisoned, fined, and even shot at by the police, illegal "pirate" taxi operators began opening up new routes, mainly from the African townships to the city centers. Bitter rivalries quickly developed between the established taxi operators and the interlopers.

In 1987, influx control legislation was repealed, the public transport sector deregulated, and taxi routes legally allocated by the regional transport authorities to the former pirates. In the Western Cape, much to the astonishment and fury of the established operators, who retained their original local routes between the townships, the former "pirates" were awarded the lucrative township–city center routes that they had pioneered. Conflict was inevitable, and it simmered through the end of the 1980s, finally erupting into full-scale war toward the end of 1990.

In the Nyanga taxi wars of 1991, no one is spared. The conflict leads only to violence.

The taxi war killings and injuries, and the loss of incomes, homes, and possessions, are devastating. Church and service organizations that want to help are at a loss for answers in the face of the complexity of the conflict. One after another, mediation attempts have failed, usually at the eleventh hour. Many people believe that they were sabotaged by "third force" agents whose motives for fomenting and maintaining the violence may be financial gain, personal power, or the destabilization of community and political organizations committed to democratization.

At the same time, the Crossroads community next door to Nyanga is being torn apart by a conflict tailor-made in apartheid South Africa. Crossroads became South Africa's most famous squatter settlement when, in 1976, the world watched on television as church leaders and others defied the bulldozers that the government had ordered to raze the community to the ground. Over the years, the community survived continual harassment, arrests, and forced removals. In the mid-1980s, a power struggle between older conservatives and progressive youth came to a head in a bitter war in which the conservative elements, supported by the police, forcibly took power and installed a state-supported local government structure. The councilors were soon accused of corrupt resource allocation, and a large section of the community responded with a violent uprising. The mayor was ousted, the local council was rendered ineffectual, and a series of warlords took control. The ANC found itself split, with sectors supporting both sides, which rendered it ineffectual too. Nothing is working in Crossroads in the middle of 1991.

CONCERNED ORGANIZATIONS RESPOND

As the violence continues into this cold, wet winter, concerned organizations are feeling helpless and useless, not knowing how best to respond. And with limited resources, what can we do anyway? A week after Mike Mapongwana's killing in Nyanga, I get a call, "This is Albert.[2] Can you come to a meeting to discuss what we can do about the violence?" The meeting will be at 9 o'clock on Thursday morning, July 18, 1991. It will last an hour. Yes, I will be there.

And so that Thursday morning we meet, a small group of NGOs invited by Albert, coming together to try to do something about the violence. We represent the women's human rights organization Black Sash; the Centre for Conflict Resolution; the Legal Education Action Program (LEAP), which informs communities about their legal rights; the Quaker Peace Centre, which focuses on grassroots peacemaking; the Urban Monitoring Awareness Committee (UMAC) established by the Democratic Party to monitor and witness the violence; and the Western Province Council of Churches.

With the rain dripping from the gutters above the metal-framed windows at the Quaker Peace Centre, we settle into a circle of chairs, eleven expectant faces, not quite sure what we are going to do. Our number includes two visitors from British universities, and I wonder what this meeting of a few well-meaning but seemingly powerless individuals must look like through what I imagine to be more worldly and detached eyes. I open my laptop computer, note the names of everybody present, and prepare to take minutes for the first time in my life.

We struggle to find our purpose, and for the next three meetings, the real question is how we can be effective. No one seems to know the answer. There is growing despondency, some members drop out, but by the fourth meeting, an operational structure has been drawn up. We call ourselves the Resource Forum, and in the months ahead we form the nucleus from which other groups are destined to emerge.

The Resource Forum

The Resource Forum proposes to provide support to people actively working to prevent violence and bring resources from organizations not easily accessible by township people. It also becomes a busy information exchange.

When we can, we try to act on what we hear. For instance, a murder incident leads us to a forum action plan:

> One woman saw her sister being murdered and gave a statement to the police identifying the killer as a special constable. Further shootings involving special constables followed. But the person she had identified was not arrested, and the woman feared for her life. The Forum decided to keep a record of who has been killed and of where statements have been made and to keep pressure on the police in these cases.[3]

Over the six months of its existence, the Resource Forum's activities cover monitoring, research, taking statements, making a representation to an ANC Peace Commission, arranging press conferences, running nonviolent action training workshops, and helping to launch other initiatives.

The Working Group

The Resource Forum almost immediately spawns the Working Group, with members from the PAC and the ANC who share a passionate desire to find an end to the violence. They ask me to be the coordinator. This small, low-key group meets semisecretly to exchange information, identify problem areas, and act as an early warning system. It is a group with a short life, because soon two of its members are on the run, hiding for their lives in the turmoil of hit lists and political threats.

I listen to the stories of township violence the group collects and write them down:

> August 21, 1991
> Sipho lives in Old Crossroads. On the night of August 15, 1991, about twenty men came at two o'clock in the morning to fetch him. One had a gun. He was taken to Ntimkulu's place, but Ntimkulu sent him to Nqala, who ordered that he should be killed and knowledge of his whereabouts denied. He was taken to the freeway to be killed. Half the group then went to ransack his shack. Sipho was stripped to his underpants. The man who was preparing the gun with which to kill him motioned with his head for Sipho to run away, which he managed to do. He hid in the bush near the airport. Eventually he reported his story to the police.
>
> He was accused of attending meetings with the enemy faction. This was the apparent motivation for the murderous attack.[4]

A man is sentenced to death for going to a meeting. In the atmosphere of suspicion and mistrust generated by the violence, everyone is someone's enemy.

But the whites, on the whole, don't want to know:

September 11, 1991
An Afrikaans [white] woman from Kuils Rivier rang UMAC to say that she was shocked by a newspaper report and her domestic worker's [maid's] account that white police were involved in the violence in the townships. This illustrates the power of the press, which should be used more by our group to get the facts out.[5]

Rachel Browne and I go to Kuils Rivier and visit the Afrikaans woman.[6] We find her, large and untidy, in her small, tidy house. She is a conservative Afrikaner living in a politically conservative neighborhood. She has no particular regard for black people, but she is incensed that whites should attack them. She had not believed what her domestic worker had been telling her: that she could no longer live in her township home for fear of night attacks, that she was living in the bush despite the bitter cold, that she lived in fear of her life. The newspaper report had challenged the "Madam's" disbelief. Now she wants to know.

We tell her. She listens. She says she will do something. "What?" we ask. She will make sure that her neighbors, and their neighbors, know too. She will phone the newspapers. She will alert her member of Parliament.

We watch her indignation and wish her luck with her campaign. Even if it is ineffective, she will never be the same again. Neither will her neighbors. We smile ruefully at the vision of this powerful, angry Afrikaans woman berating them, making them listen to a story that the neighbors will not want to hear—just as she had not wanted to hear it.

The Peace Alliance

On September 12, 1991, Black Sash and the Resource Forum jointly launch a new initiative, the Peace Alliance, which aims to bring together non–politically aligned organizations actively involved in responding to the violence in order to coordinate crisis response. Thirty organizations accept the invitation to meet at the Methodist Church Hall in the university suburb of Rosebank, and at six o'clock that evening they straggle into the cavernous hall. It is a lively meeting, raising more questions than answers:

- How can the pressure on affected communities be relieved in the long term?

- What can be done when police and council authorities do not fulfill their functions?

- How can people be educated to know their rights?

- Where is the community this evening? Why are they not represented here?

The Black Sash chairperson explains that this forum is being established to facilitate communication between service organizations that are each involved in communities in their own way.

The participants divide into three groups: Monitoring, Relief, and Preventive Action/Development. Over a series of meetings, they decide that each group will coordinate the work of its members while the full Peace Alliance will meet less frequently to cross-check areas of overlap and to coordinate responses. A steering committee is established to ensure coordination, and a communications "grapevine" is set up for crisis response.

The groups draw on one another's contacts and resources. In October, for instance, the Relief group runs out of supplies for refugees from Site B in Khayelitsha township, whose houses have been burned down and who are temporarily being housed at Sosebenza school. The Monitoring group arranges a meeting at the school with the refugees, the Preventive Action/Development group brings along the regional director of the Consultative Business Movement, a progressive business association, to hear their story, and within the next few weeks a truckload of building materials is delivered to the relief agencies to help begin the rehabilitation process.

Despite some success stories, the Peace Alliance is not as effective as its members had hoped. Our efforts do not make much of a dent in the continuing violence. The Peace Alliance also has competition. A city initiative is launched on October 10 to intervene in the taxi violence. The new Cape Town Peace Committee (CTPC) is spearheaded by the mayor of Cape Town and Archbishop Desmond Tutu, and we pin real hopes on it as both a symbolic and a practical intervention. After the excitement of the day when hundreds of people packed into the great hall in the civic center, the CTPC emerges as the new vehicle for peacemaking in the taxi violence, drawing attention and resources that drain the Peace Alliance.

Clearly, the Peace Alliance has served its purpose. We disband. Each of these forums or groups teaches the NGO community a little bit more about how to cooperate in expressing our common concern, and that the energy we generate is a healing force in its own right. Nothing is wasted. We learn another lesson too, about letting go at the right time, about not holding on to something just because it exists.

But there are times when it is right to hold on, to fight for continued existence, to protect the energy of a group . The trick is to trust yourself to know which is right! Even in the down times, I knew that the Joint Forum on Policing was something to hold onto.

The Joint Forum on Policing

It becomes increasingly clear that mutual hostility and mistrust between police and the black communities are blocking any and all peace efforts. In response, a new forum emerges. It begins with a meeting about police behavior in Khayelitsha called by the ANC Women's League and UMAC in early September 1991 and is quickly taken up by the Resource Forum. It immediately grows to involve a wider spectrum of additional organizations.[7] Ultimately named the Joint Forum on Policing, this alliance is initiated to address policing issues, and it soon absorbs the Resource Forum, which in January 1992 dissolves itself to make way for the new initiative. The Joint Forum primarily aims to monitor whether police action conforms to the Police Code of Conduct set out in the new National Peace Accord and to expose police misconduct.

The numerous allegations of police misconduct range from acts of commission, such as involvement in criminal and political activity against community members, to acts of omission, which include refusing to take statements at police stations and standing by while crimes are committed.

The monitoring groups collect over sixty affidavits. Two monitors, one of them Val Rose Christie, respond to an emergency call from the KTC neighborhood and take statements independently for later corroboration. This is the common thread in the accounts:

> At approximately 3 p.m., on hearing shots being fired, these people either rushed out of their houses or looked through windows. They saw Casspir [police armored vehicle], license number 21, followed by . . . taxis on Terminus Road close to the garage. The taxi drivers (estimated to number close on one hundred men) came across the road, some carrying petrol bombs. They

kicked in the doors of the first few shacks and threw in the petrol bombs. As a strong southeast wind was blowing, the blaze quickly spread to the other shacks. When KTC residents attempted to quell the fire, as they feared it could spread, tear gas and shots were fired. The shots were seen to be fired in what appeared to be an indiscriminate manner by both police from the Casspir and the taxi drivers. I was shown numerous bullet holes in nearly all the houses on the perimeter.[8]

In private, the police readily admit that some of their number are bad apples, men and women whose behavior is brutal, corrupt, and often racist. But they maintain that most of the force is only doing its job. The day-to-day experience of the large majority of black South Africans, however, is of a hostile and aggressive police force uninterested in effectively policing their neighborhoods. This has led to an overwhelming breakdown of black community trust in the police. The result is often violence and lawlessness in the townships, as the community takes the law into its own hands. And so the cycle spirals ever downward, as both police and community reinforce their perceptions of the other: an untrustworthy police force and a lawless community.

Now all police personnel have signed the Police Code of Conduct, committing themselves to impartial, accountable policing and respect for human rights. This is a good thing, but in itself it is not enough. The question is how to use it to reverse the spiral and start rebuilding the shattered trust between the black community and the police. Trust will be built only on experience and deeds, not on words.

One way to begin altering perceptions and building a basis for trust is for the police force to be seen to take the Police Code of Conduct seriously and to act vigorously against members of the force who breach it. Until the police are prepared to investigate allegations of misconduct against their own members and to take appropriate disciplinary action, confidence in the police will continue to be undermined.

The challenge is enormous. The big flaw is that the Police Complaints Investigation Unit, the body established by the Peace Accord to investigate alleged police misconduct, is staffed entirely by the police. The NGOs and civic organizations have little confidence that officers of the unit will investigate their fellow officers in good faith. Police culture is to be fiercely loyal, a valuable trait except where it obstructs the course of justice, as many believe it does. In addition, members of the alienated black community are often unwilling to substantiate their allegations of misconduct for fear of reprisals.

The Joint Forum sets itself the task of stimulating investigations into these allegations within the framework of the Peace Accord. The goal is not only to expose police misconduct but also to improve the basis on which investigations of police misconduct are carried out, raise public awareness of the issues, and serve as a liaison between the community and the police with a view to closing the gap between them. Ultimately, we would like to contribute to institutional change within the police force.

We try to play a facilitating role. Our activities include monitoring, investigating, informing the Investigation Unit about allegations of police misconduct, providing a channel for complaints from victims of alleged police abuse, referring cases of alleged police abuse to legal and human rights groups, intervening to promote investigation by the Investigation Unit, providing practical input to the Police Policy Group (an academic group that seeks to influence future police policy), and lobbying around policing issues.

In January 1992, when the Western Cape Peace Committee is being established, the Joint Forum applies for membership and is admitted. Albert Dayile and I are nominated as the Joint Forum delegation, and when in March we receive an invitation to join the peace committee executive, as coordinator I become the official representative.

The Joint Forum now has the legitimacy of the Peace Accord to back it up. As a member of the regional peace committee, we have the weight of national policy behind us and the nationally endorsed Police Code of Conduct against which to measure police conduct.

The concerned group that met that rainy Thursday nine months before has come a long, long way in its search for ways to address the violence.

※   ※   ※

The Resource Forum, the Working Group, the Peace Alliance, and the Joint Forum grew organically out of the NGO community's common desire to counter the violence in our region through cooperative efforts. They were more than networks, which provide a platform for information exchange, communication, dialogue, and sharing, in that their activities demanded consensus on tasks, cooperation in their execution, and commitment to a common purpose. By definition, these forums were alliances, a "joining in pursuit of common interests"[9] by independent organizations on an ongoing basis.

Working in alliance brings a number of advantages, among them:

- avoiding duplication of effort by organizations addressing similar issues;
- expanding knowledge, information, and ideas;
- increasing skills and resources;
- enjoying access to a reservoir of contacts;
- gaining a wider power base and an extended constituency;
- designing broadly based strategic planning;
- building relationships between organizations; and
- operating in a way that is cooperative, and thus energizing, rather than competitive and enervating—the better we come to know one another as individuals, the better we are able to work together as organizations.

The benefits of cooperation are a product of the independence of the organizations involved. The cooperating organizations pool resources, knowledge, skills, contacts, ideas, and information unique to each one of them, providing a multifaceted focus on, and approach to, the main purpose of the group. Usually only one or two people are nominated by each organization to attend meetings, which, along with specific tasks, absorb a few hours of each working week. The parent organization pursues its normal functions and is not affected on a day-to-day basis. However, it receives credit for the efforts of the cooperative alliance and thus expands its field of influence. It will also be affected by the failures of the alliance, but that is the risk it takes.

Alliances also present problems:

- decision making is seriously impeded if organizational consultation is required at every stage;
- the political agendas of member organizations may vary despite the common purpose of the alliance;
- accountability to parent organizations supersedes accountability to the alliance, creating divisions;
- representatives of the member organizations may be replaced at any time, breaking continuity and group cohesion;

- strategies for achieving common goals may vary wildly—for instance, from confrontation to reconciliation;
- power relationships between the bigger, more influential and the smaller, less effective organizations can be delicate;
- organizational cultures may clash; and
- personal relationships may be conflictual, but because participation in the alliance is ancillary to primary employment, there is little incentive to resolve the conflict.

Sanctions and support systems of permanent organizations do not apply. Members do not get fired for nonattendance, disapproval is the only sanction against uncompleted tasks, money and security are not at stake, and, in real terms, the alliance is dispensable as a source of work and, to a lesser extent, social identity.

We tried to overcome these problems by formulating working principles to govern decision making, conduct, accountability, attendance, and task implementation and by conducting periodic workshops to review past performance and chart the future.

Despite these difficulties, I believe alliances of NGOs, or indeed other groups, are worthwhile, mainly because they increase effectiveness and power. But there is more. Participation in an alliance is an achievement in its own right and should not be regarded merely as a means to an end. Learning to work together, pursuing a common goal, and sharing responsibility is a worthwhile process separate from the end result. I watched people discover that they too can chair meetings, assert their ideas in a group setting, and engage in cooperative efforts, often for the first time. For everyone, participation in these alliances was a contribution to the greater effort to transform South Africa from an authoritarian society to a participative democracy.

THE REGIONAL PEACE COMMITTEE RESPONDS

In April 1992, after a long and complicated mediation process, the rival taxi organizations agree to form a single taxi organization, which they call the Convention for a Democratic Taxi Association (CODETA), and to work out a constitution and common code of practice. In June they adopt a common logo. The fragile peace is holding. Soon, however, low-level conflict begins again and, although the conflict does not reach the intensity of the 1991 taxi war, it escalates over the following months as competition for business intensifies.

An oversaturated taxi industry now raises new conflicts as well. There are just too many taxis for the number of passengers, and desperate taxi operators, casting around for an answer, begin to focus their attention on the buses that lumber between the townships and into the city center, offering lower, government-subsidized fares, and regular though infrequent service. The buses are also popular because, with memories of wild rides during the taxi war still fresh, passengers think the buses are safe.

But some taxi operators and owners perceive buses as unfair competition because of the fare subsidy and try to get rid of them. It is the start of a new phase in the transport-related conflict that has destabilized the region on and off for a decade, and the cost will be counted over the next three years in yet another cycle of injuries, deaths, kidnappings, and destruction.

As the 1991 taxi war heats up again in 1992, the peace committee receives a letter. "Around 4:30 P.M. on Tuesday, August 18, 1992, one of our buses was stoned at Nyanga terminus." The letter goes on to say that fifteen minutes later, taxis blockaded all the access roads to the townships of Nyanga and Guguletu and periodically stoned the buses that were forced to turn around. Then the morning of Wednesday, August 19, 1992, the stoning began again at 5:30 A.M., and again the taxis were implicated. Bus personnel were becoming concerned for their safety, and some were threatening to counterattack the taxis. The letter asks for peace committee intervention. It is signed by Frans Mayoss, general manager of Golden Arrow Bus Services (GABS), the main bus operator for greater Cape Town.

The week before, five bus drivers and four bus inspectors had been kidnapped by about a hundred taxi drivers, who had threatened to murder them and burn buses unless the taxi drivers' demands that the bus company withdraw all services from Khayelitsha township were met. After protracted negotiations under strong police supervision, the bus company employees had been released unharmed from the padlocked shed in which they were held.

It is clear to the peace committee executive committee sitting safely in comfortable chairs around the large polished table that this dangerous and destructive conflict between buses and taxis described in the letter is not going to get better by itself. It also presents a threat to the elections that lie somewhere in our future. People need transport to get them to the voting booths. It is a serious issue in this country, where far-flung black communities are completely dependent on public transport for access to business centers. After some debate, the committee appoints a task force, including me, to meet Mayoss and make recommendations to the executive for future action.

We listen for two hours as he tells of the bus driver still in a coma since a stone hit him square in the face three days before, of taxi drivers deflating bus tires, of accidents between buses and taxis that have led to conflict, of striking workers within the two trade unions that service the bus industry, of allegations that some dismissed workers are acting in collusion with taxi drivers to divert passengers to the taxis. His face is gray and sad, his speech slow and deliberate, and his palms sweat with the effort of making sure that we understand the full impact of what he is saying.

As Mayoss sees it, the root of the problem is competition, both between taxis and buses and between taxis and taxis. There are too many vehicles and not enough passengers. Survival is at stake for the taxi industry and for the bus company. There are no easy answers to the problem.

The question is, How many people will have to be killed or injured before something is done? And who will do anything anyway? The Department of Transport far away in Pretoria is perceived as distant and uninterested, the Provincial Road Transportation Board is perceived as inefficient and corrupt, some police officers are suspected of owning taxis and of supporting one taxi organization to the detriment of the others, and the town councils that are meant to serve the black townships are virtually defunct. The recent memory of the taxi war at its height and its toll in killings, injuries, destroyed homes, and burned-out vehicles looms over us. As one, we make up our minds that the peace committee must do something.

The Transport Forum: A Policy Approach

Our recommendation to the peace committee executive is that a Transport Subcommittee be appointed to address this crisis in the transport industry. We are looking for a mandate to act, and we get it. I am appointed chairperson, and we are given the power to co-opt other members as we see fit. Within days, we swing into action.

We decide that our immediate task is to gather information in order to better understand the issues. Over the next six weeks we meet as a committee ten times, and we meet with the trade unions, the taxi organization CODETA, which is allegedly implicated in the attacks, the bus company management, the police, the Goldstone Commission, the attorney general, and the mayor of Cape Town. The conflict escalates: two bus drivers are shot and killed, and four passengers are wounded. We monitor crises as they blow up, intervening where we can, but we stay focused on our investigative task.

By the beginning of November we conclude that the conflict is rooted in four main issues. First, the history of the taxi industry, which was regulated by apartheid legislation; second, an overextended taxi industry, which has led to confrontation with the bus sector; third, lack of support for all commuter transport from central government; and finally, lack of an integrated transport policy that could provide a framework within which the transport industry could operate.

There is little that we can do about the first three issues, but we suggest that the peace committee take on the policy problem while maintaining its crisis intervention and mediation role. It seems to us that until a viable policy framework is in place, all we can do is offer Band-Aids. We propose that the peace committee convene a forum of all interested parties early in the new year to begin formulating guidelines for such a policy. The executive agrees, and we write exploratory letters to all affected parties: political parties and organizations, businesses, local and regional authorities, mayors, government, civic leaders, squatter leaders, academics, taxi organizations, bus companies, the train company, trade unions, the police, and the military.

> There is no short-cut to resolving the crisis. The peace committee therefore proposes the convening of a Forum of all interested parties early in 1993 to formulate such a policy. We believe that it is the people involved in and dependent on the [transport] industry and its environment who can best arrive at solutions and that the peace committee is well placed to facilitate such a process. The Goldstone Commission has urged us to proceed with this strategy.
>
> We would like to invite you to comment on this proposal, and to indicate your interest in joining such a Forum. We attach a list of proposed participant bodies to whom this letter has been sent, and would be grateful if you were to inform us of any additional parties who should be brought on board.

It is a carefully crafted letter:

- it offers an idea and asks for feedback from the people who are involved or have an interest in the crisis—the intent is that the idea should pass into the ownership of the recipients;
- it is inclusive and is at pains to demonstrate inclusivity by asking for additional names of people to be consulted;
- the attachment of the mailing list shows it to be an open, transparent process; and
- to enhance credibility and legitimacy, it points out that the initiative is championed by a household name, the Goldstone Commission.

The response is resounding support for the idea. We prepare meticulously for the first meeting. The planning committee holds three long planning meetings at which the high-powered committee members, including Alan Dolby, the deputy Cape Town city administrator, Paul Mann, a respected consultant to the transport industry, and Ernest Wilson, a senior business executive, good-naturedly consider everything from the venue to content. Their participation is a measure of how seriously the city and its leaders are taking this process.

On March 18, 1993, we launch the Transport Forum at the Peninsula Technikon in the great windy flatland outside Cape Town. Seventy people are spread out across the steep incline of the auditorium, looking down on the table where Jaap Durand and I sit in the middle of the stage. Jaap chairs the meeting. I guard the process.

We collect everyone's concerns about the transport industry and record them on a flipchart. The City of Cape Town administration, police, bus and taxi organizations, black business, white Chamber of Industries, independent consultants, and the mayor of Cape Town talk about their hopes, fears, and frustrations, and then we brainstorm solutions. We appoint a steering committee and adjourn with a commitment to a first steering committee meeting by the end of April.

Over the next year, this group forms the nucleus in more than a hundred meetings. The deputy director general of the ministry of transport comes to some of them, as do representatives of other transport-related institutions and organizations, and together we try to fulfill our double goal of exploring a workable regional transport policy and preventing violent conflict within the transport industry.

We engage consultants and form subcommittees to produce proposals for a transport system that would encompass all the needs of all the groups.

The members argue, protecting their interests. Participation at the meetings fluctuates. We carry on regardless, inventing the process as we go along.

We engage in mediation between taxis and taxis, taxis and the bus company, black civic associations and taxis, the local authorities, and bus and taxi organizations. We intervene in crises: when the bus drivers blockade Cape Town to protest the violence against them; when the taxi drivers blockade Cape Town to protest fines for the last blockade about routes and regulations; when a squatter area called Black City is torched and another, KTC, is attacked because of the taxi conflict; and when taxi warfare breaks out in Khayelitsha. We negotiate to get the buses back into bus no-go areas that the taxis take over. We work with the various authorities to find the perpetrators of the killing and maiming, stoning, and burning.

The Transport Forum becomes a place where people come to talk and hope for action. People hear one another's concerns and problems and find new levels of understanding. The information flow accelerates. At times, we break through and achieve agreements. But often we go round in circles; we seem to be stuck. What can this group achieve when we do not have the power to change existing policies, structures, and procedures? Only a new government will be able to do that, and the election is still months away. Frustration sets in; participation drops again; representatives of the black community in particular stop coming or arrive very late. This is a serious blow to the legitimacy of the forum, and things finally come to a head at a workshop on transport policy content in August 1993.

The workshop has barely begun when ANC representative Basil Davidson interrupts the proceedings, saying that in his view the workshop participants are unrepresentative of the wider community, that the political parties are underrepresented, that he is uncomfortable with plans for the Forum, and that he, for one, is leaving. He walks out, and the meeting dissolves into chaos. To my amazement, the Forum's stalwart supporter Deputy City Administrator Alan Dolby supports him. I realize that they are right. As the door slams behind Basil, we change the agenda for the workshop and address the issues he has raised.

GETTING THE RIGHT PEOPLE TO THE TABLE

Community representation at meetings such as these is an increasing problem. *Community*, in the language of liberation, means black community, and the emerging black leadership is in great demand precisely because their presence lends legitimacy to any proceedings. They are invited to participate, sometimes it seems for the sake of appearances, not for their substantive contribution, and because they hold the key to community co-operation. This perception is a major obstacle. In addition, they are having trouble meeting the demands for their participation on a number of counts.

First, there are too many invitations and too few leadership figures to respond to them. The choice, when it is made, is usually politically expedient, putting transport way down on the list of priorities. Second, many of the leaders have jobs, thus they are often available only in the evenings. Even then, there are competing political and civic meetings to attend, besides the demands of family and friends. Third, those leaders without jobs need to spend time seeking work or keeping themselves available for work should it arise. Further, they do not have the money for transport to the meetings. Fourth, spending hours in meetings each day is not necessarily considered the best use of time, given the stresses of the times and the demands of township life. Finally, a notable irony, the townships are so badly served by public transport that getting to meetings like the Transport Forum is sometimes out of the question.

We ask ourselves, How many citizens anywhere are prepared to give major chunks of their time to community matters? It is usually an active few, and here we are demanding that unelected, unsupported, unpaid citizen representatives should make their difficult way to venues around town at all hours of the day and night, including weekends. The discussion is delegated to a subcommittee for recommendations.

The subcommittee is inconclusive, because we do not really know what to do. One suggestion is to provide transport to the meetings, which we later try with partial success: sometimes the community representatives turn up; sometimes they do not. We also talk about attendance payments, but we argue about the ethics and pitfalls of paying people to attend meetings. We address the methodology for issuing invitations. These are faxed where possible, and a copy is also mailed. In the absence of a fax, telephone, or post office box, some are delivered by hand. During the days preceding a meeting, nonrespondees are reminded of the date, time, and place. Could this system be improved? No one had any better suggestions.

In retrospect, there were two avenues we did not pursue. We could have visited more of the black community leaders, explaining the Transport Forum and its goals, and we could have spent time with them exploring how best to facilitate their attendance. These were serious omissions. But later, in November 1993, the peace committee was asked by members of the African communities of Khayelitsha, Nyanga, and Crossroads to facilitate a Transport Crisis Forum to deal with a resurgence in the violence between buses and taxis. We merged the two forums, and for a time a balance was restored.

※   ※   ※

The story of the Transport Forum and the subsequent Transport Crisis Forum is a remarkable story about citizens banding together to try to change what is wrong in their city and their society. It is also a story about self-responsibility and about individuals believing that they could make a difference, even when the issues involved are dangerous and often life threatening. And it is a story of spirit and courage; when the existing institutions fail to resolve issues that are threatening the stability of the region, its citizens try to find an alternative solution. They are willing to break new ground without any guarantee of success, to discover the pitfalls as they go along, and to give up their enmity and work jointly with former adversaries if that is what it takes to stop the violence.

Was it a success? That depends on your definition.

We did not formulate a new transport policy for the region. At the same time, under the leadership of the peace committee, everyone connected with transport in our region came together for the first time, however imperfectly, to try to resolve a mutual problem, often in the presence of international observers from the European Community or the United Nations.

We did not stop the violence in the transport industry, but we did defuse some of it. Although it is impossible to prove a negative, and we can never know what would have happened without our efforts, the concensus is that the Transport Forum made a difference.

The stakeholders learned a great deal about what it was like to stand in the shoes of their adversaries, they formed a basis of shared information about one another, and many for the first time publicly tolerated opposing viewpoints.

We achieved a few more steps on the way to democracy. Many of the people who participated in these forums over the twelve months of their existence were practicing democratic processes for the first time in their lives. For everyone, it was a new experience to participate in discussions on issues that previously had been the preserve of government.

Relationships grew across historical divides. We made a point of serving refreshments at every meeting. We would break for tea and biscuits or, if the meeting extended over lunchtime, for coffee and sandwiches. Corridor talk is a valuable part of any process, and we consciously facilitated it.

It was an empowering process. Many of the black participants, in particular, had never before been listened to by whites, or heard their own voices in public, or experienced a process in which time and the floor were granted to all comers, not just whites and leadership. And many had never before talked together equally with the other side, black with white, ANC with government, police with black community, administrators with the people whose lives they affected.

The Nyanga Terminal Development Committee: A Developmental Approach

Hope of renewal comes to war-torn Nyanga as the winter ends in 1992 with plans to upgrade the terminus. Armed with the triumph of an uneasy peace in the taxi war, the community leadership approaches the local town council, Ikapa, and proposes a new bus and taxi terminus. Ikapa takes the idea to the Metropolitan Transport Advisory Board, which agrees to provide funds to build a new terminus on the site of the old one. But there is a condition. All the parties involved in the terminus must be involved in the negotiations around its planning and ultimate management.

My phone rings. It is Albert Dayile, the secretary of the Nyanga Civic Association. Will I, as chairperson of the peace committee's Transport Subcommittee, come to a meeting with the Nyanga Civic Association and Ikapa Town Council at the Ikapa council buildings in Nyanga to discuss the formation of a Joint Management Committee to meet this requirement? Six o'clock on the evening of November 18 will be fine.

"The problem," explains Albert, "is the taxis." I think about the last two years, about the killing of Michael Mapongwana and his wife and seventy-three others, many of them women and children, about the night attacks, the kidnappings, and the sheer terror of being caught in the middle of the taxi war. I remember sitting under a gum tree with the women sheltering their babies from the sun as they surveyed the ashes of the Black City shacks, casualties of the taxi war, that until twenty-four hours before had been their homes. I can see that for the residents of Nyanga the problem is the taxis.

But I also know that the civic association is not the only party with a problem. All the parties view one another with deep mistrust. Fatal attacks on bus drivers by taxi drivers have completely alienated the bus and taxi industries. Within CODETA, the joint taxi organization, there is dissent between the executive and the rank and file, making any agreements with the executive difficult to implement. Finally, everyone is suspicious of Ikapa municipality, as they are of all the black town councils, regarding it as illegitimate, corrupt, and inefficient. It is clear that the alliances that must be forged if the terminus is going to be upgraded are not natural or easy and will test the tolerance of the parties concerned to the limit.

We are sitting at long wooden tables in what in any normal municipality would be called the town hall. Here it is an unadorned room cut off from civic activity by security guards at the perimeter fence and in the entrance hall. The distant sounds of the Nyanga community drift through the windows into the stillness of a building abandoned for the night except for this meeting.

A cardboard model of the preliminary plans for the new terminus is perched at the end of the table. It is the center of attention. As we discuss our way through the evening, our eyes keep drifting back to it, weighing, judging, imagining what it will be like when the dust and dirt is transformed and the taxi war is a vague memory.

I suggest that there really is not any choice. A negotiating forum including all the stakeholders will have to be formed. This is not just because the funds depend on joint decision making, but also because anyone left out of the process is likely to sabotage it. It is what happens. Inclusivity is rule number one. Tolerance follows close behind.

Clearly there has been some disagreement on this issue, and I sense that I have been invited here to help tip a balance. Now everyone agrees that this is the only way forward. We consider who should be invited and end up with a list that includes two local schools, the day hospital, the Presbyterian Church located right next to the terminus, plus the black chamber of commerce, the LPC, and the four main stakeholders: taxi organizations, the bus company, Ikapa town council, and Nyanga Civic Association. We agree upon an agenda, set a date and time two weeks ahead, and define the issues that will need to be addressed: the planning process itself, interim arrangements for taxis during construction (the buses have already found another site), and the long-term management of the terminus. Ikapa will organize transport for anyone who needs it; I will issue the invitations on behalf of the peace committee. A sense of relief lifts the discussion and with smiles all round, just before eight o'clock we head out into the night. The Nyanga Terminus Development Committee has just been born.

Over the next weeks this new forum holds a series of meetings. A working subcommittee consisting of a member of each of the four main stakeholders (taxi, bus, council, and civic association) meets twice. Together they visit potential sites that the taxis could use as interim ranks, they recommend that the Nyanga Civic Association and CODETA share offices on site, and they approve the space allocated for taxi parking as per the cardboard model. Between meetings they report back to their constituencies, returning with questions, concerns, or a mandate to go ahead. It is a pattern that will be repeated over the coming months as the negotiations take their tortuous path.

Within two months, constructive agreement has replaced suspicion and mistrust to the extent the committee is able to reach a consensus. January 14, 1993 minutes: "The meeting agreed that Ikapa can proceed with the construction of the terminus."

Old and complicated enemies—some of whom talk to one another intermittently, but, in the past, never at the same time—have found common ground.

Formerly this kind of decision would have been made by the authorities without any meaningful consultation. As a result it would probably have become the cause of further conflict. Instead, the people who will have to live with the decision have spoken.

The new terminus will symbolically cleanse a place that has been at the heart of the taxi war, the battlefield where the competing taxi organizations have literally slugged it out, attack provoking counterattack, death avenged by more death. It is here that taxi drivers have killed one another, burned one another's vehicles, and threatened and harassed—and sometimes killed—bus passengers. The new terminus will be a new beginning.[10]

YOU CAN FIGHT OR YOU CAN TALK

The consensus of the four parties is an extraordinary witness to the power of joint problem solving and joint decision-making processes, and to their power as change agents. Processes that are based on inclusivity, that function through participatory approaches, that build tolerance for diverse opinions, that empower the participants to decide for themselves and to reach their decisions through consensus—these are the building blocks of democracy. And here in the battered heart of Nyanga, brick will be placed upon brick to build a terminus that is a monument to the democratic process.

The emergence of these forums and countless others like them around the country represents a choice for managing the transition constructively. The alternative is being expressed in the escalating political turmoil and rampant criminal violence. Many township youth have lost all respect for the institutions of government and lead crusades to find other functions for police stations and to evict white teachers from township schools and white professionals from neighboring clinics. At the same time, the right wing is flexing its muscles publicly, uttering dire threats and arming itself to the teeth.

These twin tracks are clearly signposted as alternate routes to the future. You can fight or you can talk. The choice is sometimes yours. More often it is dictated by political expediency, economic pressures, and societal norms. The Inkatha Freedom Party migrant laborer from the heart of kwaZulu-Natal working in the mines outside Johannesburg can no more choose negotiation with ANC townsfolk and stay alive than the Afrikaner farmer in the Northern Transvaal, bastion of frontier Afrikanerdom, can express liberal views about blacks without being branded a traitor.

Despite the headlines that describe the violence, acts of barbarism (of which there are many on all sides), and daily crime in capital letters, I am constantly surprised by the number of people who do choose to talk. Patient, attentive, concerned, they form the middle ground that is clearly going to be the country's salvation. It is here that the peace committee focuses its efforts, because strengthening the middle erodes the extremes. The rhetoric of far right and far left may be predictable and empty, but it carries weight in a country of extremes: rich and poor, powerful and disempowered, educated and deprived.

The value of forums depends on what you are looking for. For some, they are vehicles for self-expression, and the mere existence of a regular meeting in which diverse people, old enemies, the oppressed and the oppressor, sit as equals exchanging views and listening to one another is enough. For others, forums provide the opportunity to get to know the demonized, dehumanized "other" and, in this way, to start the long road to reconciliation and healing. For others still, they present serious joint problem-solving opportunities that make it possible to resolve conflict without resort to violence. Overall, forums represent a shift away from the force and bluster of the win-lose past and toward a participative win-win future.

7
POLICE

From a Force to a Service

In order for a society to transform from an authoritarian to a democratic system, the security forces must stop being a tool of government suppression and become an agent for civilian protection. This can happen only when top leadership accepts the inevitability of civilian oversight. For the South African police, the process of change was profoundly challenging. The gap was as wide as it was deep. It would take a combination of grand policy gestures and small human acts to bridge that gap. It would also take an iron political will.

A lifetime in the South African Police (SAP) has given the colonel a sense of his own power. He leans back in his chair, legs apart, an amused smile stretched across his large features. He listens with his right arm thrown along the back of his chair, but when he talks he leans forward, his forearms resting on his knees, fingers dangling and twisting a ballpoint pen that he jabs in the air to emphasize a point. He is a big man and he is impatient. He knows that the power he once wielded is diminished by this kind of meeting, and his frustration is apparent.

The police colonel is one focus of the meeting. The other is Doris Neewat. As chair of the ANC branch in Kraaifontein, she is a prominent leader and spokesperson for the thousands of Coloured and African people who live in the squatter camps of Bloekombos, Wallacedene, and Scotsdene that sprawl alongside this sleepy white town thirty-five kilometers (twenty-two miles) from the heart of Cape Town. She appears calm, sure, and steady as she stands up to address the meeting, but I wonder what this primary school teacher who is not yet thirty years old is really feeling as she faces the colonel and twelve other police officers across the crowded room. It takes practice to come face to face with the people who have for so long been the enemy, and these are early days. Later, after the national elections in 1994, she will be elected mayor of Kraaifontein, but that affirmation is well over a year in the future.

The regional peace committee called the meeting today, Wednesday, March 22, 1993, at the request of the Kraaifontein ANC. Outraged by police action and nonaction in general, by specific events of the last three months, and by the running sore that is life under apartheid rule, the ANC and community leadership mobilized and today stands ready to take on the police. The local branch of the ANC, the ANC Women's and Youth Leagues, and the local civic associations have joined forces, and the twenty-one comrades include many of their most senior representatives. They have some things to say to the local police, and they have come to say them.

The police have brought in their big guns too, figuratively speaking. The district commander, his deputy, and a delegation from the Community Relations Division at Regional Headquarters have come here to the Bellville District Command building to support the Kraaifontein station commander and his team. They have come because they signed the Peace Accord, and their highest commanders have said, "You will attend." This is all new to them, and I see from their body language that most of the police officers feel uncomfortable. Watched by international observers from the United Nations and the European Community, and shepherded by Chris Spies and me from the peace committee, people settle where they can in the overcrowded room as we begin the meeting.

Chris and I have worked together extensively, and know what to expect from each other.[1] Tonight, Chris will facilitate the meeting. I settle comfortably into a chair between a police officer and an ANC stalwart and look carefully around the room.

People give clues about themselves from their choice of seating in a meeting like this. There is that moment when a person walks into a room, hesitates, and decides where to sit, or more precisely, with whom to sit. I have watched it and can now predict what the regulars will do, but tonight is different. A number of the policemen are new to me and so are the representatives of this community that up to now has been off my beat. The room is a long rectangle; chairs have been gathered from offices all over the building and follow the shape of the room. Significantly, there is no clear dividing line between the two sides, an increasingly common setup.

Generally, the pattern is homogeneous clusters with a scattering of braver souls who mingle. I interpret the minglers as purposeful or instinctive bridge builders and make a mental note to support and encourage them if I can. Sometimes, people are just late and have to take the only available seats, and I have watched reluctant civic representatives sit very still, trying to avoid physical contact, as they find themselves between two police officers or government officials. Or a police official might find himself between two civilians. It is still a new experience for many, but for a few the choice to sit next to the former enemy can also be an act of courage and forgiveness.

Six months before I had witnessed an incident that still plays in my mind in slow motion. The setting was a workshop for the police and a number of civil and human rights NGOs that dealt with policing issues. The purpose of the workshop was to clear lines of communication between the two groups. I had facilitated a joint workshop planning process with them, and now, as they trickled in, I watched people choose their seats in the usual pattern. Then Stewart appeared.

He was an African in his early thirties, soft-spoken, quietly dressed. He seemed unremarkable, but only for seconds because then you caught something of his dignity, his stillness, his reserved strength, and you were instinctively drawn to him. Here was someone to trust. Then you discovered that he was a veteran of the struggle against apartheid, that he had been imprisoned and tortured by the police and now was working as a paralegal to help others fight injustice.

Stewart walked in, hesitated, his eyes sweeping the circle, and made his decision. He walked toward a vacant seat next to a police major. He sat down and turned to greet the police major before acknowledging the warm welcome of colleagues and friends. Only a handful of people in the room knew that he had chosen to sit beside his former torturer.

This is forgiveness in action.

※　　※　　※

Back in the police station on that warm Wednesday evening of March 1993, Chris has opened the meeting. Doris begins her presentation, reading from a two-page memo alleging nine incidents of police misconduct and making six recommendations that might improve the relationship between community and police.

She is powerful in her conviction and her courage as she stands up and faces the police colonel lounging opposite her:

The people of Kraaifontein are suspicious of the police. This is because the police are authoritarian and do not encourage the public to be party to determining policing policy. The police are seen as agents of the apartheid government rather than protectors of the people to assist with problems of crime.

The following incidents bear witness to the above allegations . . .[2]

Doris tells of tear gas, birdshot, and rubber bullets fired at squatters in the dark hours of the night; of a local police sergeant who refused to send an ambulance when it was needed and was rude into the bargain; of the mysterious shooting deaths of five people; of guns brandished in a dangerous manner and pointless arrests. She admits that the community stoned a police van after the arrest of some people for possession of *dagga* (marijuana) and states that a police officer threatened retaliation the next day.

Her comrades murmur their agreement, nodding and sighing their assent. It is true. This is how it was.

Doris continues with the recommendations. The police must adhere to the Police Code of Conduct in the Peace Accord. They must earn the respect of the people and cooperate with their representatives. They must prevent the local white right-wingers from harassing and killing people because they are black, and "the [state's] abuse of the country's police for political ends must be stopped." Finally she requests the establishment of a local peace committee "through consultation with all members of the Kraaifontein communities as well as through consultation with the police and other interested parties."

Her thoughtful presentation is woven through with peace offerings, yet the police colonel shifts uncomfortably in his seat, interjecting comments and disrupting the flow. He is not listening to find constructive solutions to these problems. He is not really listening at all but playing out a charade of head shaking and pen pointing, perhaps for the benefit of his junior officers. When he responds, he blusters, denies, defends, and keeps looking to them, perhaps for affirmation, for support, for help. It is hard to tell. The local station commander is also rude, but there is something else in the manner of these policemen that at first I can't quite put my finger on.

Then I realize what it is. Neither man has any idea what to do. They don't know how to behave in this situation, because nothing in their experience has prepared them for it. They have reached their limits, and they are out of control.

SAP AS AN INSTRUMENT OF FORCE

From the formation of the South African Police Force on April 1, 1913, until the first democratic government took power in 1994, South African governments used the police as an instrument of force to defend white minority interests. Within the first few months of its existence, the government mobilized the newly founded police force to break up a gold miners' strike on the Witwatersrand, a hunger march of Indian sugar estate workers in Natal led by Mahatma Gandhi, and a railway strike, which the government of General Jan Smuts ended by ordering the arrest and deportation of the strike leaders.

For decades of apartheid rule, law and order in South Africa primarily meant suppression of opposition to apartheid, use of force, and a perception of black areas as hostile territory. The police defended the apartheid government and its structures unconditionally. Their job was to protect white minority rule against the black majority struggle for social justice. Policing became dependent on brute force, and the police were ready and willing to use it. On numerous occasions they acted above the law even when unnecessary; two documented examples are the deaths of Steven Biko and Matthew Goniwe (see the glossary). In the name of state security, draconian state legislation sanctioned detention without trial, torture (such as extended solitary confinement), excessive use of force, exile, and harassment.

Through the use and abuse of their power, the police alienated themselves from much of civil society. Black communities saw the police as violent aggressors. Police presence aroused fear, anger, and hatred in black communities, which were underpoliced in dealing with crime and antisocial behavior and overpoliced in the search for any possible threat to the state.

By the 1980s, trust in the police by black communities had nearly disappeared. Black policemen and policewomen, 60 percent of the police force, suffered from this mistrust. Poorly paid and working long hours, black police living in the black townships increasingly were attacked and killed as the host communities expressed their long-held disgust at black police collaboration with the enemy.

Low levels of arrest and prosecution of criminals in black townships fueled the perception that the police were unwilling or unable to render effective service. The conviction that there was a vast difference in the level, intensity, and promptness of police investigations and arrests between black areas and white areas was prevalent. Communities consistently complained that the police were rude, arrogant, and disrespectful. There was also a widespread perception in black communities that the police were unwilling to investigate allegations of misconduct against their members and to take disciplinary action against them, a perception that completely undermined any vestiges of confidence there may still have been in the police.[3]

And on top of all this, the blurred line between the police and the justice system in the eyes of the public meant that the police shouldered the blame for a justice system that on the whole lacked legitimacy in the eyes of most South Africans. Blacks widely experienced the justice system as a white one, unfriendly to them. In an overloaded system that was cracking at the seams, known criminals were systematically released on bail pending investigations and trials months, if not years, into the future. Witness protection programs barely functioned, and potential witnesses often refused to testify, as criminals, released back onto the streets on bail, threatened them and their families with death. In a country where the official unemployment figure was 40 percent, but in many communities reached over 70 percent, where there was minimal welfare provision, and where the differential between rich and poor was judged to be the highest in the world, crime was rampant. In some areas, gangs reigned through terror, and criminals slipped through the net down the shadowy alleyways that snaked between darkened shacks.

The police also came to personify the apartheid system for black communities. They represented the state to the people, embodying the illegitimate order that they enforced. The police would regularly thwart the will of black communities, whether a community wished to depose the local councilors as puppets of an illegitimate government or to demonstrate community opposition to the building of a police station rather than a creche (daycare center) or clinic or to use an empty white school to relieve an overcrowded African one. Almost without exception in these crises, the police acted as protectors of state agents and properties, intervening between the people and their goals.

Apartheid legislation institutionalized the police as government instruments. Psychologically, policemen and policewomen needed to believe that apartheid was right because they were asked to enforce it every day. From the black majority perspective, the police were the enemy, and there was widespread skepticism about whether they had the will or the wherewithal to be anything else.

❋   ❋   ❋

Back at the overheated Kraaifontein meeting, I watch the colonel and the station commander metaphorically shooting themselves in the foot. I ask myself whether the police can transcend this heritage. Can they conquer their racism and authoritarianism? Are they willing to put aside personal biases and provide an effective and efficient service irrespective of race? Will they be prepared to enter into relationships based on accountability to the black communities where they work? Can they make the transformation from a police force to a police service? And, more poignantly, if they are willing to try, can they do it before it's too late?

Rereading Doris's list, I note that the majority of the complaints are about the attitude of the police toward the community and how that attitude affects police behavior. For me, the recommendations hint at a future in which the police will show respect, offer cooperation, behave responsibly, prevent harassment by racist white folk and by the police themselves, and, finally, stop "the abuse of the country's police for political ends." With this last, somehow this impoverished community finds it in their hearts to acknowledge that the police, too, have suffered the abuse of their political masters.

To fulfill Doris's wishes, we must change the attitudes and behavior of the entire police force. It is a daunting prospect, and as this dreadful meeting makes its slow progress through the evening, I keep coming back to it. How do you go about changing attitudes? I remember reading some research papers arguing that, although it is virtually impossible to change attitudes, you can change behavior. If we could only find a way to change the behavior of the police toward the community, the response might be so rewarding that a change of attitude would follow. A kind of feedback loop would keep reinforcing new behavior patterns, which in turn would support the new attitudes. This could result in permanent change, in transformation of the police from a force to a service.

What if the colonel truly listened to the views of the community, demonstrated verbally and through body language that he took their complaints seriously, and said he would take positive action? What if he suggested a joint committee to investigate ways in which the police and this community could better cooperate? What if he expressed concern for the conditions in which the community must live and offered his commitment to doing everything possible to make improvements?

If he behaved as though he genuinely cared, the response of the community representatives would undoubtedly be welcoming, even if initially tinged with disbelief. And if the behavior of the police followed their colonel's lead, over a period of probably only a few short weeks the response of the community to the police would be revolutionized. Stones would be transformed into handshakes, aggression into cooperation, scowls into smiles. Individual police officers, my musing continued, would be so overcome with relief and joy at being received as human beings, at being greeted as friends and protectors, that their attitudes would change to complement their new behavior—and presto, they would be transformed. The lions would lie down with the lambs—or so I fantasized.

But, I thought, watching the station commander floundering red-faced through the mire of complaints, the police would need to know what to do. They would need tools for change. They would need to be taught listening, problem solving, mediation, negotiation, and facilitation skills. That is a tall order. Could it be done through training?

Gerrit Nieuwoudt is at the meeting.[4] His face is, as usual, impassive, but I now know him well enough to be sure that he too is appalled by the behavior of his colleagues. After the meeting, we confer. He agrees that it is worth trying some training. It is worth trying anything that can ensure that this kind of behavior fades quickly into the past. (Much later, he tells me how ashamed he felt about the meeting.) We agree to try to get some kind of training program off the ground.

TRAINING: TAKING THE PLUNGE

The design is two half-days of training for station commanders from all over the region. I attend the first training session, interested in this experiment in which I have invested so much hope. Twenty-five station commanders are already drinking coffee in the foyer of the hotel when I arrive just after 8:00 A.M. (I immediately notice that there is only one woman among them and sigh inwardly but realize that we must choose our battles carefully.) Deep inside, I never for one moment doubt that we will make it, but in moments of exhaustion, overwhelmed with the sheer magnitude of the task that we have embarked on, I sometimes wonder how.

The workshop seems to be going well, even though one officer is determined not to cooperate, perhaps in case anyone assumes he has something to learn. I am amused and only a little irritated by his performance. Others make up for him with their attentiveness and willingness to participate, especially in the role plays.

One station commander who plays an aggressive and disruptive community leader in a simulated police/community meeting admits afterward that he enjoyed himself enormously. He also suddenly understood what it might feel like to be a disempowered civic leader facing up to the all-powerful police force.

But it is some months later that the story really ends. Stef Snel, director of UMAC and a leading figure in the peace process, says, "I met a policeman who said that he had been in the [Centre for Conflict Resolution's] training workshop for station commanders. He said that it had changed not only the way he handled his professional life, but also the way he relates to his wife and family; in fact, he said that it had changed his life."

These are the moments that keep the peace workers going through what seems like continuous conflict and crisis as the power struggle sharpens and we face a marked escalation of violence throughout our torn land.

POLICE CODE OF CONDUCT

The signing of the Peace Accord toward the end of 1991 signals to the police that the old order is indeed over and a new one must be designed and constructed to take its place. It is a significant moment, and the challenge is formidable: a top-to-bottom transformation of police structure, practice, training, and culture. The Peace Accord also provides an extraordinary opportunity for police redemption in the eyes of the black community. If there is going to be one shot at beginning to establish the police force as a respected public institution, this is it.

For the police, the provisions of the Peace Accord are unprecedented, committing them to protect and serve all the people of South Africa in a rigorously nonpartisan fashion; to use minimum force; to adhere to high personal standards of conduct free of racial prejudice, corruption, and unlawful action; and to believe that they are accountable to society. South

Africa now expects every policeman and policewoman to render an efficient service in an accountable manner to all South Africans.

Put yourself into the shoes of a police officer when the Peace Accord
and its Police Code of Conduct is presented to you as the new way of doing
your job. For as long as anyone can remember, the role of the police has
been to eliminate opposition to the government, one way or another. Then
one day the political leaders huddled with those communists and terrorists
from the ANC, egged on by liberal priests and self-interested businessmen,
and before you can say *goeie more* (good morning) they have promised that
the police will change themselves, so fundamentally that they will even
call a black man "Sir."

I remain optimistic that the Peace Accord will make a difference, even
if the process is flawed. Every single police officer across the land signs it,
committing to seven pages of general provisions and a detailed code of
conduct. Yet many of the policemen and policewomen we meet in the field
say that they are not committed to it. A Police Board of eleven civilians
and eleven senior police officers is established to make policy recommendations on policing that will "reconcile the interests of the community
with that of the police."[5] Initially, at least, it appears to have no teeth.
A Police Complaints Investigation Unit is designated to each region to
follow up complaints of police misconduct, and police reporting officers
(PROs) will be appointed to channel the complaints. But the investigation units are staffed only by police officers, some of them from a security
branch background. Without civilian oversight, they lack credibility, and
the PROs are not appointed for nearly two years.

But all this provides a structure for change, and as the struggle for the
hearts and minds of the police gathers momentum, more and more individual police officers surrender to the inevitable. Some begin to try on new
ideas like a new coat, testing the language of service, respect, and humility
for comfort and effectiveness. Their motivations vary, from a genuine will
to reform to a pragmatic assessment of how best to keep their jobs under
the future ANC government to a wait-and-see attitude of keeping all options open while the politicians play their fateful game. But the majority
seem to be grimly hanging onto the world as they know it, reluctant to
accept change.

Police delegates to the peace committee show deep suspicion for the
first few meetings. It is hardly surprising. Every moment of their training,

every instinct, every shred of their history as police officers and, in most cases, as Afrikaners (senior ranks, which were almost entirely white Afrikaners, are assigned to the Peace Accord structures) is violated by this engagement with the enemy.

They are not alone in their unease as for the first time, long-time political opponents from every sector of society sit around a table to talk, a new event in our divided society. Within a remarkably short time, the brick walls in our minds begin to crumble, and alongside our clear perceptions of the values and issues that alienate us, we get the first glimpses of the humanity and commonality that bind us. The Peace Accord is first and foremost a vehicle for bridge building.

For many, transformation of the police seems a pipe dream. Yet it is the cornerstone of South Africa's quest for a democratic future. Police force must become police service. We will never achieve the multiparty democracy we want without this fundamental shift. We have to find ways to overcome individual and collective resistance to change.

It is a time of deep uncertainty for the police as a whole and for individual policemen and policewomen. They are fearful about the future and its effect on their careers. No one has prepared them psychologically or tactically for the new style of policing. They feel great stress facing escalating violence with insufficient resources. They know of the deep-seated community anger boiling over after years of repression. They see their fellow officers killed, and die by suicide, at the highest rate in South African history. The police administration cannot provide adequate psychological support for dealing with this sudden surge in stress levels.

I find it difficult to judge how the transition is proceeding, as conflicting accounts tip the seesaw of evidence this way and that. Monitors report that members of the infamous ISD stood impassive for hours while demonstrators danced in front of them, waving sticks and spitting at them, making faces. That sounds encouraging. Community leaders in Khayelitsha report that the ISD raided two hundred houses at four o'clock in the morning, breaking down doors, using foul language, arresting residents apparently at random, using excessive force just the way they used to. That sounds discouraging. A report says a station commander spent hours in meetings with the community to assess community policing priorities, yet I witness a colonel ordering a baton charge when an angry crowd of taxi drivers gathers to air their grievances. I try to make sense out of this confusing picture, but there is no sense to be made.

There is also dissent among the NGOs, academics, clergy, advocacy groups, community leaders, and conflict resolution practitioners involved in policing issues. Many of them suffered directly at the hands of the police or witnessed daily police brutality during the hard-line days of the 1970s and 1980s. Understandably, they suspect a covert agenda every time the police announce a change. I believe that the police force as a whole, and particularly those police officers brave enough to attempt change, should be encouraged and supported in their efforts even if it cannot be proved that they are sincere. And they should be challenged and criticized when necessary.

We learn to live with the ambiguity. My stomach knots when some fellow NGO and church peace workers are suspicious of the few of us who work with the police to transform them. It is hard to do things that colleagues misunderstand, criticize, and even condemn. I want the approbation of my peers, and I want to be liked. But I know that for me this is the right way. I know that the police cannot make the transition on their own. I am committed to conflict resolution methodology as an effective tool for change, and I am reminded by daily events that the transformation of the police is crucial to the transformation of South Africa as a whole. I see our work focused on two tiers, the institutional and the personal. I apply the old conflict resolution adage and try to be "hard on issues, soft on people."

Reaching out to another human being and making a connection carries enormous power. Kindness is a nondenominational currency, and I believe there is good hidden somewhere in each human being. I do not believe that one person can ever change another, but that we can help each other where there is the will to change.

In the end, we all do what we believe in and what we can do best. The monitors from various human rights NGOs and church organizations play a key role, working day in, day out as watchdogs of violence in general and police activity in particular. Together with a spectrum of concerned organizations, they file meticulous reports on every deviation, from the absence of nametags to allegations of murder. In crises, we rush to the scene, summoned through our radio pagers, and scrutinize police response.

The peace committee, its subcommittees, and LPCs draw a broad constituency into meetings with the police on a regular basis. In October 1992, with a planned demonstration by thousands to mark the opening of the last white parliamentary session looming just a few days away, a group of independent monitors meets with the Regional Command of the police to agree upon lines of communication. The transport crisis escalates as the war between minibus taxis and buses erupts yet again, and the various stakeholders, including the police, start meeting on a regular basis to try to find a solution. Local and regional authorities hold crisis meetings about protest marches. Members of Parliament are drawn into conflicts. Police representatives attend this growing round of meetings, and as they learn to engage as equals rather than as authority figures, barriers crumble, personalities emerge, and relationships start being built in defiance of the stereotypes.

COMMUNITY POLICING

As the country's 114,000 policemen and policewomen contemplate an uncertain future in December 1992, the police proudly announce the formation of a Community Relations Division within the police force to become operational immediately.

This marks the public launch of the community policing idea. Later, people will ask, What made them change? Why did they agree to do it? The answer is that they had no choice. The pressure to change pushed up from the bottom and pressed down from the top, and history was propelling them forward. At the top, the political will to transform South Africa, led by de Klerk and Mandela, set the agenda, and as government servants, the members of the police force had to fall into line. Political necessity succeeded where no amount of coercion could have.

At the bottom, policing had become a more and more dangerous, difficult, and unrewarding job as black communities flatly refused to cooperate with a police force that they viewed as the enemy. The generals packed their bags and trekked to Europe and America to inspect different models of progressive policing that they thought might work and came home with community policing.

Community policing is a new philosophy that evolved as a response to the inability of traditional policing philosophy to prevent or control the civil rights riots and anti-Vietnam War protests of Americans in the 1960s and 1970s.[6] Traditional policing emphasizes reaction to incidents, enforcement of law and order, and authoritative management with little community input. Community policing emphasizes "the joint process in which communities, through representative structures, and the police work together toward the creation of safe, secure environments."[7] It stresses problem solving as a process, community involvement and input, and decentralization. Community policing is a service, it responds to the community, and it is everyone's business.

The key is joint police-community action. In the community policing philosophy, the police are just one of the agencies necessary for order in society. Other agencies, such as neighborhood watches, community courts, and self-defense or self-protection units,[8] reside in the community. The formation of the Community Relations Division enshrined the Liaison Forum, in which the police and the community confer about policing matters, as the cornerstone of its new policy. It consolidated the order that in March 1992 had gone out to every station commander throughout the country to hold regular monthly meetings with interested organizations in his or her precinct and set it within a structural and procedural framework. It represented a forward leap conceptually, but it did not provide the conclusive solution that the police hoped for. In hindsight, although it proved to be a significant stepping stone in the process of transformation, precipitating a genuine forward momentum, the real work had only just begun.

The first attempts at police liaison forums in response to the March 1992 order were haphazard and unsuccessful. The station commanders called the meetings, set the agendas, and chaired the proceedings. It was the only way they knew how to do it. Needless to say, the community organizations were unimpressed by this display of old-style, authoritarian police culture, and they withdrew from the process. They saw it as yet another government whitewashing attempt: changing the appearance but not the reality of their lives. To the police, this proved that consultation with the community was pointless and impossible.

The problem was that neither the police nor the communities knew how to do community policing. There was little understanding of the concept, and few had the skills to put it into practice. The principles that underpin it were foreign and worthy of suspicion on both sides, and there was serious doubt that the relationship between the police and the people could ever be mended. For the police, it was also alarming; they questioned in their own minds and among themselves how it would be possible to do their jobs if they were to be accountable to the communities they were meant to police.

A TRIAL BALLOON IN MANENBERG

As community policing stalled in many areas across the country, news got out that something extraordinary had happened in the uneven streets of a Coloured neighborhood of Cape Town called Manenberg. There, a social worker called Chris Ferndale was quietly achieving what the rest of the country was still talking about. Since early 1992, Chris had been working with the police and the local community. Together, they had traveled through the valley of the shadow between old-style policing and community policing and had come out the other end, ready to foster the safety and security of the community and the police. It was pioneering work that everyone was proud of.

Manenberg is a blue-collar, Coloured neighborhood where drug-dealing, family violence, gangsterism, and alleged police corruption had for many years plagued the ordinary people who were just trying to get on with their lives. There had been many attempts to resolve local problems, but time and again the initiatives came up against the lack of accountability and cooperation from the local police. The relationship between the community and the police was at an all-time low when in March 1992 Chris was asked to help.

Chris, the son of a Coloured policeman, grew up with the derisive shouts of *polisie kind* (police child) ringing in his ears. It was the taunt hurled at children whose Coloured or African parents joined the police in the apartheid years. To add to his humiliation, Chris noticed that his father, a noncommissioned officer, was denied promotion when whites whom his father trained raced up the ranks. His father's trainees included Nic Acker, who in the early 1990s became the top-ranking policeman in the Western Cape. Chris's father remained a sergeant at a suburban police station for thirty years.

Chris distanced himself from his father the policeman and went into social work. In time, he reconciled with his father the man, but it was only in 1992 that the story came full circle when, through his involvement in Manenberg, Chris discovered that what he really wanted to do was "to change the cops in a real way." At exactly the same time, their families having touched briefly thirty years before, the son of the young Coloured police sergeant came face to face with the Western Cape regional commissioner of police. As the new South Africa emerged, they sat as equals on opposite sides of the negotiating table. Chris's dad was proud that Nic Acker knew who his son was.

Serious socioeconomic problems in Manenberg forced the community to act.[9] The local service and community organizations asked the National Association for the Care and Rehabilitation of Offenders (NICRO), a national NGO promoting social and criminal justice, to help find solutions. NICRO appointed Chris, then one of their fieldworkers, to the project. "Week after week a colleague and I walked the streets," he remembers. "We consulted everyone, asking, 'How do you see the relationships among youth, how can we control development, how can we resolve family violence?'" One overwhelming response was that the police were taking sides in the conflicts that racked the community and that this should stop. Another was that the conflict between the community organizations and the police had to end.

For four months, thirty organizations met regularly: churches, mosques, businesses, advice offices, taxpayers associations, civic organizations, anti-drug networks, and neighborhood watches. They formulated a common vision that committed the community to developing a democratic relationship with the police. A delegation met with the local police to test their reaction to the idea of a democratic partnership. Others visited fledgling liaison structures in neighboring areas to evaluate their progress. By June they were finally ready for the first police-community meeting.

It was to be the start of a determined battle of wills as the police tried to control the process, and the community resisted. But the discussion was frank, and in the end the two sides found common ground, consolidated at a meeting in August 1992 when they formed a joint secretariat and adopted the Peace Accord as the guiding document. It was the only community policing forum in the country that chose to operate through a secretariat instead of electing a chairperson. At the public and in-house meetings that followed, the police and community representatives alternately hosted and chaired meetings.

The forum took its role seriously. It held educational public meetings on the Peace Accord, legal and judicial systems, and family violence, rape, battering, and other issues. At the start of 1993, a series of workshops tackled the doubts, fears, and perceptions local police harbored in building this new relationship with the community. The forum held a joint training course for police and community members on family violence and battering.

Early consultations with the broader community and ongoing feedback highlighted family violence as one of the most pressing issues in a basket of pressing issues. The forum made this a priority. Police officers were specially trained to respond and, together with a network of health workers, psychologists, priests, and volunteers, were able to offer effective family violence service. As an unexpected consequence, reported incidents of family violence increased, since, for the first time, community members felt confident in talking to the police. This newfound trust, built around the painful personal conflict that infects every community, became generalized and spread to other issues too.

In his article entitled "Democratizing the Police," Chris outlines the lessons learned:

- a democratic relationship with the police can be forged only if organizations are strong;
- the will and hearts of community representatives and police must change;
- structured programs need to be developed with set goals;
- there must be active participation in the agreements reached;
- regular assessments of community-police relations need to take place;
- debate and the ability to disagree and develop are integral to the process;
- the broader community needs to be kept informed; and
- local police officers can change through education.

Chris ends his article on an optimistic note: "Communities are patrolling their own streets, making peace and jointly educating themselves and the police. There is still a long road ahead, but people have begun to own their police station and the peace process."

CHANGE AT POLICE HEADQUARTERS

While Chris helps the Manenberg community make their liaison forum work, a tidy world is turning upside down on the sixth floor of police Regional Headquarters in the center of Cape Town. This is where the regional management team has its offices, and in regional offices like this around the country, the December 1992 announcement of the formation of the Community Relations Division has its greatest effect. It will be some time before the full impact of this new-style policing trickles down to the rank and file.

The guidelines for community policing have been circulated. Researchers at National Headquarters in Pretoria had defined and refined the principles and theory and conjured them into a step-by-step guide for practical application. It was a difficult task, because apartheid-style policing was based on force and aggression, whereas community policing is based on service and cooperation. The police now contemplate their imminent transformation from a police force to a police service.

National Headquarters underlines the serious intent and importance of the new Community Relations Division in a mission statement: "We undertake to develop a policing style based on accountability and human rights as well as a policing system based on cooperation and support of the community, through purposeful interaction and with the purpose of promoting higher-quality service by the South African Police."[10]

The guidelines document is discussed endlessly in the sixth-floor corridors and around the conference table. In the end, it is sent to skeptical police managers whose main reservation is about how to implement it—or if it can even be implemented.

In March 1993, ten officers are dispatched from Cape Town to Pretoria for a workshop. When they get back, their job will be to immediately implement community policing in the Western Cape. It is an order.

Gerrit Nieuwoudt, one of the ten, feels that the guidelines are still too impractical to work with. Together with some of his colleagues, he rewrites them as a manual for distribution throughout the region. My copy has my name printed on the lower-right corner. At that time, it is an extraordinary document to come from the police.[11]

It is realistic about their political future: "If the SA Police intends to survive effectively and wants to be accepted, it will have to adapt to the external environment and the accompanying changes."

It is realistic about their track record: "An attitude of antagonism and hatred toward the Police still prevails. . . . the SA Police is still viewed as a political instrument. . . . a section of the community questions our ability to meet their needs."

It doesn't pull any punches: "The SA Police has been responsible for the enforcing of discriminatory legislation in the past. . . . a subculture of brutality and bias actually developed. . . . the above has led to a situation in which the Police policed the community in isolation without any consideration concerning the needs of the community. This also contributed to a situation in which the community no longer trusts the SA Police and a large section of the community even hates the SA Police."

It says what needs to be done: "It is, therefore, clear that the SA Police is not acceptable to the largest section of the population and will have to change in order to survive. The new approach which we are going to adopt must be acceptable in any political dispensation and at the same time it must lead to effective policing. The SA Police has decided on Community Policing as the policing style of the future."

COMMUNITY POLICING GATHERS MOMENTUM

On Wednesday, June 30, under the auspices of the Peace Accord, 150 police officers; political, NGO, and peace committee representatives; church and civic leaders; and international observers gather in a conference room at a Johannesburg airport hotel for a consultative workshop on community policing. A block away at the World Trade Centre, the multiparty negotiating process is recovering from an attack the previous Friday, when heavily armed right-wing militia members drove an armored car through the heavy plate-glass facade, sending splinters and security personnel flying in all directions. We skirt the considerable security presence that has collected in the wake of the attack and settle in for a long day of our own tough talking.

The police have taken the workshop very seriously indeed and have sent the commissioners and deputy commissioners from eight of the eleven regions created by the National Peace Accord and senior officers from the other police divisions. Four keynote speeches are given by high-level officials from the main political organizations and parties, all endorsing the need for a new, improved brand of policing. NGO and grassroots political representatives have gathered from every corner of the country.

At ten o'clock that night when we close the meeting, the walls are papered with ideas about community policing captured on flipcharts with red, blue, black, and green marker pens. This raw material consolidates six key principles that the police adopt as the framework for the implementation of community policing:

1. Structured consultation between the police and communities, in other words, the liaison forums

2. Joint planning and responsibility between the police and the community
3. Mobilization of all resources available to the community and the police to resolve problems and promote security and safety
4. Acting as an integral part of the criminal justice system and the community, not apart from them
5. Accountability, transparency, and professionalism
6. Broadening of the police mandate from a reactive focus on crime control to a proactive problem-solving focus on the underlying causes of crime and violence. [12]

What does the community need from the police? The Police Board commissions Laurie Nathan and me to write a paper.[13] These needs and recommendations, together with the ideas and suggestions emanating from the June workshop and others, are taken up with the Multi-Party Negotiations Forum at the World Trade Centre and eventually culminate in the constitutional provisions on community policing forums enshrined in the New Police Act.

At the same time, Malibongwe Sopangisa,[14] the LPC grassroots fieldworker based in Nyanga, makes his contribution to the dialogue with a paper on police-community relations based on his experience in the front line of conflict:

> The number of unresolved murder cases of political activists in the area has not assisted in improving relations between the police and the community. For many people the question has been: what is the role of the police if people are killed with no arrest of perpetrators? Another area of concern for ordinary people has been the release of people who have committed serious crimes. People in the community have no faith in the system of justice. For them someone can kill today, to be released the next day. This introduces a sense that the police are not there to protect them. It also acts as a stumbling block to good community-police relations.

It seems clear that despite the best efforts of the police leadership, police operations on the ground lag far behind their goals. Malibongwe's suggestions, though, encourage me by the extent to which they parallel police strategic thinking. He proposes communication between the police and the community, real accountability by police to the community, a workable complaints system so that "the people feel that their complaints are going somewhere," and a campaign to educate police and community about community policing.

Why, when the police establishment has committed to community policing, and developed policy and enacted laws to support it, is the translation
of these efforts into active policing so poor? Laurie Nathan and I address
this in our paper, concluding that there are at least six good reasons why
the police are failing to meet their objectives.

First, many police members lack the technical, political, and interper-
sonal skills to apply the policy in practice. They do not understand fully
what is expected of them, and they are resistant to the proposed changes.
Second, police and community groups on the whole lack necessary skills in
communication, negotiation, and problem solving. Third, community policing has not as yet permeated the entire police establishment, and divisions such as the ISD frequently undermine the work of the Community
Relations Division. Fourth, the high level of community mistrust remains
a constant barrier, and communities are fearful of being seen to collaborate
with the police. Fifth, communities are not homogeneous and cohesive,
and as they often lack representative leadership, it is sometimes unclear
with whom the police should liaise. Finally, community policing is being
introduced in a top-down manner with little effort to promote a bottom-up
approach and build a more equal partnership with communities at the local level.

WORKING GROUP ON COMMUNITY POLICING

Mid-1993, the Centre for Conflict Resolution convenes the Working Group
on Community Policing to develop policy guidelines for community policing in the Western Cape. The working group includes academics, a social
worker, peace workers, an international observer (a police officer), and
regional police officers ranging from general to captain.

At the first meeting, we sit around the table in the seminar room at the
Centre and look at one another. I am by now used to mixed gatherings like
this through my involvement in the peace committee, but for others this is
a first. One academic shakes his head in astonishment, saying, "I never
thought I would sit down with the police like this to calmly talk about—
well, anything, and certainly not to shape their future." Later, when community policing is well on its way to normalcy, a police colonel confides,

"We could never have done it without you," meaning civil society. "We needed you," he says, as we talk about those difficult days when most of the police force were still unconvinced that they should change and were uncertain about what was expected of them.

But with each meeting it gets easier, and we end up like any committee, arguing, conceding, persuading, rewriting. By October, we agree on a nine-page document that we send to police headquarters for approval by the Regional Police Management Committee. At the same time, we present it to a large gathering of NGOs. Both consultations are successful, and soon the paper is circulating throughout the country, spurring on police and NGOs in the ten other regions to similar exercises in a fundamental principle of community policing and joint problem solving.

Our paper lays out what both sides can expect. Community policing principles will radically affect policing policy, regulation, and action, shaping the daily lives of the nation's policemen and policewomen, even in small ways. It will transform criteria for promotion, management style, and the underpinnings of police culture. Community organizations will rethink their position on community courts and anticrime committees, which currently exclude the police, and instead begin to forge partnerships with the police.

Policing activity will become tuned to community priorities, and joint problem solving will become the familiar tool that the baton has been, as local police replace authority and force with negotiation and consultation. The police will be accountable to the communities that they serve as this major shift from a police force to a police service gathers momentum.

Community policing is a process, not a product.[15] We remind ourselves of that as 1993 turns into 1994 and the difficulties continue. The police are committed to it, but they still struggle to make it stick. They have allocated massive resources to it, and reordered police structures to encompass it. They have designated the Community Relations Division the new elite. In the past, the path to promotion was through the Security Branch. The new path is through community policing. It is a subtle but significant shift, signaling that the old ways have no future.

Elrena van der Spuy, a sociologist and member of the Police Board based in the Western Cape, defines the problem, "The rhetoric of community policing outstrips the reality, as many in the townships and elsewhere will testify. But," she continues, "that the police has taken it seriously . . . is not to be denied."[16]

This transformation to a philosophy of community policing was dramatic. Even in societies where policing is generally perceived as legitimate, the switch to community policing can be traumatic. In South Africa, the contrast in style produced shock waves that caused some police officers to leave the police force because they knew that they just couldn't do it.

The success of community policing rests on the attitudes and behavior of the policemen and policewomen who implement it. At the time of this writing in 1999, attitudes and behavior of large numbers of the police still remain enormous barriers to community policing. NGOs allege old-style harassment and even torture in some police stations, and senior police officers responsible for its success admit that they still fight an uphill battle. Many black communities report little change.

Yet, community policing is now in place in South Africa. The key factor was political will. National leadership decided that the police should henceforth operate under civilian control and adhere to a long list of new principles and values, and it was done. However, as that police colonel said to me in 1994, "We couldn't have done it without you"—meaning the NGO community and our insistence that the police become a service for the entire South African community, no exceptions. Also meaning the black community leadership that so bravely tried to make community policing work, as in Manenberg. Also meaning the National Peace Accord that provided a forum within which police-community relations could be forged and sustained. Also meaning the regional and local peace committees where police and civilians jettisoned the stereotypes and got to know one another as human beings.

The corps of policemen and policewomen committed to community policing is growing steadily. The police force is demilitarized and reconstituted as a police service, and stories of the new-style policing practice sit alongside the complaints. To monitor the very real, but admittedly slow, progress that has been made, frustrated police reformists both inside and outside the police need to remind themselves daily how things used to be and that the shadow of apartheid will hover over all government institutions for a long time to come. And they need to recommit themselves daily to making sure that how things used to be becomes, as quickly as possible, only a memory.

8
UBUNTU, THE SPIRIT OF AFRICA

Example for the World

The story of South Africa's transformation is many things, but above all, it is a story of hope. It tells of a brutally divided society that found it in its heart to come together and negotiate a political future that held a place for all its people. It was not necessarily the place that everyone wanted. Extreme right Afrikaners wanted, and still want, their own whites-only "homeland." Extremist blacks wanted whites removed from power and out of the country, forthwith. Grudgingly, both regrouped to strategize their future, or, having lost in South Africa's first ever democratic election, generally fitted in.[1] The story of the new South Africa began to unfold.

Before the election was possible, before the new South Africa was possible, the voices of its painful history demanded that reconciliation begin its long, slow journey. The Peace Accord provided the appropriate tools and techniques, but tools, techniques, and mechanisms are not enough. Reconciliation is about people and about their willingness to bring spirit and truth and feeling to the reconciliation table to give it meaning. Many were willing, and they came and broke bread with their old enemies.

They came, black and white, because they wanted to build a new future. If black, they could come only if they were willing to *forgive* (although, as Mandela would often remind them, this did not require them to forget). And they found that they could forgive when they understood that forgiveness does not mean condoning what has been done, but letting go of that burden of resentment and anger that always sits so heavily on our shoulders when we do not forgive. Whites could come only if they were willing to *give up* power, position, and privilege. And they found that they could only give up what they considered their right when they saw that it too released a burden, of guilt, injustice, and shame. Reconciliation meant *mutual giving*, and it will be needed for a long time to come as this beautiful country heals its deep and ancient wounds.

In this mutuality of purpose, the spirit of Africa leveraged the high ground with its culture of acceptance. Africa tolerates mistakes, accepts weakness and failure, embraces good in others, and forgives the rest. The West harshly enforces what it calls high standards, punishes those who fail to meet them, and prides itself on being right at all costs. This false pride cannot admit wrong. Can the West learn from Africa?

At the reconciliation table, people rooted in the African ways of forgiveness were able to carry South Africa across the abyss. They were black and white, but they were mostly black, because the black people had so much to forgive. The decades of oppression, humiliation, limitation, and loss hovered overhead as the first contacts were made, the first stories told—and listened to—and the first steps taken into the void that was the future. In the process, individuals discovered that they could make peace and that they had the power to change the world around them. They no longer needed to wait for the authorities of one sort or another to do it for them. Empowerment took on a South African identity as hundreds, then thousands and millions, of people began to trust in themselves and their own wisdom.

Peace workers shepherded the peace process. Peace workers are generally optimists, because by believing in good, one makes the good possible. You cannot make, keep, or build peace if you do not believe that it is possible.[2] Peace and the human spirit wither in the face of negativity.

A white policeman encouraged to be his best starts to relate to black people as individuals who need his protection, respect, and access to justice. A black activist encouraged to be her best begins to relate to whites as individuals rather than as the generic oppressor. The commonality among the six peace workers profiled in chapter 2—the Robben Island prisoner, the apartheid government politician, the activists, both black and white, the Security Branch policeman—was that they all came to a point in their lives where they were willing to find the good in others, even in erstwhile enemies. It was one of the ways that they set about healing both South African society and themselves, and it worked.

UBUNTU

This, then, is the real spirit of Africa. In Xhosa and Zulu it is called *Ubuntu*. In Xhosa, *Ubuntu ungamntu ngabanye abantu* means "People are people through other people." In Zulu, *Umuntu ngumuntu ngabanye* means "One is a person through others." In Sotho, it is called *Botho*, in Venda, *Vhuthu*. It resonates through centuries of African communitarian tradition. It speaks of community building, a basic respect for human nature, sharing, empathy, tolerance, the common good, and acts of kindness. It is African humanism.

"Ubuntu is about the essence of being human; it is part of the gift that Africa will give the world," says Archbishop Desmond Tutu. "It embraces hospitality, caring about others, being willing to go that extra mile for the sake of others. We believe a person is a person through another person, that my humanity is caught up inextricably in yours. When I dehumanize you, I inexorably dehumanize myself. The solitary human being is a contradiction in terms."

Khaba Mkhize, a black journalist for *The Natal Witness*, has become something of an Ubuntu evangelist. He writes with passion and conviction about this African quality that he believes provides South Africa's salvation as it seeks to heal the terrible wounds of the past and forge a shared future. "There's no gatecrashing in an Ubuntu setting," he quips. "No invitations. Everyone is welcome."[3]

Mkhize says, "Ubuntu is about feeling for your fellow brother and sister." He recites the Cs that come from Ubuntu. They begin with open communication and direct contact. "For starters," he declares, "learn to greet me and I will learn to greet you . . . after we greet we shake hands. A handshake is a great unifier of beings. Shaking a hand is another way of knocking on your heart, another way of cultivating common humanity."

The other Cs include consultation, compromise, cooperation, camaraderie, conscientiousness, and the biggest C of all, compassion. Mkhize notes that kiSwahili speakers use the slogan *Harambee* (To win together). "It is when people are reawakened to the prerogative of pulling together for a common purpose, which is a winning formula, that we'll all be clear about what Madiba [President Mandela] means when he pleads, 'Help me to build a better South Africa for *All!*' And the cement," Mkhize concludes, "is Ubuntu."[4]

In one of his regular columns about Ubuntu, Mkhize reproduced a letter from a white who, in an echo of John F. Kennedy's famous challenge, wrote, "Time to stop saying what is the government doing for me, and start saying what can I do for my country and fellow people. Ubuntu. We have so much going for us, not least of which has been due to the incredible forgiveness, good-naturedness and sheer decency of the vast majority of black South Africans."[5]

Back in 1989, Aggrey Klaaste, the (black) editor of South Africa's highest circulation black newspaper, Sowetan, started to talk about Ubuntu through his newspaper. "Foreigners are always remarking on the goodwill that seems to exist between the races here. There is something indefinable in black South Africans, springing from an ethic that has come down over many, many years from our lost civilizations. I wish to see this ethic, this Ubuntu, as it is called, as the answer for attaining what the world has always craved for—the brotherhood of man."[6]

Klaaste, who describes himself as an idealist, understood then that South Africa was destined to show the world what a multiethnic, multicultural, multiracial country would look like. He also sensed that the vigor of the antiapartheid movement worldwide was to some degree an expression of buried racist feelings that needed a focus. "I have a feeling," he wrote then, "that, while world-wide outrage is being expressed against apartheid, the world is secretly wishing that South Africans can show it how to deal with this problem." He continued prophetically, "The political leaders of South Africa, from the far right to the far left, cannot be expected to provide the solutions on a plate. In fact, the political leaders will be led by the people of South Africa, those who march together for peace. . . . we will force the leaders, people like F. W. de Klerk, to think like modern men."[7]

The corporate sector and academia have also found Ubuntu. At the end of 1991, the Black Management Forum and the (white) Institute of Directors sponsored with others a conference to explore the possibility of integrating Ubuntu into business management. In 1994, South African Airways restructured its organization to embrace Ubuntu values and launched a marketing campaign to reflect its new Ubuntu-based policy of a caring airline. In early 1995, coauthors Lovemore Mbigi (black) and Jenny Maree (white) published a book about the role of Ubuntu in management in the new multicultural South Africa.[8] In parallel with this flurry of Ubuntu ideas, an independent think tank was established to disseminate the spirit of Ubuntu. Named the Council for African Thought, it provides a platform for black academics to articulate the African experience and influence formerly Eurocentric public policy.[9]

As the spirit of Ubuntu became recognized in the public arena, black people like the Rev. Barney Pityana began to voice a widespread longing for moral reconstruction and spiritual development to accompany the physical and material Reconstruction and Development Program, the new Government of National Unity's policy centerpiece. Pityana, a close friend of the late Steven Biko and former head of the Program to Combat Racism at the World Council of Churches in Geneva while in exile from South Africa, said in a speech to the seminarians of a college in Grahamstown that he was worried that South Africans were in danger of losing their humanity. He was worried that black people were adopting the white values of money and materialism. He was worried that the churches, which had done so much during the battle against apartheid, were failing their people now as they struggled to frame a coherent vision for the future and provide the leadership that the new dispensation so desperately needed.

"What we need is a society with new values, a new moral community," he said. "No national life is possible without some common moral values. Otherwise, we will just kill one another, cheat one another, and lie to one another all the time.

"The African moral principle of Ubuntu will have to become something more than a mere catch-phrase," he continued. Then he spoke directly to the future clergy, who were listening spellbound: "How ready are you, ministers-in-training, to take up this new and challenging task? In a way the task is simple enough. We need to teach the basics of love and care for one another. We need to insist upon honesty and compassion, upon sharing and generosity of spirit. We need to teach the ten commandments and to get the milk of human kindness flowing again in our communities."[10]

When South Africans meet, they should greet one another not with "How are you?" but with "Tell me your story," says Chris Mann, a white Durban-based development specialist. He is talking about ways of breaking the entrenched stereotypes that underpin relationships in South Africa. "A common bond begins to develop and the diversity starts to unify only when our individuality as humans is recognized, in law and in the workplace as well as in our personal relations," he says. But he is careful to define the kind of individuality he is talking about. "[Western individuality] leads to the individualism that Africans so often criticize as inhuman . . . when the family and the community are replaced by lonely, self-absorbed individuals."

The African connection to the ancestors, or "shades," is key to understanding the African form of individualism, which sees the individual as the product of and influenced by an assembly of presences. In addition, many living beings affect our daily lives. Mann concludes, "Our souls by this belief, while cored by an energy that is the self, are neither closed-in solitudes nor personal *bantustans* [homelands under apartheid]. They are better described as communities of shades."

Ubuntu, Mann says, "challenges the inward and spiritual apartheid that still afflicts so many." He says that the New South Africa can flourish only when we deal with both this inner and the outer segregation.[11]

�֎   �֎   ✖

In many ways, the Peace Accord was a tangible expression of the spirit of Ubuntu. It provided a mechanism for South Africans of all races, as individuals, to take responsibility for our collective reconciliation and healing. We had to find within ourselves empathy, generosity, humility, hope, and a willingness to try and to risk. We had to face fear, a sense of inadequacy, and that legacy of apartheid, the inner pain of both the oppressed and the oppressor. We had to learn to love instead of to fear one another, and translate that love into action, as, for the first time, we began to really know one another.

The transformation of South Africa also had a dramatic impact across the world as antiapartheid activists found themselves bereft of the cause that for some had defined their lives. The end of apartheid signaled the end of the long, hard struggle that had seen activists arrested in Washington, camped outside the door of the South African embassy in London, and demonstrating against the sale of South African oranges and wine in stores across Europe and against illegal sports tours in New Zealand.

Those were the heady days when activist voices had traveled on the wind into the draughty corridors of power in Pretoria and had made a difference. Now apartheid was finished, and for some, so was their life's work. One day, eighteen months after Mandela's election, when I was speaking about the transition in Washington, D.C., a man got up and said, "No, this is not true. We have to keep fighting; there is no change."[12] I understood his panic as the issue that had given his life meaning slipped through his fingers. I hoped that one day he would visit South Africa to see the transformation he had helped create.

SACRIFICE

On August 25, 1993, in the early evening light of the bustling African township of Guguletu, a young American met her destiny. Amy Biehl was giving three African friends a lift home when she was attacked and brutally murdered by a mob of about thirty young African men. She was twenty-six years old, and she was killed because she was white. Paradoxically, her murder would break the cycle of violence by young blacks that had spiraled dangerously out of control and was threatening to send a spear through the heart of the peace process.

Nelson Mandela had been Amy's hero since high school. She studied South Africa as a college student at Stanford University and took up the "Free Mandela" cause. In 1992, Amy won a Fulbright scholarship to attend the predominantly black University of the Western Cape.

Every Sunday, she phoned home. "She was committed, excited, and involved," says her mother, Linda Biehl, remembering those high-energy conversations in which Amy tried to tell her family about another week in her new life.[13] But it was only later, after her death, when her family visited the scene of her life there, that they fully understood what she was talking about. Being there, in Cape Town, seeing what she had seen, meeting her friends and colleagues, visiting the black townships and experiencing the squalor of the squatter camps where she had worked to improve conditions, hearing about their daughter, their sister, from voices that were black and white—then, only then, did they understand the power of who she was in the context of South Africa. "It was all a little bit overwhelming that my daughter had actually done this with her life," says Linda about that trip. "I was in awe of my daughter; how she affected people half way around the world, and how they were celebrating her life."[14]

Amy's death was not in vain. The racially motivated killing of Amy Biehl shocked South Africans to the core. "Even the radical township youth were shocked," says Stef Snel in a letter to me about that time. "She was murdered in and by members of a community I know well. I had been working in those areas for some years. Not long before her death, Pro Jack, a well-loved activist who was later killed by his own people, saved a white journalist from knife-wielding ANC and PAC youth in the Guguletu area. I had also curtailed my exposure to the townships as I knew that antagonism towards whites was growing among the youth. A PAC friend from Khayelitsha had asked me to stay out of that area for the same reasons. This brutal killing of a comrade broke the spell of the boiling, indiscriminate hate towards whites, and resulted in much introspection by the black youth."[15] In Guguletu, the community responded with guilt, anguish, and deep shock, and mothers marched through the uneven streets, praying out loud for their sons' redemption.

"If there is any comfort for the family," church and political leader Allan Boesak said during the Biehl family's visit, "it is this, that Amy's death now becomes an inspiration for those very young people to make sure that the ideals that she had, and the inspiration that she found here, that those things will actually be achieved."[16]

"It was not a senseless murder," says Linda. "I feel that there are reasons for things. Amy was led down a path to her involved role in Cape Town at a crucial time." "Amy went there to change things," says her father Peter Biehl. "Her death is completely understandable in the context of struggle and completely understandable in terms of the background of disenfranchised young black people. As horribly as we miss her and as empty as we feel without her, her death is consistent with her purpose for being there."[17] Linda adds softly: "Physically, she's not here, but the spirit, her personality, the sense of who she was leads us on."[18]

The Biehl family has established a private foundation, Peter says "for the twenty-dollar giver,"[19] to encourage people, especially young people, to help themselves. They say that the message of reconciliation is important for young people. So far, the Biehls have identified a few small, grassroots NGOs in Amy's territory, the Western Cape, that they support with money, contacts, and resources. They take a human and pragmatic approach. As Peter says, if people need shoes, they give them shoes.

※　　　※　　　※

While they were in South Africa retracing Amy's footsteps, the Biehls visited another family grieving their own devastating loss, the widow and daughter of Chris Hani. Fourteen-year-old Nomakhwezi was with her father when he was gunned down in cold blood four months before Amy was killed. When the Biehls and the Hanis met a year later, this extraordinary teenager said, "My father . . . wouldn't have liked us to be bitter and live in hatred, and start hating white people. That doesn't help anything at all, and that's not what he lived for." As Limpho Hani comforted her distraught daughter, she too said through her tears, "Whoever decided to kill Chris, that was the motive. He wanted our leadership to be bitter, he wanted our leadership to be angry. They can kill all of us but we will continue on our peaceful route to democracy."[20]

Amy had revered Chris Hani. When he was killed, and her parents had rung in concern to ask, "Are you all right," she had responded sharply, "Why ask about me?"[21] Their question was a response to the television pictures of anguished violence that were flashing around the world as black youth lashed out at the system that had oppressed them and their parents and their parents' parents, back and back through generations. Now it had killed Chris Hani, and the lid blew off.

In his autobiography, Nelson Mandela describes Chris Hani as one of South Africa's greatest sons, and, just weeks before his assassination, a leadership opinion poll had ranked him second only to Mandela in popularity.[22] Mandela writes that, at the time, there were very real fears that his death would provoke a racial war, because the white Polish immigrant who pulled the trigger did much more than kill a man, or even a great leader. As he and his coconspirators had intended, the bullets that struck Chris Hani also struck at the soft center of African experience. Once again, the white man had come with his guns and taken that which was most precious to the black man—just taken it at will, brutally, viciously, and with finality. It was the story of the last 350 years, the recurring nightmare of the African continent. It was, psychologically and spiritually, a body blow, and it knocked black South Africa right off balance.

At the time, black confidence in the negotiating process was at a low. The downward spiral had started with the breakdown of negotiations in May the previous year. In June, a massacre had left forty-nine ANC supporters dead, and the ANC had withdrawn from negotiations in protest and shock, alleging police complicity in the killings. In September, twenty-eight ANC protesters had been killed by Ciskei security forces as they marched on Bisho, the Ciskei capital.[23] In October, Buthelezi and some white extreme right-wing groups had formed a curious alliance opposing negotiations. As the old year turned into 1993, uncertainty hung in the air like soupy fog. The people felt alienated from their leadership, who more and more seemed to be too busy with national affairs to keep adequately in touch with their grass roots. And all the while, the conditions of everyday life—the grinding poverty of the townships, the absence of services and facilities, the ingrained discrimination—remained very much the same.

Stef Snel says that he had felt the sense of pressure building in the nation. "It was the feeling of apprehension you get in Africa before a big storm. I got the same feelings about the sociopolitical situation. It's easy to say these things in hindsight, that the murder of an individual, however tragic, had some kind of cathartic effect on the nation or the region, but say it I must."[24]

It is a concept as old as religion, and as deep, that the greatest sacrifice of all is to give up one's life for another, or for the common good. The deaths of Chris Hani and Amy Biehl, and countless other deaths, each in its own way changed the course of South African history, bleeding the abscess of pain and anger, shocking people to their senses, mobilizing the silent majority to find its voice in protest, taking us step-by-step to the national elections of April 1994 and irreversible democracy. It was a spiritual journey of immense proportions, and it touched us all.

�֍   �֍   ✖

Each day of South Africa's transformation process brought with it little miracles of the human spirit. The stories in this book describe reaching out, breaking through, forgiveness, and reconciliation, not by saints and pious leaders, but by ordinary people. None of it was easy, everyone was struggling with the past, with pain and fear, anger and resentment, loss and fear of loss. In the context of their experience, the people of South Africa were heroic in their willingness jointly to reinvent their society. Especially black people. Robert Schrire, a political scientist at the University of Cape Town, says, "Any social scientist would expect 98 percent of blacks to hate whites and wish retribution, and yet the reality is the reverse. And since we cannot explain it rationally, we will have to regard it as one of the great miracles of the South African dilemma."[25]

The story of South Africa's transformation needs to be told, and retold, to be listened to, and, finally, understood as one of the great miracles of our world today. It grew out of the long, hard, dangerous struggle for freedom from oppression by a remarkable stream of men and women, many of them unrecognized for their valor, who determinedly held onto their sense of humanity in the face of the inhumane. It was nurtured as leaders of extraordinary stature emerged to clear the way through the debris of apartheid, and it flowered in the sunlight of its own brand of democracy. But most of all, it tells of individual men and women drawing on the strength of spirit within themselves to reach one another and to begin the process of making their peace. This is their story. *Abande* (Xhosa: Let it increase).

EPILOGUE

In March 1995, just eleven months after South Africa's first-ever democratic election, an American businessman raised his hand at a conference in Johannesburg to ask a question of the speaker, Roelf Meyer, the minister of constitutional development. Meyer, an Afrikaner who had been a key negotiator for F. W. de Klerk's government during the transitional negotiations, listened attentively as the American said that in all negotiations there have to be winners and losers. In what ways, he asked, had the ANC and the National Party each won and lost during the negotiations process? Roelf Meyer smiled before he replied, "We realized at a very early stage that we had to achieve a win-win solution."[1]

It was a conversation that the Americans in the audience had rarely heard before between opposition politicians. In South Africa, it was also a new voice, a voice that had been born during the transition from apartheid to democracy. As I listened, I wondered at how this nation that had represented everything that was divisive, oppressive, and exclusionary had become a model for transformation. In the course of four years, we had shifted our worldview and embraced a win-win, nonadversarial culture embedded in a multiracial democracy.

This is not to say that every aspect of the South African nation was transformed overnight. It will take many years for balance to be restored and for apartheid to fade into memory. What we had done, though, was to shift the model, or paradigm, and begin building our brave new world from a completely fresh blueprint.[2]

This book is not about the national negotiations that shaped South Africa's new political structure but about the national peace process that underpinned them, informed them, and provided a framework for collective civic expression of the new South Africa. Can others learn from our experience? I believe it is an extraordinary offering to the world. Nothing like it had ever been tried before, and our achievement has become a beacon of hope to troubled communities everywhere. Now the international community knows that it is possible for a whole society not just to change political structure and leadership but also to transform itself in the process.

Given the extraordinary work of the peace committees and peace work-ers, it was a shock when South Africa's new democratic government closed down the Peace Accord structures in December 1994. Everyone associated with the peace process was outraged. The peace committees had under-stood that after the 1994 election their role would change, and they had worked together to propose a trimmed-down, reoriented, realistic vision for their future. Instead, within six months, they were disbanded, despite the protests of communities such as Crossroads that depended on the com-mittees for their stability.

Theories vary as to why the government did it. It certainly was not the money; the annual budget for the entire country was R 44 million, or about U.S. $7 million, and the peace committees had already found some inde-pendent funding to see them through 1995. And it was not because their role had ended with the demise of apartheid. It was clear that South Africa would need buffers between authorities and the black community, and fo-rums for consultation, negotiation, joint decision making, and relationship building, far into the future. Local government elections loomed a year ahead, and it was unthinkable that they should not be monitored. Addi-tionally, the peace committees were, with exceptions, successful, so it was not a question of effectiveness.

"The motivation is a bit of a mystery," says Peter Gastrow. "To my knowl-edge, there was no definitive statement from the government explaining their action." He talked with individuals who said that the new constitu-tion provided democratic structures at all levels. The local levels—the town councils—would soon be run by these democratic structures. This is where conflict should be dealt with, they said. A separate Peace Accord structure would not be necessary.

"In reality, I think they were concerned about competitive structures and competition for funds and power," Peter concludes.[3] And this is in-deed the conventional wisdom, that the politicians wanted control and that it was precisely because the Peace Accord was so successful that it was closed down.

The signs had been there in the everyday life of the peace committees. Chris Spies believes that we achieved success in the peace structures in spite of the politicians. "It was absolutely crazy how red tape and party political interests hampered the peace process," he says. He talks about the infighting that was going on between the political parties "while we were working our nails off to just get something done," and is convinced that politicians should never be entrusted with an institutionalized peace process.[4]

For one thing, politicians, generally speaking, do not have the experience to handle a large project like this. He suggests that professionals should have been hired to furnish management services, allocate resources, and provide infrastructure. He says that official support for the peace committees was actually very small.

In retrospect, the relationship between the peace committees and their political masters was doomed from the start. The peace committees, operating in crisis mode to deal with daily, ongoing violence, required flexibility, resources, and quick responses, whereas the politicians who administered them gave priority to their party political interests. These incompatible goals were a sure recipe for conflict. In a way, control of the peace process by party politicians represented a contradiction in terms.

Despite the short shrift accorded it by the politicians, outgoing National Party and incoming ANC alike, the legacy of the peace process is indelibly written on the new South Africa. In the old South Africa, adversarial, win-lose systems prevailed. Mandela modeled nonadversarial, win-win approaches during his presidency, informing the emerging society, even though imperfectly.

People got used to participation in the forums that sprang up all over the country, at local, regional, and national levels. It was clear that when interest groups come together in a spirit of collaborative problem solving around an issue of common concern, they have the best chance of finding sustainable goals, solutions, and formulations for the future. Some forums even functioned in an executive capacity. The National Economic Development Forum (NEDF) dominated the financial sector with real-time decision-making powers, so that when in 1993, the then minister of mineral and energy affairs unwisely announced a petrol (gasoline) price increase without consultation, creating a violent rebellion in the minibus taxi industry, the matter was eventually referred to the NEDF for resolution.

Third-party intervention, instead of confrontation, became an accepted and often preferred way of responding to conflicts and crises, to the extent that at the eleventh hour before the April 1994 election, IFP leader Buthelezi insisted on international mediation to resolve the crisis.

Wide consultation informed decision making in defiance of the deep-seated tradition that power was vested in the authorities alone. Much of it was a consequence of necessity; people were demanding to be involved in decisions that affected their political futures and their civic lives. For instance, the growing recognition that development was a source of conflict because of the top-down way that it had always been implemented prompted consultants to seek new methodologies. In 1993 in Port Elizabeth, the Urban Foundation successfully managed the largest upgrading of a squatter settlement in the country, providing ten thousand freehold serviced sites, conflict-free. They did it by involving the community from day one, when their regional and national directors went to regional ANC leader Govan Mbeki, recently released from Robben Island, to seek his advice. What are the priorities for the area, they asked? School facilities and squatter areas, came the response, and so this project grew from the hearts of the people and was shaped to include their views through broad consultation at every stage.

Conciliation has become mainstream. At the end of May 1998, Justice Minister Dullah Omar opened a specialist Labor Court that employs conciliation as a technique, calling it "one of the proudest achievements of post-apartheid South Africa." He described it as a great achievement because "it is legitimate, efficient, employs conciliation as a technique to cut down the number and intensity of disputes, and it is accessible."[5] It also has equal status to the High Court.

There are no shortcuts to making, keeping, and building peace and no quick-fix solutions. It is a long and sometimes tedious process. "People who come into a conflict situation with a once-off [one-time] program shouldn't expect results," says Chris Spies. "Just spreading training courses like you sow seed on the land and hope that some fertile ground will take them in and let them bear fruit—it is simply not good enough."[6]

We can learn a lot from one another's experience. The principles and skills that worked for us in South Africa, in my experience, are equally useful in the Balkans, or the Middle East, or Northern Ireland. Their application will change with the culture and the particular circumstances of the conflict. Chris Spies learned not to sow trainings like seeds. It is a universal lesson, and it is this universality that I believe is transferable.

So what does this look like, this transfer of principles and skills? It might mean that the peace process that worked so well to bridge the ANC-Afrikaner divide could encourage Burundians to find inclusive, participatory mechanisms to bridge between Hutus and Tutsis. It might mean that the peace committees that became the melting pot for apartheid adversaries could inspire ethnic groups in Macedonia to reach out to one another through conversation and joint action. It might mean that the long hours spent in forums, building relationships and breaking down stereotypes, could be a model for Israelis and Arabs to find their common humanity and shared goals.

At Search for Common Ground, the Washington, D.C.–based non-profit NGO where I work, we reckon that maybe 50 percent of what works in one place may be transferable to another—but we are never sure which 50 percent it is!

There is no one formula, model, or blueprint, but in certain circumstances there might be something close. A methodology might just need to be tweaked, not bent, into a new cultural or political shape. In 1999, a Northern Irish delegation went to South Africa to consolidate their commitment to their peace agreement, and a South African sat on the Northern Irish police commission, telling of the struggle to turn apartheid police into community police. Northern Irish, South African, and Middle Eastern politicians, conflict resolution practitioners and academics, and civic leaders have been exchanging experiences since the mid-1990s.

My work at Search for Common Ground now takes me to some of the most violent and conflictual places on earth, and in each of them I hear the same human voices. I listen to the demand for inclusion and relationship building and the need for bottom-up approaches to complement the top-down heavy hand of government. I see the longing for an end to war and violence and the need for healing. I weep at the devastation that the world's win-lose ways wreak in the lives of millions of men, women, and children. I hear, in every language, "It is not we the people but our leaders who are making this war." I dream of the possibility of a win-win future, jointly crafted by governments and their people.

We *can* do it better. I believe we have the opportunity to learn, by trial and error, what works and what doesn't. One day we will know how to prevent conflicts from turning violent, and that day will come sooner if we learn from one another. There is no time to keep reinventing the wheel. Pick over the processes of the South African peace accord, and see what works for you. Dissect civil society's profound contribution to the reconciliation process in Northern Ireland. Adapt the example of "Oslo," where an unlikely third party created the conditions in which Israelis and Palestinians could look beyond their past and present enmity toward new possibilities. Discard what doesn't work or fit, or keep it on a shelf for another time.

Our experiences can also be inspirational. The work we do in one place, and our communication about it, can inspire others to say, " So there is another way to respond to conflict. Peace is possible. We can do it too." And that is where this book began.

The Peace Accord provided an institutional home for peacemaking, wove it into the fabric of society, and imprinted it on the hearts of countless South Africans. Despite its imperfections, it was an agent for societal transformation that, during the course of its short, sharp life, supported the people and politicians of South Africa as they crossed their Rubicon. For the first time in history, the methodology of conflict resolution was used to transform a nation. This book is a tribute to that peace process and to all the South Africans who chose to make it work. Particularly, it is a tribute to the peace workers who collectively formed the mighty wind that swept through our country, transforming it as they went.

To you I say: *Ubuntu*. This book is our book.

NOTES

INTRODUCTION

1. Heribert Adam and Kogila Moodley, *The Negotiated Revolution* (Johannesburg: Jonathan Ball Press, 1993).

2. Allister Sparks, *Tomorrow Is Another Country* (Johannesburg: Struik Book Distributors, 1995).

3. Guillermo A. O'Donnell and Phillippe C. Schmiter, *Transitions from Authoritarian Rule* (Baltimore: Johns Hopkins University Press, 1986).

4. Peter Gastrow, *Bargaining for Peace* (Washington, D.C.: United States Institute of Peace Press, 1995), 16. Gastrow's book offers a full description of the process that led up to the establishment of the National Peace Accord. This section draws heavily on his book.

5. Often called simply the "Peace Accord." The full text of the accord is reproduced in Gastrow, *Bargaining for Peace*, 113–154.

6. Interview, by telephone, with Peter Gastrow, September 1999.

7. By *conflict resolution methodology* I mean the application of constructive, collaborative approaches to conflict using mediation and facilitation techniques to resolve, manage, and transform conflict and prevent violence.

8. Laurie Nathan, "An Imperfect Bridge: Crossing to Democracy on the Peace Accord," *Track Two* (Cape Town) 2, no. 2 (May 1993).

1. THE PEACE ACCORD

1. Signatories to the National Peace Accord: African National Congress, Amalgamated Union of Building Trade Workers of South Africa, Ciskei, Confederation of Metal and Building Workers of South Africa, Congress of South African Trade Unions, Congress of Traditional Leaders of South Africa, Democratic Party, Dikwankwetla Party/Qwaqwa Government, Federation of Independent Trade Unions, Ximoko Progressive Party/Gazankulu Government, Inkatha Freedom Party, Intando Yesizwe Party, Inyandza National Movement/KaNgwane Government, KwaNdebele Government, KwaZulu Government, Labour Party of South Africa, Lebowa Government/United People's Front, Merit People's Party, National Forum, National Party/Government of South Africa, National People's Party of South Africa, Solidarity Party, South African Communist Party, United Workers' Union of South Africa.

2. Wessel Nel, "Voices from the Field," *Track Two* 2, no. 2 (May 1993). At the time, Nel was the Democratic Party member of Parliament for Mooi River, Natal.

3. Pofadder is named for a Khoi or Nama headman, Captain Pofadder, who lived there. It does not refer to the puffadder snake, as is commonly believed.

4. See chapter 2, "Peace Workers."

5. This story was told by Chris Spies in a series of interviews by telephone in November 1995.

6. Player/referee was a common metaphor during those times, usually directed at a government that was accused, often justly, of trying to play both roles at the same time.

7. International observers played an important role in the peace process, acting as the eyes and the ears of the international community. The various factions were usually on their best behavior in the observers' presence. See chapter 2, "Peace Workers."

8. This story was told in 1996 by Andries Odendaal, then coordinator of the Southern Cape Peace Committee. He has since joined the Centre for Conflict Resolution in Cape Town, where he coordinates a project on rural peacemakers.

9. Durand is an Afrikaner and an ordained minister in what is now called the United Reformed Church. At the time of these events he was deputy vice chancellor of the (black) University of the Western Cape.

10. Retief Olivier is an Afrikaner and an ordained member of the Dutch Reformed Church.

11. See the glossary for more information about civic organizations (SANCO) and WECUSA.

12. See chapter 6, "Forums."

13. The full R 6 million required for the construction of the new terminus was allocated by the RSC just before South Africa's first-ever democratic elections in April 1994.

14. The description of this meeting, including the quotations, is drawn mainly from my personal notes.

2. PEACE WORKERS

1. These profiles are based mainly on interviews that Lesley Fordred taped in Cape Town between October and December 1995.

2. There are no women clergy in the Dutch Reformed Church.

3. See chapter 1, "The Peace Accord," 26–28.

4. Members of the PAC were subsequently convicted and sentenced for mounting this attack.

5. See chapter 3, "Planned Intervention."

6. Lu Harding, Black Sash Monitoring Group, Statement, August 29, 1992.

7. As I close the file that starts with Lu Harding's report and ends with a newspaper cutting announcing occupancy of Tafelberg School by Thandakulu School on October 1, 1992, I remember the near violence of the previous week and wonder what would have happened if Lu hadn't sounded the alarm. Lu died in 1994, and this story is a tribute to this gentle woman's commitment, courage, and longing for peace in our land.

8. During the 1980s, a number of human and civil rights NGOs emerged with a monitoring component. With the crisis of violence in the early 1990s, the various groups formed themselves into a national network operating outside the peace structure. Police Colonel Gerrit Nieuwoudt said in an interview in March 1995 in Cape Town that the presence of outsiders definitely prevented violence. He also said that the NIM report after Chris Hani memorial day (March 14, 1993) directly contributed to a change in police behavior.

9. Letter from Val Rose Christie, March 14, 1996.

10. See chapter 7, "Police."

11. Val learned to live with the duality of also representing NIM on the regional peace committee. It was not unusual for us to play multiple roles at a time when violent incidents outnumbered the people able to respond. What counted, as Gerrit Nieuwoudt emphasized, was that we be transparent about our agenda.

3. PLANNED INTERVENTION

1. We later adopted a jacket with the Peace Accord dove logo and "Observer" in large red characters, which made a bit more sense.

2. A Danish policeman, one of the international observers sent by the European Community on a six-month mission.

3. Report compiled by Chris Spies, regional organizer, Western Cape Peace Committee, April 15, 1993. Included with the minutes of the Western Cape Peace Committee Executive Committee Meeting, April 28, 1993.

4. This account of this meeting, including the quotations, is drawn mainly from my own notes.

4. CRISIS RESPONSE

1. The description of these conversations, including the quotations, is drawn mainly from my own notes.

2. *Cape Times,* April 17, 1993.

3. These impressions of the mediation in Langa are my own and do not necessarily reflect the views of Chris Spies or Vincent Diba.

4. Joseph Montville argues that you build trust by confirming, that is, removing doubt. In a dialogue between adversaries, confirming implies accepting the other person's fundamental values and personal worth. "The goal is to establish working trust . . . and the role of a third party, like that of a therapist, is to involve and confirm individuals representing groups in conflict who for a variety of reasons find it difficult to reach out directly to their adversaries." I like this description because it confirms my own experience in the field. Joseph Montville, "The Healing Function in Political Conflict Resolution," in Denis J. D. Sandole and Hugo van der Merwe, eds., *Conflict Resolution Theory and Practice: Integration and Application* (Manchester: Manchester University Press, 1993), 112–118.

5. Letters from Sean Tait, written in December 1994 and January 1995.

6. The paragraphs about neutrality draw extensively on Ron Kraybill's thinking and specifically on his article "The Illusion of Neutrality," *Track Two* 1, no. 3 (November 1992).

7. A serviced site provides electricity, water, and sewerage, but no housing.

5. TRAINING

1. The account of the Voeldrif and Verdrag trainings, and Craig Arendse's personal story, are drawn mainly from an interview with Craig in Cape Town, March 1995.

2. An Afrikaans-speaking Coloured who began antiapartheid activities in high school.

3. Speeches made at the Young Presidents' Organization Conference, Johannesburg, February 26–March 3, 1995.

4. An American, Ron came to us as a seasoned conciliator and was the Centre's first training director. Working with South African trainers, he adapted his methodology and approach to South African ways and became recognized as an authority on conflict resolution and training. After seven years at the Centre, he returned to America.

5. This and other quotations in this chapter are taken from entries for July 1993 in Ron's personal journal, to which he kindly gave me access.

6. See the glossary for a description of the ANC and the PAC and their widely different political perspectives.

6. FORUMS

1. *Sunday Times*, March 31, 1991.

2. Albert Dayile is a fieldworker at the Quaker Peace Centre. His job is to find ways of making peace in Nyanga and the other townships around Cape Town where violence is currently spiraling out of control. He is also secretary of Nyanga Civic Association.

3. Resource Forum minutes, August 29, 1991.

4. Working Group minutes, August 21, 1991.

5. Working Group minutes, September 11, 1991.

6. Rachel has just joined UMAC. We will work closely together over the next three years, but now we are new to each other, and as she drives, fragments of her life unfold. Her childhood on an idyllic apple farm in the distant mountains, her marriage to a television cameraman and musician, her university degree in drama. It all seems a far cry from the dusty, violent streets that we will walk together so often as we go about our work.

7. Including the Legal Resources Centre, Lawyers for Human Rights, the Church of the Province of South Africa, the Human Rights Commission, the Institute for a Democratic Alternative for South Africa, and the National Association of Democratic Lawyers. Besides these NGOs, the regional ANC leadership, local civic associations, and township community groups also participated.

8. Affidavit sworn by Val Rose Christie, 1992.

9. Susan Collin [Marks], "For Better or for Worse: Alliances as an NGO Response to Conflict" (paper presented at SAACI Fifth National Conference, University of Port Elizabeth, November 25–28, 1992).

10. The new terminus was built according to the cardboard model. I visited it in September 1999 and watched the hurry of the buses and taxis moving in and out. I felt very proud of the peace committee's role in turning a place of violence into a bastion of noisy, bustling normality for buses and taxis and for the community they serve.

7. POLICE

1. See chapter 2, "Peace Workers," for more about Chris Spies.

2. Memorandum of Kraaifontein Community Organizations, March 1993.

3. Susan Collin [Marks] and Laurie Nathan, "From a Police Force to a Police Service: What the Community Needs from the South African Police," *Track Two* 2, no. 4 (November 1993). This is a shortened version of a paper commissioned by the Police Board in 1993.

4. See chapter 2, "Peace Workers," for more about Gerrit Nieuwoudt.

5. National Peace Accord, 3.3.3.

6. Lee P. Brown, "Community Policing: A Practical Guide for Police Officials," no. 12 in the series *Perspectives on Policing* (Harvard University, September 1989).

7. Working Group on Community Policing, "Discussion Document" (Capetown, October 18, 1993). This section of the chapter draws on this document, the product of four months' deliberations by a group of police officers and civilians, including myself. It formed the basis for regional policing policy and was also used nationally to kick-start similar discussions in other parts of the country.

8. The self-defense units (SDUs) of the ANC and the self-protection units (SPUs) of the IFP emerged as a response to the breakdown in effective policing in black communities during the 1980s. Composed mainly of militant youth, they took it upon themselves to mete out their own brand of street justice, some of which was excessive and brutal.

9. Chris Ferndale, "Democratizing the Police," *Track Two* 2, no. 4 (November 1993). This section of the chapter draws on this article and on an interview with its author in Cape Town, March 1995.

10. Quoted in Elrena van der Spuy, "Community Policing," *Track Two* 2, no. 4 (November 1993).

11. Community Relations Division, Western Cape, *Community Policing: Manual for Implementation* (issued by the Community Relations Division; undated).

12. Briefing to the Select Committee of Safety and Security, National Assembly (Cape Town) by Lieutenant-General L. C. A. Pruis, November 1, 1994.

13. Laurie Nathan is internationally acknowledged as an expert on peace and security. He was appointed executive director of the Centre for Conflict Resolution, Cape Town, in 1992. At that time, I held the position of senior researcher at the Centre. The paper for the Police Board was subsequently published as: Susan Collin [Marks] and Laurie Nathan, *From a Police Force to a Police Service: What the Community Needs from the South African Police* (Cape Town: Centre for Intergroup Studies, September 1993).

14. See chapter 2, "Peace Workers," for more about Malibongwe Sopangisa.

15. Van der Spuy, "Community Policing," 7. This section of the chapter draws on the ideas in this article.

16. Ibid., 8.

8. UBUNTU, THE SPIRIT OF AFRICA

1. The violence continued in KwaZulu-Natal and in the townships of Gauteng province (the Johannesburg area), where members of the IFP and ANC still wage war despite leadership demands for peace. Now much of the violence is a struggle for access to economic benefits and local positions of power rather than for the power to shape the national political agenda.

2. This idea should not be confused with positive thinking, which is useful and effective but stops short of the heart and soul that, together with the mind, create the "wholeness" or healing that is the essence of peace work. I am talking about looking for the good, finding it, nourishing it, and cherishing it. I am talking about goodness in action.

3. Khaba Mkhize, "It's Time to Blend Our Cultures," *Natal Witness*, August 2, 1995.

4. Excerpt from a speech delivered by Khaba Mkhize in Pietermaritzburg and published in *Natal Witness*, July 13, 1995.

5. Khaba Mkhize, "Beyond Thought and into Action," *Natal Witness*, July 12, 1995.

6. Aggrey Klaaste, "Good Chemistry," *Leadership SA* (October 1989).

7. Ibid.

8. Lovemore Mbigi and Jenny Maree, *Ubuntu: The Spirit of African Transformation Management* (Johannesburg: Knowledge Resources, 1995).

9. " 'Ubuntu' Council's Born," *Sowetan*, November 1, 1994.

10. "The Urgent Need for Moral Reconstruction" (summary of an address by Barney Pityana at the College of the Transfiguration in Grahamstown), *Challenge*, August 1994.

11. Chris Mann, "Building a Nation of Individuals, Not Warring Nationalists," *Business Day*, November 9, 1994.

12. Comment from participant in a seminar at the United States Institute of Peace, Washington, D.C., October 1995.

13. Interview by telephone with Peter and Linda Biehl, March 1996.

14. "Inside the Struggle: The Amy Biehl Story," *Turning Point*, ABC broadcast, April 20, 1994.

15. Letter from Stef Snel, February 1996. At the time, Stef was director of the Urban Monitoring Awareness Committee, established to monitor violence in the townships. He would roam the townships, watching, listening, talking to people from all walks of life. Wherever he went, Stef was welcomed and trusted. Everyone knew that he worked day and night to still the anger that so much injustice and violence was being done on a daily basis, and everyone knew that he was doing all that he could to discover the truth in the violence-racked townships.

16. "Inside the Struggle."

17. Biehl interview.

18. "Inside the Struggle."

19. Biehl interview.

20. "Inside the Struggle."

21. Biehl interview.

22. Gastrow, *Bargaining for Peace*, 82.

23. Ciskei was one of the African homelands.

24. Letter from Stef Snel, February 1996.

25. "Inside the Struggle."

EPILOGUE

1. Speech made at the Young President's Organization conference in Johannesburg, March 1995.

2. Jennifer Bowler, "Changing the Paradigm," *Track Two* 3, no. 1 (February1994).

3. Interview, by telephone, with Peter Gastrow, September 1999.

4. Interview by Lesley Fordred with Chris Spies in Cape Town, October 1995.

5. *Business Day*, June 1, 1998.

6. Spies interview.

GLOSSARY

Afrikaner Weerstandsbeweging (AWB). The Afrikaner Resistance Movement, a paramilitary organization, renowned for its swastika-like symbols and stiff-arm salutes and the rousing oratory of its leader, Eugene Terre'Blanche. The AWB participated in violent disruptions at several points during the transition but was unable to seriously derail negotiations.

African National Congress (ANC). An organization founded as the South African Native Congress on January 8, 1912, to resist the Land Act that prohibited ownership of land by blacks; it soon became the lead voice in the struggle against white domination. In 1923, it changed its name to the African National Congress. In 1955, with the launch of the Freedom Charter, it reaffirmed its commitment to nonracialism and nonviolence, despite escalating oppression by the white authorities. Then in June 1961, after forty-eight years of nonviolent efforts had failed to bring about any change of heart by successive white governments, the ANC formed a military wing called Umkhonto we Sizwe (Spear of the Nation) to begin an armed struggle. The ANC was banned by the government in 1960 but continued to operate in exile from its headquarters in Lusaka, Zambia. After its unbanning in 1990, the ANC began a difficult transition from liberation movement to political party. In the April 1994 elections, the ANC won over 62 percent of the seats in Parliament and dominated nine of the eleven regions; its leader, Nelson Mandela, became president of South Africa. In 1999, the ANC once again won the elections with a landslide vote.

Azanian People's Organization (AZAPO). The primary political vehicle for the philosophy of the Black Consciousness movement in South Africa. It was founded in 1978 after most of the original Black Consciousness organizations had been banned. Black Consciousness arose in the 1970s around a philosophy advocating psychological liberation through "conscientization."

Biko, Steven. Founder of the South African Students Organization (SASO). Born in 1946 in King William's Town, Biko founded SASO in 1968 and dominated black politics for the next decade, even after his banning orders were issued in 1973. Through this organization and other mediums, Biko became known for his articulate formulation of the Black Consciousness philosophy. Biko and the Black Consciousness movement focused on liberating the minds of blacks by challenging the psychology of apartheid and the self-image it imposed on the oppressed. Biko argued that apartheid's racial categories were socially constructed and artificial, and he worked toward redefining *black* to be used as an indicator of oppression rather than of race. His theories and slogans became the basis for the student organizing that contributed to the Soweto uprisings of 1976. In 1977, he was arrested and jailed for violating his banning orders after he was captured at a police roadblock returning to Port Elizabeth from Cape Town. A few days later, on September 12, 1977, Biko died from massive head trauma suffered while in police custody.

black consciousness. A philosophy that stressed the psychological impact of racism in reaction to the nationalist philosophies that preceded it. Black Consciousness supporters challenged the racial categories promulgated by the state, extending the term *black* to cover all those racially oppressed under apartheid. The movement encouraged black self-reliance and assertiveness.

Black Sash. A women's human rights organization founded in 1955 to protest governmental restructuring to remove Coloured voters from the common voters' roll. It took its name from the black sashes that the women wore as a sign of mourning for the constitution as they stood in silent but articulate protest in public places. These nonconfrontational protests were designed to embarrass governmental officials, and the backlash against the protesters was immediate. Startled whites spat and sneered at these "*kaffir* lovers" (*kaffir* is a derogatory term for blacks) in public and shunned them (and sometimes even their children) in private. In the 1960s, "Sash" established educational programs and advocacy and advice centers directed against the pass laws and other apartheid legislation and, in the 1980s, began to monitor the escalating violence, creating a Monitoring Group with members trained to observe, take statements, and write reports.

Botha, Pieter Willem (P. W.). "The Old Crocodile," prime minister from 1978 to 1984 and state president from 1984 until 1989. Botha began his tenure as leader of South Africa by instituting a series of reforms designed to placate discontent without seriously threatening National Party hegemony. He pushed through parliamentary reform that gave Asians and Coloureds their own Houses of Parliament, but this reform only inflamed black opposition groups and provided a national issue as a rallying point for the formation of a unified opposition. Botha then retrenched and instituted various states of emergency through the 1980s. In February 1989 he suffered a stroke and in August was forced to resign by his own cabinet.

Broederbond. The "Band of Brothers," a secret organization formed in 1918 by Afrikaner nationalists intent on preserving the Afrikaner culture and entrenching the use of the Afrikaans language. In 1938 the Broederbond staged elaborate celebrations to mark the hundredth anniversary of the Great Trek. Nationwide, this pageant of the Afrikaners' past hardship and endurance helped coalesce nationalist support and led to the National Party victory in 1948. The Broederbond served as a think tank for Afrikaner intellectuals, and it directed the Nationalist government's strategy. Its core commitment was to the survival of the Afrikaner through apartheid ideology.

Buthelezi, Mangosuthu Gatsha. Heir to the chieftainship of the Buthelezi tribe and founder and leader of Inkatha. Born on August 27, 1928, he became chief executive officer of the newly established kwaZulu Territorial Authority in 1970, a position that evolved into the post of chief minister of the "self-governing" kwaZulu homeland in 1976. Buthelezi was very close to many of the leaders of the ANC and took the position of chief minister with ANC approval, but a rift arose when Buthelezi, angered by the ANC leadership's refusal to censure members who were condemning him as a "collaborator" with the government, broke with the ANC. Subsequently, he came to be seen as a moderate opposition leader, somewhat less radical and more pro-business than the ANC. On this basis he began to build Inkatha to rival the ANC. During the 1980s, Inkatha feuded with the United Democratic Front over political influence in kwaZulu. After the release of Nelson Mandela, Buthelezi and Inkatha continued to compete with the ANC for political power. But Buthelezi's political position deteriorated as the government and the ANC found common ground. He often withdrew both himself and Inkatha from constitutional negotiations in protest at the direction the talks were taking. He agreed to participate in the April 1994 elections seven days prior to the first day of voting. Inkatha won the kwaZulu-Natal administrative district, and Buthelezi became minister of home affairs in Mandela's Government of National Unity.

Centre for Conflict Resolution (CCR). Formerly (until 1994) the Centre for Intergroup Studies, CCR is an independent NGO that "seeks to contribute toward a just peace in South Africa by promoting constructive, creative and cooperative approaches to the resolution of conflict and the reduction of violence."

Centre for Intergroup Studies (CIS). Predecessor to the Centre for Conflict Resolution. Established by the University of Cape Town in 1968, CIS's goal was to facilitate communication between groups in conflict. Through its work—in mediation and facilitation, research, education, and training—it played a unique role in efforts to establish a just peace in South Africa. It was directed by Professor Hendrik Willem "H. W." van der Merwe until his retirement in 1992.

civic organizations. Locally organized, grassroots, civil society groupings that often functioned as governing bodies for the townships in opposition to the state-erected structures of the early 1980s. The "civics" formed the backbone of the United Democratic Front. In the 1990s they evolved into a grassroots support for the ANC under the umbrella of the South African National Civic Organization.

Congress of South African Trade Unions (COSATU). An umbrella organization formed in 1985 by the black labor unions. In 1987, COSATU and the United Democratic Front, with sixteen other organizations, formed the Mass Democratic Movement. Later, when the ANC was unbanned, an ANC-SACP-COSATU alliance was formalized, bringing the weight of the black labor movement behind the ANC's political negotiations. It also injected gifted union negotiators into the political arena and kept economic issues firmly on the agenda.

Conservative Party (CP). A party formed in 1982 by Andries Treurnicht and other National Party members unhappy about Prime Minister P. W. Botha's reform measures, which granted limited political rights to Coloureds and Asians. The Conservative Party's platform was a return to the heyday of "grand" apartheid. In the 1987 parliamentary elections the CP became the official opposition party when it won 26.4 percent of the vote. In 1989 it won 31.2 percent. Although the CP did not participate in the 1994 elections, some of its most important members, led by General Constand Viljoen, broke off and hastily formed a right-wing party called the Freedom Front immediately prior to the deadline for party registration. The Freedom Front won 2.2 percent of the vote in 1994.

Convention for a Democratic South Africa (CODESA). The vehicle for South Africa's first attempts at multiparty negotiations. The inaugural meeting, on December 20, 1991, of CODESA was hailed as the start of formal negotiations. Two hundred twenty-eight delegates from nineteen parties participated, representing the widest variety of political leaders to convene up to that point in South Africa, even though the extreme right and left refused to come to the table. The largely ceremonial CODESA I was given substance by the appointment of five working groups charged with resolving particular issues. CODESA II, which was scheduled for May 15, 1992, was expected to provide the breakthrough; however, negotiations collapsed when it became clear that the government's and the ANC's visions for the future were widely divergent. The ANC was committed to majority rule; the government was seeking a way to retain power. A massacre at Boipatong in June 1992 prompted the ANC, which accused the government of complicity in the violence, to withdrawn from the talks.

de Klerk, Frederik Willem (F. W.). Last state president of the old South Africa. Born on March 18, 1936, "F. W." grew up in a very political family. His father held several high cabinet and National Party posts. First elected to Parliament in 1972, de Klerk subsequently held several cabinet posts, heading the Ministry of National Education through 1989. He also became leader of the Transvaal National Party in 1982. He was elected state president in September 1989. At the time, de Klerk was considered the most conservative of the four National Party candidates to replace P. W. Botha. However, in February 1990, de Klerk opened Parliament with a speech that, in one fell swoop, unbanned previously sanctioned rival political parties, including the ANC, the South African Communist Party, and the PAC; freed Nelson Mandela and other political prisoners; and pledged to end "grand" apartheid. De Klerk oversaw the dismantling of the apartheid regime and negotiated the new constitution with the ANC and other opposition parties. In March 1992, de Klerk called a whites-only referendum on his policies and won over a two-thirds majority, silencing right-wing critics who had been claiming that he was acting without a mandate. In 1993 he shared the Nobel Peace Prize with Mandela. In the April 1994 elections, de Klerk and the National Party won over 20 percent of the vote, entitling de Klerk to the position of second deputy president of the Government of National Unity.

Democratic Party (DP). A party formed in 1989 through the merger of three liberal parties, including the Progressive Federal Party. Although it received a significant minority of the votes in 1989, it found itself in a state of limbo after the National Party U-turn that adopted many of its policies. In response, DP leader Zach de Beer sought to carve out a niche as a mediating force in the negotiations. This role became institutionalized when de Beer was chosen to head the working group of parties preparing for the Convention for a Democratic South Africa. The DP received 1.7 percent of the vote and seven parliamentary seats in 1994.

Department of Education and Training (DET). Under apartheid, when education for blacks and whites was administered by separate government departments, the department was responsible for black education within the Republic of South Africa, excluding the homelands.

End Conscription Campaign (ECC). A group formed in July 1983 to campaign against compulsory conscription (of white males) and support war resisters in a number of practical ways. The ECC grew rapidly in 1984 and 1985 in the wake of Pretoria's decision to deploy conscripts in the townships, both because of revulsion at fighting fellow South Africans and because of increased casualties. The state cracked down under the 1986 state of emergency, and many ECC members were restricted and detained.

Goniwe, Matthew. One of the United Democratic Front's most successful and magnetic organizers. Born in 1948, Goniwe became a high school science teacher in Lingelihle, the township for the town of Cradock in the Great Karoo desert. From that position, he helped found the Cradock Residents Association (CRADORA), one of the first examples of the grassroots organizing that came to be called "people's power." The respectful values that Goniwe preached and the organizational structures he helped to pioneer empowered people and made the UDF a formidable force all over the Eastern Cape. In June 1985, he and three colleagues were brutally murdered while driving home from a meeting. On the day of his funeral, the government imposed a partial state of emergency on the country (the first since 1960) and used the event to arrest UDF leaders who were among the fifty thousand people in attendance.

Government of National Unity (GNU). The transitional governing structure designed to ease the process of incorporating majority rule. It was a coalition of all parties that received more than 5 percent of the vote in April 1994, with the delegation of cabinet seats based upon the proportion of votes each received. The GNU hierarchy included a state president and two deputy presidents, one from the party that came in second, and the other from any other party that received more than 20 percent of the vote. Because no other party received more than 20 percent, the second deputy presidency was awarded to the victorious party. This compromise structure broke the logjam of constitutional negotiations by ensuring a transitional framework in which power sharing was practiced. In the 1999 elections, the government was formed by the winning party, the ANC.

hostels. Single-sex dormitories used to house migrant laborers, particularly miners, in township areas. The philosophy behind the hostel system was to bring black labor to the cities and mines while leaving their families and psychological homes in the rural areas. Men spent eleven months of the year in the hostel, returning home for one month before repeating the cycle. Hostels became a source of intense township conflict in the late 1980s and early 1990s, especially in the Johannesburg area, because many hostels housed mainly rural Zulu men loyal to Inkatha, while the surrounding townships often supported the ANC or PAC.

Inkatha Freedom Party (IFP). A party with roots in a Zulu cultural organization, Inkatha YeNkululeko Ye Sizwe (National Cultural Liberation Movement), founded by Buthelezi in 1975. During the 1980s, many observers, both at home and abroad, perceived Inkatha and its leader, Mangosuthu Gatsha Buthelezi, as potential alternatives to the "extremism" of the ANC. Inkatha officially became a political party after the opening of the South African political arena in 1990. It sought to protect "group rights" and supported a strong, decentralized federalism. It relied primarily upon its traditional power base among the Zulu population, using traditional Zulu power structures and symbolism. In 1994, Buthelezi and the IFP entered the election at the last minute but still managed to receive 10.5 percent of the overall vote and won the right to govern the KwaZulu-Natal province. Buthelezi served as minister of home affairs.

Internal Stability Division (ISD). A division of the South African Police. In 1991, in an attempt to change its image, the South African Police disbanded the Riot Police, a division notorious for its use of brute force, particularly in black townships, and reconstituted it as the ISD. Local units were known as internal stability units (ISUs). The ISD operated through its own chain of command and was unaccountable to local or regional police, and it quickly became as feared and hated as its predecessor. When the police force was restructured as the South African Police Service under Nelson Mandela's government, the ISD was dissolved altogether.

Joint Forum on Policing. A group formed in January 1992 as an alliance of NGOs and community and political organizations with the primary goals of monitoring police behavior and activity for adherence to the Police Code of Conduct as set out in the National Peace Accord and exposing police misconduct. In addition, it sought to improve the basis on which investigations of police misconduct were carried out, raise public awareness of policing issues, and liaise between the community and the police with a view to closing the gap between them. Ultimately, it hoped to contribute to institutional change within the police force. In 1993, with the launch of the Network of Independent Monitors, which took over much of this monitoring work, the Joint Forum switched its focus to the facilitation of community policing. At the time of writing, it is still the primary forum for civilian involvement in community policing in the Western Cape.

laager. Literally, a defensive encampment surrounded by a circle of wagons; it was the traditional method of defense for the large wagon trains of the Afrikaner "Great Trek" into the interior of the country in the early and mid-eighteenth century. Under apartheid, the laager became a metaphorical description of the white, especially Afrikaner, response to perceived threats to the apartheid order, whereby whites were urged to come together to defend their common interests against a common threat. This reactive unity emphasized similarity within the group, ignoring or covering over intragroup differences while overemphasizing differences between the group and the perceived threat.

Mandela, Nelson Rolihlahla. The first democratically elected president of South Africa. Born on July 18, 1918, near Umtata, Mandela was educated at a boarding school and then went on to Fort Hare University, from which he was expelled in 1940 for his part in a student strike. He completed his B.A. by correspondence and then studied law at the University of the Witswatersrand. He helped to found the ANC Youth League in 1944. In December 1952 Mandela was arrested and charged under the Suppression of Communism Act. He was subsequently banned. In 1956, Mandela was arrested with 155 others and charged with high treason. He was found not guilty after a trial that lasted four-and-a-half years. He then went underground, avoiding charges of incitement related to a strike protesting the proclamation of the Republic in 1961. But fifteen months later he was arrested and imprisoned, and shortly after that, government forces raided the ANC underground headquarters in Rivonia, arresting most of the leadership of the ANC. Mandela was included in their trial and was sentenced to life imprisonment. He was immediately transferred to Robben Island. In 1982, he was transferred to Pollsmoor Prison. During a hospital stay in 1985, Mandela met for the first time with Hendrick Jacobus (Kobie) Coetsee, minister of justice, police, and prisons. This contact began four years of secret contacts between Mandela and the government, and also between the external leadership of the ANC and government officials, that eventually led to the release of Mandela and the unbanning of the ANC in February 1990. After twenty-seven years in prison, Mandela led the ANC delegation that negotiated with the National Party government on the transfer of power and the end of minority rule. He shared the Nobel Peace Prize for 1993 with then President F. W. de Klerk. On May 10, 1994, Mandela was installed as president of South Africa.

National Council of Trade Unions (NACTU). The trade union organization of the Pan-Africanist Congress (PAC), formed in October 1986 through the merger of the Council of Unions of South Africa and the Azanian Congress of Trade Unions.

National Party. A party founded in 1914 by J. B. M. Hertzog that came to power in 1948 as an Afrikaner nationalist party led by D. F. Malan. It was the political party responsible for implementing the policies of apartheid and for proclaiming the Republic of South Africa in 1961. In 1989, after president and party leader P. W. Botha suffered a stroke, F. W. de Klerk was selected as party leader and installed as president. The National Party received 20.4 percent of the vote in the 1994 election, winning the Western Cape province and entitling de Klerk to the position of second deputy president in the Government of National Unity.

National Peace Accord (NPA). An agreement signed on September 14, 1991, by the major South African political parties and organizations (with the exception of those on the extreme right and left); business, trade union, and "homeland" leaders; and others that established a network of peace committees at the local, regional, and national levels to facilitate conflict resolution with the aim of alleviating political violence and intimidation. This unique agreement also set up codes of conduct for political parties, police, and security forces and attempted to contribute to socioeconomic reconstruction and development. The structures of the NPA were officially dismantled by the Government of National Unity in December 1994.

Network of Independent Monitors (NIM). A network formed as a nongovernmental organization in September 1992 to coordinate the monitoring components of several human rights and church-based organizations. NIM's objective was to provide independent monitoring aimed at reducing political violence. Its primary focus was to monitor marches, demonstrations, rallies, campaigns, and situations of politically motivated community conflict. It also sought to generate effective investigation that could lead to the prosecution of the perpetrators of violence.

no-go areas. The colloquial term for areas deemed too dangerous for whites (regardless of their beliefs or goals) to enter because of rampant violence and hostility.

Pan-Africanist Congress of Azania (PAC). A group formed in April 1959 as an offshoot of the ANC by Robert Sobukwe that for many years was the major political alternative to the ANC for black South Africans. As a means of empowering blacks, the PAC's ideology excludes whites. After sponsoring a series of protests against the pass laws in 1960, one of which resulted in the infamous Sharpeville Massacre in which police killed 69 and wounded 180, the PAC was banned and Sobukwe imprisoned. It was unbanned in 1990. It failed to attract significant support in the 1994 elections, garnering only 1.2 percent of the vote. The Pan-Africanist Student Organization (PASO) is the student association of the Pan-Africanist Congress.

racial terms. I have used the racial designations of the apartheid era because I want to convey what it was like, and how it all worked. Thus, *black* refers to all people who are not white, and *white* refers to all people who are not black. Within the black group, African blacks are called *African*, people of mixed race are called *Coloured*, and the predominantly Indian Asians are called *Asians*. The term *nonwhite* was widely used in the earlier days of apartheid to refer to all the black subgroups, but is not used in this book. There were no official subgroups of whites. However, there were some strange and arbitrary designations for non-African groups; for instance, Chinese were considered black whereas Japanese were regarded as white.

Regional Services Council (RSC). A government agency set up to control resources and coordinate services for municipal regions, which were often politically divided because of the racial boundaries of the Group Areas Act. It became notorious for its heavy-handed application of apartheid legislation and resistance to changes prompted by the negotiations process and the Peace Accord.

Security Branch. A branch of the South African Police that served as the apartheid government's intelligence service for crimes directed against the state.

South African Communist Party (SACP). A party formed in July 1921 as the Communist Party of South Africa (CPSA). The CPSA was banned in 1950 and the organization disbanded, but it re-formed underground as the SACP in 1953 and since then has had very close ties with the ANC, the latter being somewhat of a refuge for the SACP and the former providing much of the ANC's intellectual guidance and leadership. Many of the ANC's most prominent leaders were members of the SACP. With the ANC having transformed itself into a political party, the SACP has sought to carve out its own niche in the political terrain of postapartheid South Africa. In April 1993, Chris Hani, secretary general of the SACP, was assassinated by a member of a right-wing organization who was conspiring with a leading member of the Conservative Party.

third force. A term used to characterize groups believed to be responsible for activities intended to destabilize negotiations between the National government and the ANC. Suspicions about third-force activities, focused on the security forces and other right-wing groups, were vindicated when the Goldstone Commission found enough circumstantial evidence to hold that government forces were complicit in many instances of political violence in black areas.

townships. Poorly serviced black neighborhoods that were built outside white towns and cities to house blacks with the legal right to urban residence and employment. The populations of these areas were substantially enlarged by the growth of huge and illegal squatter communities, which further taxed the already inadequate amenities. *Township* became a pejorative term consistent with poverty, overcrowding, and, later, criminality and defiance of the apartheid authorities.

Umkhonto we Sizwe (MK). "Spear of the Nation," the military wing of the ANC. It was launched in 1961 and worked inside the country for two years. In 1963, its internal leaders were arrested and its networks destroyed. Operating in exile, MK was largely ineffective until the 1976 riots provided it with a flow of militant exiles. Although MK never presented a formidable military threat to South Africa, its rhetorical uses were very significant. It was a powerful symbol for the mobilization of support in the townships and represented an important bargaining chip in early negotiations with the government. MK was key to breaking down white control of the military establishment in South Africa. During the transition, MK leaders were trained to take over leadership roles in the postapartheid South African military, and MK troops have been integrated into the postapartheid South African National Defence Force.

United Democratic Front (UDF). An umbrella organization formed in 1983 in response to the government's proposed constitutional reforms. Encompassing township organizations, particularly civic associations and youth groups, the UDF functioned as a stand-in for the ANC. In addition to organizing resistance campaigns, the UDF was particularly successful in intimidating the town councils that the government had set up in an attempt to give the appearance of popularly elected local governance for black areas. In 1987, the UDF joined with COSATU and others to establish the Mass Democratic Movement. The UDF was banned in February 1988. When it was unbanned with the ANC and other political organizations in 1990, it was unable to find a niche alongside the ANC and officially ceased to exist in August 1991.

GLOSSARY SOURCES

Davies, Robert, Dan O'Meara, and Sipho Dlamini, eds. *The Struggle for South Africa: A Reference Guide to Movements, Organizations, and Institutions.* London; Atlantic Highlands, N.J.: Zed Books, 1988.

Gastrow, Shelagh. *Who's Who in South African Politics: Number Two.* Johannesburg: Ravan Press, 1987.

Ohlson, Thomas, and Stephen Stedman. *The New Is Not Yet Born: Conflict Resolution in Southern Africa.* Washington, D.C.: Brookings Institution, 1994.

Ottoway, Marina. *South Africa: The Struggle for a New Order.* Washington, D.C.: Brookings Institution, 1993.

Sisk, Timothy D. *Democratization in South Africa: The Elusive Social Contract.* Princeton, N.J.: Princeton University Press, 1995.

INDEX

Susan Collin Marks is a South African who worked as a conflict resolution practitioner and peacemaker during South Africa's transition from apartheid to democracy (1990–94). During those tumultuous years, on a daily basis she and her colleagues intervened in crises and mediated conflicts between the police and the black community, opposing political groups, enemies in the taxi wars, demonstrators and security forces, government and angry youth. She served on the executive committee of the Western Cape Regional Peace Committee under the auspices of the National Peace Accord, and worked as senior researcher at the Centre for Conflict Resolution in Cape Town. In 1992, she founded the quarterly publication *Track Two*. In 1994, she was awarded a Jennings Randolph Peace Fellowship at the United States Institute of Peace. She now lives in Washington, D.C., where she is executive vice president of Search for Common Ground, a nonprofit nongovernmental organization working in conflict resolution internationally, with offices in the Middle East, Balkans, Africa, Europe, and the former Soviet Union. She was born on a mission station in kwaZulu-Natal and grew up in the Eastern Cape Province of South Africa.